Step-by-Step

Resumes

SECOND EDITION

Build an Outstanding Resume in 10 Easy Steps!

Evelyn U. Salvador

Certified Resume Writer and Career Coach

Step-by-Step Resumes, Second Edition

© 2011 by Evelyn U. Salvador

Published by JIST Works, an imprint of JIST Publishing
7321 Shadeland Station, Suite 200
Indianapolis, IN 46256-3923
Phone: 800-648-JIST   Fax: 877-454-7839   E-mail: info@jist.com

Visit our Web site at **www.jist.com** for information on JIST, tables of contents, sample pages, and ordering instructions for our many products!

> See the back of this book for additional books and ordering information. Quantity discounts are available for JIST books. Please call our Sales Department at 800-648-5478 for a free catalog and more information.

Acquisitions and Development Editor: Lori Cates Hand
Interior Designer: Marie Kristine Parial-Leonardo
Page Layout: Toi Davis
Proofreaders: Laura Bowman, Jeanne Clark
Indexer: Kelly D. Henthorne

Printed in the United States of America
15 14 13 12 11 10   9 8 7 6 5 4 3 2 1

Library of Congress Cataloging-in-Publication Data

Salvador, Evelyn U., 1952-
  Step-by-step resumes : build an outstanding resume in 10 easy steps! /
Evelyn U. Salvador. -- 2nd ed.
      p. cm.
   Includes index.
ISBN 978-1-59357-778-0 (bound-in CD : alk. paper)
 1. Résumés (Employment) I. Title.
HF5383.S25 2010
650.14'2--dc22

                              2010025503

ISBN 978-1-59357-778-0

About This Book

My goal in developing this workbook is to give you precisely what you need to write a top-notch, high-impact resume so you don't have to wade through tons of books, making an already daunting task more complex.

My mission is to help you catapult your career as painlessly as possible via a simple how-to resume-building process, so that you can achieve the highest-level result possible by writing your resume yourself. My goal is to impart upon you the methods, techniques, and proprietary information I have successfully used in my private practice that have helped clients advance their careers and improve their quality of life, and to coach you side-by-side as you complete each step.

The amount of effort you put into preparing your resume is commensurate with the level of success you will achieve when you send it out. The greater the effort, the greater the interview results, and the more satisfied you can be with the type of job you land and, ultimately, your lifestyle. So pay particular attention as you review each step to make your resume the best it can possibly be! The end result will show prospective employers why you are the best candidate for the job.

As resume writers and career coaches, we take every little bit of information from our clients to capitalize on their strengths and their competitive edge; and we weigh every word in the resume before we consider it complete. So to get the most out of this process, take your time with each step to be sure you have left no stone unturned in making yourself shine!

All you need to do is follow each step carefully to develop your winning resume. And when you're reading your final draft, don't be surprised if you say, "Wow! I'd hire me!" as clients of professional resume writers often do.

Let's get started on *your* road to success!

Contents

STEP 3: LIST YOUR GENERAL INFORMATION AND JOB RESPONSIBILITIES 33

STEP 4: IDENTIFY YOUR ACHIEVEMENTS 75

STEP 5: PUT TOGETHER YOUR FIRST DRAFT 135

STEP 6: ROUND OUT YOUR RESUME WITH CLIPBULLETS™..159

STEP 7: WRITE YOUR COVER LETTER 197

STEP 8: CREATE A PERSONAL BRAND FOR YOUR JOB SEARCH 209

STEP 9: PULL TOGETHER, EDIT, AND DESIGN YOUR RESUME 243

STEP 10: READY YOUR RESUME FOR JOB BOARDS AND E-MAIL 257

APPENDIX: SAMPLE RESUMES.................................265

INDEX 291

INTRODUCTION:
How to Use This Book

I have written, designed, and produced numerous promotional materials and sales tools for businesses and individuals over the past 19 years. I actually came into the profession of resume writing and career coaching out of designing and writing brochures and self-promotions for businesses. My nature is to tackle challenges through creative problem-solving techniques. So when family and friends came to me to write their resumes, I automatically wrote and designed them as I would any other sales tool—around the product (the applicant), the market (the profession), and the targeted audience (the prospective employer).

I wrote the resumes by infusing the number-one marketing technique: selling the benefits of the applicant's (the product's) services by showcasing why they were an asset to prospective firms. Then I designed their resumes to match their targeted audience (the employer).

These family members and friends instantly received job interview calls. At first, I chalked it up to luck or being in the right place at the right time. However, when the results continued to be the same every time, I realized it wasn't luck at all. What I didn't realize at the time (because it was an innate and subconscious process from my advertising experience) was that selling benefits was a success quotient—for not only businesses, but for job seekers as well.

After becoming very involved with resume and career organizations, I found that my colleagues were in fact doing the same thing…selling the benefits of their clients' services to meet their targeted audiences' needs. And this is one of the reasons resumes prepared by expert professional resume writers are far more successful than resumes written by applicants on their own. I want to pass that knowledge on to you, so that you, too, can prepare a highly successful resume that sells and showcases the benefits of your product and services… you!

EVERYTHING YOU NEED TO PUT TOGETHER A WINNING RESUME

The *Step-by-Step Resumes* process contains everything you need to write your resume like a professional resume writer—one step at a time. It includes all of the worksheets, assessment tools, and instructions you will need to craft a winning resume specific to your profession—without having to do a lot of reading or research. You will also find the worksheets and Resume ClipBullets™ on the CD at the back of the book.

Easy-to-follow instructions are right where you need them: when you are completing a particular step. This workbook contains in-depth but very concise information (no fluff—only what you need to know) so that you can define and target your goal, assess your skills and attributes, document your responsibilities, identify your achievements, write your professional summary and cover letter, design your resume presentation, and pull it all together to develop a successful resume that gets interviews. It includes hundreds of industry-specific keywords, action verbs (your bullet starters), and descriptive adjectives and adverbs to write your resume effectively…everything you need to build your customized, interview-generating resume.

Step-by-Step Resumes is meant to be used as a worksheet process; so please delve right into the worksheets, and don't hesitate to write in the book. Or you can pop the accompanying CD into your computer to locate and complete the Achievements worksheets and ClipBullets™ to build your resume.

Once you complete the assessment tools and worksheets, I will show you how to convert your answers into resume bullets and transfer the information over into your final resume format—bullet by bullet. This is the same process that professional resume writers use when we consult with clients in our private practices, and the techniques we use to create their customized resumes. You are basically getting into the mind of a professional resume writer and gaining the inside knowledge and expertise, which you can use to your advantage.

Completing this process thoroughly will provide you with an extremely professional resume that can help you significantly increase your interview odds. It will also prepare you for interviews because many of the questions you will answer during the resume process will be asked by employment professionals.

WHAT DOES A SUCCESSFUL RESUME CONTAIN?

Most job seekers write task-oriented resumes and do not document their responsibilities and achievements around their targeted profession. By contrast, a successful resume does the following:

- ✔ Targets employers' needs.
- ✔ Targets your goals and desires.
- ✔ Contains powerful marketing phrases.
- ✔ Relays your qualifications in a compelling way.
- ✔ Engages the reader and maintains interest through content and design that have impact.
- ✔ Plays up your strengths and minimizes weaknesses.
- ✔ Incorporates relevant information and omits irrelevant information.
- ✔ Omits negative red flags and converts them into positive assets.
- ✔ Identifies and correctly targets key transferable skills (those you've used in one position or profession that work well in another).
- ✔ Incorporates effective marketing, design, and presentation strategies.
- ✔ Portrays how you can help prospective employers reach their goals.
- ✔ Demonstrates the fit between your qualifications and the employer's needs.
- ✔ Ensures correct placement of relevant qualifications.
- ✔ Incorporates industry-specific keywords and language.
- ✔ Meets current resume-writing standards.
- ✔ Uses CAR (Challenge-Action-Result) statements in quantifying your accomplishments.
- ✔ Utilizes the most suitable resume format for you.
- ✔ Turns bland responsibility bullets into action-packed achievement bullets.
- ✔ Gets interviews—and a lot of them!

WHAT ARE THE 10 STEPS?

Following the 10 steps in this book will guide you in developing a winning resume. The 10 steps in this resume-building process are as follows:

Step 1: Assess Yourself

Step 2: Set Your Resume Strategy

Step 3: List Your General Information and Job Responsibilities

Step 4: Identify Your Achievements

Step 5: Put Together Your First Draft

Step 6: Round Out Your Resume with ClipBullets™

Step 7: Write Your Cover Letter

Step 8: Create a Personal Brand for Your Job Search

Step 9: Pull Together, Edit, and Design Your Resume

Step 10: Ready Your Resume for Job Boards and E-mail

Along the way you'll encounter personal assessment tools, resume strategizing methods, specialized skills by profession (keywords), action verbs, numerous worksheets for your specific situation, Resume ClipBullets™ with easy fill-in-the-blank answers, writing and editing guidelines, resume format templates and how and when to use them, professional summary foundations, cover letter templates, sample resume designs, and resume and cover letter samples.

This how-to resume process will allow you to incorporate cutting-edge professional resume-writing strategies without having to be resume-communication savvy. If you don't think you have the writing skills, achievements, or confidence to do this, don't worry. I will show you simple methods and techniques I have successfully used for my clients throughout the years; and I will help you write your resume. In the end, I will even critique it for you personally if you'd like (complete the order form at the back of the book and send it to me for your critique).

The process is easily adapted to each profession and precisely customized to each individual, whether you are a file clerk or a chief executive officer. Everyone who completes this process—no matter how similar their positions are to each other—will end up with a very different, unique resume.

WHAT ARE THE BENEFITS OF COMPLETING THIS 10-STEP PROCESS?

The information and guidelines in this workbook have helped job seekers do the following:

- ✔ Increase their interview odds
- ✔ Heighten their confidence level
- ✔ Gain renewed enthusiasm for the job search
- ✔ Feel empowered in the interview stage
- ✔ Land the position they seek sooner
- ✔ Obtain higher salaries

The assessment tools and worksheets in this book will help you discover the following:

- ✔ All of your personal attributes and how they help you in your profession
- ✔ Your areas of expertise (also known as keywords)
- ✔ How to develop an effective, targeted resume strategy
- ✔ Your achievements: what you accomplished, how your achievements benefited your employers, and the tangible results of your efforts
- ✔ How to identify and quantify your achievements in a compelling way
- ✔ How to be objective about yourself and sell that precious commodity called "you"
- ✔ Industry-specific action verbs to jump-start the bullets in your Professional Experience section
- ✔ How to develop your competitive edge using personal branding strategies

✔ How to infuse expert resume-writing techniques and meet resume-writing standards

✔ How to choose which resume format to use for your situation

✔ How to write a compelling cover letter

✔ How to design a professional sales tool that stands out from the crowd

✔ How to craft a winning, interview-generating resume that gets calls

HOW DO I USE THE WORKSHEETS IN THIS BOOK?

Step-by-Step Resumes contains worksheets specific to many types of job functions, responsibilities, and achievements for many professions. To use the components successfully, you will select and complete the appropriate general worksheets along with the worksheet components that are specific to your field. As you complete each worksheet, you will build upon your resume; and in the end, all of the pieces will come together.

Using the Assessment Tools

You will find assessment tools to help you determine your targeted goal, your personal attributes, and keywords to complete your resume professionally. Taking a personal inventory of all of your skills, talents, and attributes will also serve to build your self-confidence during the interview stage (a very positive "side-effect" of going through this process!).

Using the Resume Strategizing Tools

Resume strategizing is your first and most important step. After you complete the resume strategizing phase, you will know exactly what your resume should include and exclude, and you will be on the right track when completing the worksheets. These tools include the following:

✔ **Define Your Job Objective and Its Requirements (Step 1):** For documenting the type of positions or titles you seek and the requirements and keywords of specific job openings.

✔ **Your Work History Worksheet (Step 2):** For listing all of your places of employment along with any additional experience you have in your targeted field in order to decide which positions to include on your resume and which to exclude.

✔ **Your Resume Foundation (Step 2):** After you have determined which jobs to include in your resume, you will compile basic information related to each of your employers so that you can easily determine which worksheets to complete in later steps.

Using the General Worksheets

Documenting your responsibilities and achievements is the next important step. Steps 3 and 4 include various worksheets to help you catalog your generic information, document your responsibilities, and identify your significant achievements. The first three of the following general worksheets are for all job seekers; you will complete the latter three only if they are applicable. Details on each worksheet are as follows:

1. **General Worksheet** (Step 3): For your generic information (personal, education, certifications/licenses, employment, affiliations, related interests, and computer skills).

2. **Job Responsibilities bullets** (Step 3): Various exercises are included in Step 3 to help you develop your job responsibilities bullets, one by one.

3. **General Achievements Worksheet** (Step 4): Includes generic achievement questions that are applicable to almost any position.

4. **Entry-Level/New Graduate Achievements Worksheet** (Step 4): You will complete this worksheet if you do not yet have any job-related experience in your field.

5. **Supervisory Achievements Worksheet** (Step 4): For those who supervise others (with the exception of managers and executives).

6. **Management and Executive Achievements Worksheet** (Step 4): Powerful achievement questions for all who are in a management capacity.

Using the Achievement Worksheets by Profession

Step 4 also contains industry-specific worksheets, which include questions relating to a variety of position types and business functions found in most workplaces. Please do not feel intimidated by all of the worksheets. They are all-inclusive so that everyone can use this workbook; not everything is applicable to everyone. However, it is a good idea to review each worksheet and answer all questions that *are* applicable to your positions and targeted job. You will later include the bullets that are applicable to your situation and list them in order of importance to your targeted profession.

Using the Resume-Bullet Conversions

Once you answer the worksheet questions, because the questions are formulated using resume-ready language, you can easily convert the questions and answers into final resume bullets. Step 4 explains how.

Using the Action Verbs Lists

The most complete set of action verbs found anywhere is included in Step 3. The action verbs you select that are applicable to your job functions will become your bullet starters for the Professional Experience (or Employment) section of your resume. You will build on that process to create each of your resume bullets.

Using Descriptive Adjectives and Adverbs

You can use these never-before-published lists of descriptive resume adjectives and adverbs in Step 9 to further quantify your expertise, job functions, and achievements. The lists are provided to help you infuse additional descriptive word choices into the Professional Summary and Professional Experience sections of your resume and cover letter to describe how well you performed various functions.

Using the Resume ClipBullets™

Something you have not seen anywhere before, Step 6 contains easy-to-copy achievements by job function or position type with actual prewritten customizable bullets for you to select and fill in the blanks with your own unique job information. Infusing the ClipBullets into the Professional Experience section of your resume will help you perfect your resume.

CREATING YOUR PERSONAL BRAND

Infusing personal branding strategies and making your resume visually appealing can put you in a better light—if prepared professionally. Steps 8 and 9 include formatting and design instructions as well as other elements you can add into your resume to "wow" recruiters and help establish your personal brand. These strategies have consistently worked for my clients—from entry-level to executives.

DESIGNER RESUME SAMPLES

I have included in Step 9 and on the CD some unique resume designs from my *Designer Resume Gallery* that have proven to generate outstanding interview responses—much greater than the norm. These designs are the secret competitive edge I have used in my resume-writing business throughout the years to help bring clients significant results.

Because these professional designs stand out from the crowd of plain, bland resumes that employers are accustomed to receiving, clients report that prospective employers tell them they immediately stop to look at their resumes, show them around the HR office, and read them over and over. Combined with a compellingly written resume and cover letter, job seekers who use these designs frequently get called for interviews much more often than the norm.

In other words, *Step-by-Step Resumes* contains everything you need to target your resume and profession correctly, document your responsibilities, identify your achievements, design a professional sales tool that stands out from the crowd, and "wow" employers—all the elements of an interview-generating resume!

A CONFIDENCE-BUILDING SELF-DISCOVERY PROCESS

In addition to helping you write the best resume for your profession, the *Step-by-Step Resumes* process is also an empowering personal growth tool that can ultimately help you land the position you want and be more fulfilled with your job regardless of your professional level or position title.

Once you complete your customized, compelling, interview-generating resume, you will have in your hands a high-end marketing sales tool to sell your product—yourself. And like any other salesperson, knowing the product thoroughly helps one to better sell it.

Many clients have told me that completing these worksheets became a catharsis for them—an in-depth self-discovery learning process that provided them with full product knowledge of their most precious commodity: themselves.

Why? Because it is soul-searching. It is confidence-building. The simple how-to process itself is revolutionary and groundbreaking. It makes people think of—and helps them to reflect upon—everything they have learned and accomplished through the years—their vast store of knowledge in their field and their many personal attributes, skills, and talents that have helped them to get there. And as a result, they realize their full worth and potential.

Excellent Interview Preparation

What does all this do for you? It is also excellent interview preparation. Full product knowledge about yourself helps you to prepare for the interview *before* you are in front of the prospective employer. It has helped clients catapult their careers and lives forward by empowering them to walk into interviews knowing they are highly capable, which in turn helps them demonstrate that they are the right candidate for the job. And when my clients have felt that confident about themselves, their commanding presence has helped them prove they are capable and deserve a higher salary than other candidates. It has also given them renewed enthusiasm for the job search and the ability to land the job they really want sooner.

There are reasons for this. Did you know that it is usually not the more skilled applicant who wins the job, but the one who presents himself or herself in a better light? The one whose resume stands out from the rest? The one who performs better in an interview? Putting in your best effort when you complete this 10-step process will help you reap these rewards!

The Key to Catapulting Your Career

Having a highly crafted resume that stands out from the rest, feeling confident about your abilities, and being prepared for the interview are the keys to catapulting your career and leading a more fulfilling life.

Will this be you? You might not think so now, but ask yourself that question again after you go through this 10-step process and have in your hands your completed, highly customized, well-thought-out, comprehensive, and compelling marketing tool—your resume, the end result of your efforts!

As you go through each of the self-assessment check-off lists and worksheets, stop at the end of each section to reflect upon all of your abilities, skills, talents, and knowledge. Let them entrench themselves in your psyche, fill you with self-esteem and confidence, and propel and empower you.

ACKNOWLEDGMENTS

I'd like to acknowledge Liz Benuscak, CPRW, JCTC, Executive Director of Bi-Coastal (www.bi-coastalresumes.com; 800-813-1643), who worked with me for over three years writing resumes and cover letters for clients of Creative Image Builders (formerly Desktop Publishing Plus). Some of her verbiage is inherent in my own, and hence in this book, as we worked together closely sharing ideas, strategies, and content to tackle many different client challenges.

I'd also like to acknowledge three wonderful resume and career organizations that have helped me through the years in my private practice to advance my own writing and keep abreast of changing times. They are the National Résumé Writers' Association (www.nrwa.com), the Career Management Alliance (www.careermanagementalliance.com), and Career Directors International (careerdirectors.com). All three organizations are the créme de la créme in the field. If you seek a resume writer or career coach in your area or are interested in entering this field as a resume writer or career coach, I'd highly recommend all of these organizations.

I dedicate this book to my husband, John Salvador, and five of my children (Leroy, Elisabeth, Jacqueline, Johnny, and Bruce), who have either been there for total support, provided ideas, or just endured my absence during this endeavor. Also my sister, Debra Crespi, who has provided visionary entrepreneurial strategy and expertise in my current business of selling groundbreaking resume and career products.

WHAT DO YOU WANT FROM THIS PROCESS?

Many of you are working in a profession you have become skilled at, yet you feel you are not compensated for your worth, or the job you have is not fulfilling to you in some way. And when you venture to look for other possibilities, you may find it difficult to get another job that will either help you feel more satisfied or make more money than you are currently. In a difficult economy, some of you have lost your jobs and are competing with many others for the same positions.

Others are no longer happy in the profession in which you have been working and want to change careers. Some of you are seeking a promotion, while others are entry-level and need to get your foot in the door. Whichever your situation, decide precisely what you want from this process and wholeheartedly go for it!

USING THE CD

The CD at the back of this book will save you a lot of typing, as well as provide 24 resume design templates that I have used as my secret weapon for getting clients noticed.

Installing the CD

Put the CD in your computer's CD-ROM drive and open the window for the drive. You will see a set of folders labeled **Foundations, Resume Design Templates, Sample Resumes,** and **Worksheets.** When you double-click a folder, you will either see another set of folders or a list of Word filenames. All files on the disc are in Microsoft Word format and are compatible with versions 97 and later. Double-click a filename to open the file in Word.

Using the Resume Foundations

Access these files by clicking the **Resume Summary Foundations** folder within the **Foundations** folder. You will see a set of summary foundations for writing your professional summary. Click the **Resume Format**

Foundations folder to see a foundation for each of the five main types of resumes: **Reverse-Chronological, Combination, Functional, E-mail,** and **CV.** Select the foundations that work best for you, fill in the blanks, and then use them as the starting point for your resume.

Using the Cover Letter Foundations

Click the **Cover Letter Foundations** folder within the **Foundations** folder and you will see four different templates for starting your cover letter. Use the one that works best for your situation as a basis for starting your cover letter.

Selecting Your Worksheets and Resume ClipBullets™

Personal information, employment, and generic achievement questions are contained in the General Worksheet. You can access this worksheet by clicking the **Worksheets** folder and then clicking the **General Worksheets** folder. Another general worksheet on this menu that everyone will use is the Resume Draft Worksheet.

The **Achievements Worksheets** folder contains questions from Step 4 related to specific professions and levels. Click the **Worksheets** folder and then the **Achievements Worksheets** folder. Then click the **Levels** folder and select a level-specific achievements worksheet: **Entry-Level/New Graduate, Supervisory, Management and Executive,** or **General.**

Then select one or more worksheets from the **Professions** folder as appropriate to your profession.

To access the Resume ClipBullets™, click the **Worksheets** folder and then the **Resume ClipBullets** folder. Then access the ClipBullets™ files (from Step 6) that correspond to the achievements worksheets you selected earlier.

You can open these Word files, modify the bullets as appropriate, and then copy and paste them directly into your resume.

Using the Personal Brand Worksheets

Click the **Personal Brand Worksheets** folder within the **Worksheets** folder. Follow the directions in Step 8 to use these worksheets to develop the elements of your personal brand and incorporate it into your resume.

Using the Resume Design Files

You can access all 24 of the sample designs shown in Step 10 by clicking the **Resume Design Templates** folder. Most of the resume designs are three-page documents containing a cover letter page and a two-page resume. You can add or delete pages as needed.

Sample Resumes

The sample resumes from the appendix are also available in PDF format on the CD-ROM, in the **Sample Resumes** folder.

Links to Job Boards

Also on the CD-ROM is a Word file titled **Links to Job Boards**. Open this file, press the Ctrl key, and click each link. You will be taken directly to the job boards discussed in Step 10. This saves you the work of typing each URL from the book.

step 1

Assess Yourself

- Define Your Targeted Job and Its Requirements
- Assess Your Personal Attributes
  - Instructions for Assessing Your Personal Attributes
  - How Your Primary Personal Attributes Will Be Used in Your Resume
- Assess Your Skills
  - What Are Keywords and Why Are They Important?
  - Your Areas of Expertise
  - Transferable Skills
  - Skills Assessment Areas
  - Skills Assessment Instructions for Compiling Your Areas of Expertise Section
- Compile Your Customized Areas of Expertise

DEFINE YOUR TARGETED JOB AND ITS REQUIREMENTS

The very first thing you must do before you do anything else in the resume process is to define your goal, which is simply the position title(s) you seek. In order for your resume to be effective, you need to target it toward that goal by including your most relevant skills and experience.

> **note** If you are targeting various positions that are in different fields, you will need to develop a resume variation to target each of the other positions.

Because employers hire the applicants who come closest to matching their available job descriptions, your mission in developing your resume is to show how your qualifications match as closely as possible the qualifications that your targeted position requires. A resume that is not targeted cannot achieve this, and is therefore not as effective in landing interviews.

In the box that follows, fill in the primary position title you are seeking, as well as any others you might consider in the same field.

What position(s) are you seeking? (List all possible titles within the same field.)

_____

_____

_____

_____

If you don't already have information about your target job available, you will need to do some research. Review various job postings, classified ads, Internet job boards, job descriptions, company Web sites, and so on to find position-related information regarding required qualifications, skills, and attributes for the position(s) you seek. Jot down this information in the following box. Be sure to include all important buzz words (industry jargon, also known as keywords) because those will be important *keywords* to include in your resume. Keywords are addressed later in this step.

Describe the qualifications required for the position(s) you seek.

_____

_____

_____

_____

_____

_____

_____

_____

_____

_____

Keep your goal and these qualifications in mind as you go through the resume process throughout this book. Remember, you need to come as close as possible to matching your experience and skills with these requirements.

ASSESS YOUR PERSONAL ATTRIBUTES

First, you will assess your personal attributes—your positive personal characteristics that make up who you are. Attributes help provide a personal touch and add character to your resume. They help the reader get a feel for who the person is behind the piece of paper. This list will play an important role when you're putting together your resume.

Instructions for Assessing Your Personal Attributes

1. Review the list of personal attributes on the next page. Important attributes for managers and executives are in bold.

2. Check off all attributes you feel come closest to who you are.

3. Think carefully about your profession and underline the top 10 attributes that you feel will be the most helpful to you in performing your targeted position. These will become your primary attributes.

How Your Primary Personal Attributes Will Be Used in Your Resume

You will use your primary personal attributes to build the "Professional Summary" section at the top of your resume (discussed in Step 5), when you develop your cover letter (in Step 7), and when you select some descriptive adjectives and adverbs to infuse into your resume (in Step 3). So keep them in mind for when you start to draft your resume.

Your primary attributes will also be very helpful for you to showcase during interviews and exemplify success stories of how those attributes have helped you succeed in your work. Job seekers often find completing this particular worksheet to be a self-discovery process that helps to develop or strengthen their overall job candidacy confidence. Appearing confident in any job search is a huge plus in securing the job you want.

Selecting from this comprehensive list is much easier than trying to think of attributes on your own. You will probably be surprised at just how many of these attributes apply to you!

 caution Be careful not to infuse too many attributes into your resume. A nice mix blends personal ability with professional know-how.

YOUR PERSONAL ATTRIBUTES

Check off the attributes that you feel come closest to who you are. Then review each checked item and determine which 10 attributes will help you the most in your target profession. Think in terms of which attributes set you apart from your competition—those that help you achieve successful results. Underline those. They are your primary attributes, which you will use later in the process. Boldfaced attributes are particularly important for managers and executives.

- **Able to develop loyalty in staff**
- Able to exhibit conviction
- Able to handle ambiguity
- Able to help others solve problems
- **Able to overcome adversity**
- **Able to overcome barriers and obstacles**
- Able to show good judgment
- Able to show initiative
- Able to streamline operations
- Accepting
- Accessible
- Accommodating
- Accountable
- Accurate
- **Action-driven leader**
- Active
- Adaptable
- Adventure-seeking
- Advocate
- Aesthetically inclined
- Agile
- Alert
- Ambitious
- Analytical
- **Approachable/ nonthreatening**
- Articulate
- Artistically inclined
- Assertive
- Astute
- Attentive to detail
- Authoritative
- Autonomous
- Balanced
- Budget conscious
- Calm/level-headed
- **Candid**
- Career-preneurial
- Caring
- Cautious/careful
- Challenge seeker
- Chameleon-like

- Cheerful
- Child focused
- Client focused
- Client service–oriented
- Collaborative
- Comfortable with ambiguity
- **Commanding presence**
- Committed
- Committed to excellence
- Communicative
- Community-oriented
- Compassionate
- Competent
- Competitive
- **Composed**
- Comprehensive
- Computer literate
- Conceptual
- Conciliatory
- Concise
- Confident
- **Conflict manager**
- Congenial
- Connected
- Conscientious
- Conscious of my health
- Considerate
- Consistent
- Convincing
- Cooperative
- Coordinator
- Courteous
- Crafty
- Creative
- Credible
- Critical thinker
- Cultivator
- Curious
- Customer focused
- Customer service– oriented
- Deadline conscious
- Decisive
- Dedicated
- Degreed
- **Delegator**
- Dependable

- Detail-oriented
- Devoted
- Diligent
- Diplomatic
- **Director of high- producing teams**
- Disciplined
- Discreet
- **Diversity manager**
- Down to earth
- Driven
- Dynamic
- Easy to get along with
- Easygoing
- Economical
- Educated
- Effective
- Efficiency-oriented
- Efficient
- Empathetic
- Empowered
- Empowering
- Encouraging
- Energetic
- Engaging
- Entertaining
- Enthusiastic
- Entrepreneurial
- **Ethical**
- Expeditor
- Experienced
- Expert
- Expressive
- Facilitator
- Fair
- Flexible
- Focused
- Followup-oriented
- Forward-thinking
- Friendly
- Future-oriented
- Generous
- Genuine
- Globally focused
- Goal-driven
- Good at working under pressure
- Good listener
- Hardworking

- Healthy perspective
- Helpful
- Honest
- Humanistic
- Humorous
- Imaginative
- Impartial
- Implementer
- Inclusive
- Independent
- Influencer
- Initiator
- **Innovative**
- Inquisitive
- Insightful
- **Inspiring to my team**
- Instructor
- **Integral**
- Intelligent
- International
- Intuitive
- Inventive
- Investigative
- Kind
- **Leader**
- Learning oriented
- Likable
- Logical thinker
- Loyal
- Mechanical
- Mediator
- **Mentor**
- Methodical
- Meticulous
- **Morale builder**
- Motivated
- Motivator
- Multiskilled
- Multitalented
- Multitasker
- Negotiator
- Nonjudgmental
- Nurturing
- Objective
- Observant
- Open
- Open-minded
- Open to change

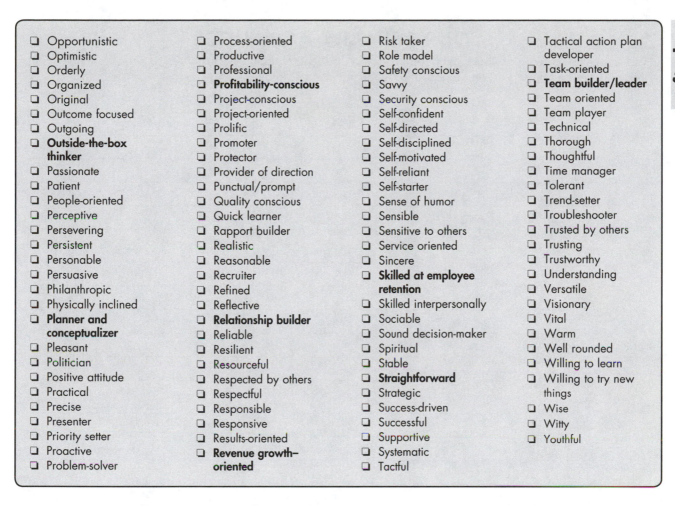

- ❏ Opportunistic
- ❏ Optimistic
- ❏ Orderly
- ❏ Organized
- ❏ Original
- ❏ Outcome focused
- ❏ Outgoing
- ❏ **Outside-the-box thinker**
- ❏ Passionate
- ❏ Patient
- ❏ People-oriented
- ❏ Perceptive
- ❏ Persevering
- ❏ Persistent
- ❏ Personable
- ❏ Persuasive
- ❏ Philanthropic
- ❏ Physically inclined
- ❏ **Planner and conceptualizer**
- ❏ Pleasant
- ❏ Politician
- ❏ Positive attitude
- ❏ Practical
- ❏ Precise
- ❏ Presenter
- ❏ Priority setter
- ❏ Proactive
- ❏ Problem-solver

- ❏ Process-oriented
- ❏ Productive
- ❏ Professional
- ❏ **Profitability-conscious**
- ❏ Project-conscious
- ❏ Project-oriented
- ❏ Prolific
- ❏ Promoter
- ❏ Protector
- ❏ Provider of direction
- ❏ Punctual/prompt
- ❏ Quality conscious
- ❏ Quick learner
- ❏ Rapport builder
- ❏ Realistic
- ❏ Reasonable
- ❏ Recruiter
- ❏ Refined
- ❏ Reflective
- ❏ **Relationship builder**
- ❏ Reliable
- ❏ Resilient
- ❏ Resourceful
- ❏ Respected by others
- ❏ Respectful
- ❏ Responsible
- ❏ Responsive
- ❏ Results-oriented
- ❏ **Revenue growth–oriented**

- ❏ Risk taker
- ❏ Role model
- ❏ Safety conscious
- ❏ Savvy
- ❏ Security conscious
- ❏ Self-confident
- ❏ Self-directed
- ❏ Self-disciplined
- ❏ Self-motivated
- ❏ Self-reliant
- ❏ Self-starter
- ❏ Sense of humor
- ❏ Sensible
- ❏ Sensitive to others
- ❏ Service oriented
- ❏ Sincere
- ❏ **Skilled at employee retention**
- ❏ Skilled interpersonally
- ❏ Sociable
- ❏ Sound decision-maker
- ❏ Spiritual
- ❏ Stable
- ❏ **Straightforward**
- ❏ Strategic
- ❏ Success-driven
- ❏ Successful
- ❏ Supportive
- ❏ Systematic
- ❏ Tactful

- ❏ Tactical action plan developer
- ❏ Task-oriented
- ❏ **Team builder/leader**
- ❏ Team oriented
- ❏ Team player
- ❏ Technical
- ❏ Thorough
- ❏ Thoughtful
- ❏ Time manager
- ❏ Tolerant
- ❏ Trend-setter
- ❏ Troubleshooter
- ❏ Trusted by others
- ❏ Trusting
- ❏ Trustworthy
- ❏ Understanding
- ❏ Versatile
- ❏ Visionary
- ❏ Vital
- ❏ Warm
- ❏ Well rounded
- ❏ Willing to learn
- ❏ Willing to try new things
- ❏ Wise
- ❏ Witty
- ❏ Youthful

On the following two pages, list the top 10 primary attributes that you underlined in this checklist.

note Not all attributes are helpful to all professions, so take some care in your selection. For example, being nurturing, flexible, accepting, and client-oriented might be excellent assets for a social worker; however, they would be a red flag for an IRS examiner. Similarly, someone who is entertaining, artistically inclined, and agile could be a good recreation therapist but not necessarily a good stockbroker. Other assets, such as work ethics, troubleshooting, productivity, and dedication, could be excellent attributes for almost any employee and profession.

Step 1

YOUR PRIMARY ATTRIBUTES

List the top 10 primary attributes that you underlined on the preceding pages. Then explain how these attributes are helpful to you on the job and beneficial to an employer.

1. _____

2. _____

3. _____

4. _____

5. _____

6. _____
_____
_____
_____
_____

7. _____
_____
_____
_____
_____

8. _____
_____
_____
_____
_____

9. _____
_____
_____
_____
_____

10. _____
_____
_____
_____
_____

ASSESS YOUR SKILLS

Selling the benefits of your product and services (you!) and matching those benefits to your target job's requirements are how you will achieve success with your resume. I want to emphasize how critical it is to target your audience correctly and identify the benefits of your services to sell to that market. Even though this is mentioned in many resume books, it is not something most people who prepare their own resumes take into consideration. Either they choose to ignore it or they do not know how to put it into effect. Not targeting your position correctly is self-defeating.

The first step in determining the benefits of your services is to assess all of your skills and identify those skills that match the needs of the prospective employers you are targeting. After you check off all of your applicable skills from a list of the most important keywords for many business functions and professions, you will know the skills you are selling, just as a successful salesperson has in-depth product knowledge about the product he or she is selling.

Successful marketing is all about first identifying the features of a product and then about determining the benefits of those features to the targeted audience. After you determine the features (skills) of your product (you), you can determine the benefits to use in selling you to your prospective employer (your target market). And that's what the resume process is all about. Most people who write their own resumes are not aware of this strategy. Instead they take a look at their background and list the job functions they have performed. That's hit and miss—usually miss.

As you continue the process in this step-by-step guide, keep in mind the following success quotient:

The Success Quotient of a Highly Successful Resume

The Product = You

The Targeted Market = Your prospective employer

The Features = Your skills, attributes, experience, achievements, education, and other qualifications

The Benefits = What will sell your product (you) to your targeted market

The Result = A highly successful resume that generates interviews

---

You know the product and the targeted market; now let's start with your features—your skills—by taking an inventory of everything you know. You will use these areas of expertise in your resume as keywords.

What Are Keywords and Why Are They Important?

Keywords are your skill areas, industry jargon, or buzz words, which are critical components of your resume, especially for larger firms that use scanning software to look for these words in your resume and determine whether to screen your resume in or out based on their presence or absence. Many employers today use this technology to determine whether you are a qualified candidate. If your resume does not contain the necessary keywords for your profession, your resume might never be seen by human eyes. Keywords are also important visual information because they qualify your expertise.

tip Use job descriptions, performance evaluations, job postings, classified ads, Web site searches, or other sources to glean important keywords to include in your Areas of Expertise section.

Your Areas of Expertise

Your Areas of Expertise section will be the second section of your resume following your Professional Summary (or Profile). It will include all of your primary skill areas (keywords) in list form. You will also infuse keywords throughout your resume and cover letter when explaining your responsibilities and achievements. When you complete this skills assessment step, you should have almost all of the keywords you will need…and probably many more.

Transferable Skills

Transferable skills are skills you have used in one profession that you can transfer over to and use in another. These and other skills could be *innate skills, learned skills,* or *function-related skills.* They are addressed in various sections of this book depending on the purpose they will serve in your resume.

✔ **Innate skills** (such as organization, creativity, leadership, diplomacy, time management, multitasking, or resourcefulness) address your personal attributes, self-management, and moral skills. These skills are the primary attributes you discovered in the preceding exercise.

✔ **Learned skills** are the specific skills you learned in your current position, another profession, college, or another part of life that are applicable to the position you are now targeting (such as research and analysis, sales, budgeting, advertising, financing, Internet marketing, production, project management, or contract writing). These job-related learned skills are addressed in this exercise, under their corresponding skill titles.

✔ **Function-related skills** can be a mix of both innate and learned skills (such as reviewing, drafting, coordinating, estimating, fabricating, managing, translating, troubleshooting, negotiating, monitoring, and surveying). You will capture these skills later in the action verbs section of Step 3, where you will use them to develop the responsibilities and achievements components of your Professional Experience section.

Skills Assessment Areas

This skills assessment section covers skill areas that will become a part of your Areas of Expertise section of your resume. This section is broken down into several main categories including the following:

✔ Management Skills

✔ Supervisory/Human Resources Skills

✔ Business Areas of Expertise

✔ Computer Skills

✔ Profession-specific Keywords

Skills Assessment Instructions for Compiling Your Areas of Expertise Section

Follow these steps to assess your skills and compile your Areas of Expertise section.

1. Review all Areas of Expertise categories on the following pages and check off all skill areas in which you have knowledge. This includes knowledge from professional experience, volunteer work, education…even hobbies and day-to-day life experience.

2. Review each of the skills you checked and underline those skills that directly target your resume objective and in which you have a high level of proficiency. The underlined skill areas—your primary areas of expertise—will become your Areas of Expertise section (in list form) in your resume.

 note You might have garnered skills within certain specialized areas (skill sets) that were not the main focus or function of your actual position. But they *are* applicable to your targeted job, so be sure to review each of the skill assessment areas. For example, you might not be a manager, but you might have performed managerial functions; you might not be in marketing, but you might have conducted market research; and so on.

3. If your Areas of Expertise section includes a list of about 12 to 20 items (more for technical or managerial professionals), you are in great shape! You might actually end up having far more than 20 items. If this is the case, there are a few ways to handle it depending on the circumstances. I will get to that later.

Go ahead and check off all skill areas with which you are familiar on the following worksheets.

Step 1

KEYWORDS/AREAS OF EXPERTISE

Review the lists of keywords and check off all skills in which you have knowledge. Double-check those skills in which you are highly proficient and that directly target your resume objective.

All keywords for your Areas of Expertise section were excerpted from Evelyn Salvador's *12,000+ Keywords by Profession Book on CD* (Creative Image Builders, $39.95). You can order the complete book containing profession-specific keywords for more than 1,300 positions using the order form at the back of this book.

Management

- ❏ Administration management
- ❏ Advertising direction
- ❏ Asset and liability management
- ❏ Budget development
- ❏ Building strategic alliances
- ❏ Business analysis
- ❏ Business case development
- ❏ Business plan development
- ❏ Business reengineering
- ❏ Business start-up
- ❏ Business strategizing
- ❏ Capital equipment budgets
- ❏ Capital improvements
- ❏ Capital projects direction
- ❏ Change management
- ❏ Client needs assessment
- ❏ Communication technology management
- ❏ Competitive analysis
- ❏ Competitive edge
- ❏ Compliance direction
- ❏ Consortiums
- ❏ Contract negotiations and development
- ❏ Corporate administration
- ❏ Corporate development
- ❏ Corporate image development
- ❏ Corporate missions
- ❏ Corporate reorganization/ restructuring
- ❏ Costing and budgeting
- ❏ Cross-functional direction
- ❏ Customer referrals and retention
- ❏ Customer service improvement and initiatives
- ❏ Customer service management
- ❏ Decision-making direction
- ❏ Directing high-producing teams
- ❏ Distribution management
- ❏ Diversity management
- ❏ Divestiture
- ❏ Due diligence
- ❏ e-commerce management
- ❏ Efficiency improvement

- ❏ Executive management
- ❏ Facilities management
- ❏ Financial management
- ❏ Financial strategies
- ❏ Fiscal management direction
- ❏ Forecasting marketplace trends
- ❏ Global markets
- ❏ Human resources management
- ❏ Information delivery systems direction
- ❏ Information technology direction
- ❏ Information technology initiatives
- ❏ Inventory management
- ❏ Leadership development
- ❏ Logistics management
- ❏ Long-range planning
- ❏ Low staff turnover
- ❏ Management by objectives
- ❏ Manufacturing direction
- ❏ Market strategy
- ❏ Marketing direction
- ❏ Media involvement
- ❏ Mergers and acquisitions
- ❏ Mission statements
- ❏ Multimillion-dollar profit and loss direction
- ❏ Multisite management
- ❏ National/regional account management
- ❏ National/regional sales
- ❏ Negotiations
- ❏ Networking
- ❏ New business development
- ❏ New market identification
- ❏ New product lines
- ❏ Office management
- ❏ Open lines of communication
- ❏ Operations management
- ❏ Organizational restructuring
- ❏ Personnel management
- ❏ Policy formulation
- ❏ Proactive management
- ❏ Procedure development
- ❏ Product analysis and development

- ❏ Production management
- ❏ Productivity improvement
- ❏ Profit and loss management
- ❏ Profit margin increases
- ❏ Program development
- ❏ Project management
- ❏ Public relations
- ❏ Public speaking
- ❏ Purchasing management
- ❏ Quality assurance/quality control management
- ❏ Quality improvement
- ❏ Relationship building
- ❏ Research and development
- ❏ Return on investment
- ❏ Revenue growth
- ❏ Risk management
- ❏ Safety and risk management
- ❏ Sales and marketing campaigns
- ❏ Sales and pricing analysis
- ❏ Sales direction
- ❏ Sales forecasting
- ❏ Servant leadership
- ❏ Staff coaching and mentoring
- ❏ Staff leadership development
- ❏ Staff recruitment
- ❏ Staff scheduling
- ❏ Staff training and development
- ❏ Start-up operations
- ❏ Strategic alliances
- ❏ Strategic planning direction
- ❏ Strategic vision
- ❏ Strategizing client needs
- ❏ Team building
- ❏ Technology planning and direction
- ❏ Telecommunications direction
- ❏ Training and development direction
- ❏ Turnaround management
- ❏ Venture capital financing
- ❏ Visionary strategies
- ❏ Warehouse management

Supervisory/Human Resources

- Affirmative Action laws
- Affirmative Action program plan development
- Allocation of staff resources
- Applicant screening and testing
- Benefits administration
- Benefits and risk management
- Budget development and management
- Career counseling
- Career development activities direction
- Childcare/elder care
- Claims administration
- Coaching and motivating winning teams
- Collective bargaining agreements
- Compensation programs
- Delegation and follow-up
- Disability insurance
- Discipline issues
- Dispute resolution
- Diversity management
- Drug testing
- Employee assistance and wellness programs
- Employee benefits program administration
- Employee contracts
- Employee evaluations
- Employee grievance systems
- Employee incentive programs
- Employee orientation
- Employee records systems
- Employee relations
- Employee selection
- Employee suggestion systems
- Employment marketing programs

- Equal Employment Opportunity (EEO)
- Equal Employment Opportunity grievance investigations and resolution
- Executive development programs
- Fair and equitable pay rate policies
- Federal and state legislation
- Interviewing
- Health insurance packages
- Human resource administration
- Human resource management consultation
- Human resource program management
- Human resource systems planning and implementation
- Interviewing
- Job analysis
- Job classification concepts
- Job descriptions
- Job evaluation methods
- Labor arbitration
- Labor laws
- Labor policies
- Labor relations
- Lawsuit settlements
- Long-term disability
- Low staff turnover
- Management advisement
- Management training and development
- Manpower forecasting and planning
- Maximizing employee potential
- Medical examinations
- Mergers and acquisitions assistance

- New hire training
- Occupational Safety and Health (OSHA) standards
- On-the-job training
- Orientation sessions
- Payroll operations
- Pensions
- Performance appraisal development
- Personnel handbook
- Personnel management
- Policy formulation
- Position classifications
- Problem-solving
- Productivity improvement
- Program compliance
- Recruitment
- Recruitment initiatives
- Regulatory affairs compliance
- Reward systems development
- Salary administration systems
- Settlement negotiations
- Staff scheduling
- Staff supervision
- Staff training and development
- Strategic planning
- Team building
- Train-the-trainer programs
- Training and development programs
- Transportation programs
- Unemployment insurance
- Union negotiations
- Union practices
- Union relations
- Wage and salary administration
- Wage negotiations
- Workers' Compensation
- Workshops

(continued)

KEYWORDS/AREAS OF EXPERTISE (continued)
Administrative, Operations, and General Business

- Budget administration
- Budget development
- Building/lease contracts
- Business analysis
- Business plans
- Business start-up
- Client relations
- Communications
- Contract development
- Contract negotiations
- Correspondence
- Customer service
- Goods transfers
- Manufacturing

- Materials scheduling
- Merchandising
- Negotiations
- Networking
- Operations
- Policy and procedure development
- Product/service delivery
- Production
- Productivity improvement
- Project development
- Project life cycle
- Project prioritizing
- Project scheduling

- Purchasing
- Quality assurance
- Quality control
- Recordkeeping
- Research and analysis
- Stock distribution
- Strategizing client needs
- Transportation
- Travel arrangements
- Vendor relations
- Word processing
- Workflow management
- Writing

Advertising

- Account management
- Ad development
- Advertising promotions
- Advertising sales
- Animation
- Communication media
- Conceptualizing
- Coordination of audience, message, and medium
- Copy writing and editing
- Corporate image projection
- Creative problem-solving

- Desktop publishing
- Digital video recording
- E-commerce
- Graphic design
- Idea generation
- Layout and design
- Maintaining account base
- Marketing campaigns
- Media selection
- Multimedia advertising
- Multimedia production
- Newspaper advertising

- Photo composites
- Photography
- Presentations
- Print technology
- Public relations
- Radio advertising
- Retail advertising
- Scanning and retouching
- Television advertising
- Typesetting
- Visual communications
- Web site development

Compliance

- Analytical instrumentation troubleshooting
- Audit plan development
- Biological functions
- Documentation review
- Environmental protection
- Equipment maintenance, validation, and calibration
- FDA compliance
- Finished goods testing
- Finished product releases
- Good manufacturing practices
- In-process testing
- Internal and external review processes

- Inventory audits
- Labeling audits
- Laboratory testing review
- Manufacturing audits
- Methods development
- Microbiology testing systems
- Packaging audits
- Pollution control
- Preformulation studies
- Product inspection programs
- Product liability lawsuits
- Product quality concerns
- Product test data
- Production
- QA Performance Reports

- QA/QC conceptualization
- QA/QC documentation
- QA/QC implementation
- QA/QC programs and systems
- Quality assurance audits
- Quality control product review process development
- Raw materials testing
- Recall risk elimination
- Release specifications testing
- Stability testing and studies
- Statistical QA programs
- Technology transfers
- Validation
- Vendor indemnification programs

Finance and Accounting

- ❏ Accounts payable
- ❏ Accounts receivable
- ❏ Auditing
- ❏ Bank reconciliations
- ❏ Bookkeeping
- ❏ Budget analysis
- ❏ Budget development
- ❏ Cash control
- ❏ Cash-flow projections
- ❏ Client investments
- ❏ Compliance
- ❏ Corporate governance
- ❏ Corporate taxes
- ❏ Costing
- ❏ Data collection
- ❏ Due diligence
- ❏ Estate taxes and planning
- ❏ Federal tax laws
- ❏ Financial audits
- ❏ Financial management
- ❏ Financial planning
- ❏ Financial statements
- ❏ Financing
- ❏ General accounting
- ❏ General ledger
- ❏ Government accounting
- ❏ Income tax returns
- ❏ Information technology consulting
- ❏ Inventory control
- ❏ Invoicing/client billing
- ❏ Job estimating
- ❏ Journal entries
- ❏ Lines of credit
- ❏ Management accounting
- ❏ Market analysis and assessment
- ❏ Mergers and acquisitions
- ❏ Negotiations
- ❏ Payroll processing
- ❏ Payroll tax returns
- ❏ Payroll worksheets
- ❏ Portfolio profitability retention
- ❏ Product/service delivery
- ❏ Productivity improvement
- ❏ Profit and loss responsibilities
- ❏ Public accounting
- ❏ Quality assurance
- ❏ Recordkeeping
- ❏ Research and analysis
- ❏ Revenue growth
- ❏ Sales forecasting
- ❏ Sales tax returns
- ❏ Schedules of depreciation
- ❏ Stock exchange recorder
- ❏ Tax and compliance audits
- ❏ Tax planning and consulting
- ❏ Taxes
- ❏ Workers' Compensation
- ❏ Year-end tax closings

Manufacturing and Production

- ❏ Assembly
- ❏ Automated manufacturing
- ❏ Blueprint reading
- ❏ Capacity planning
- ❏ Capital budget
- ❏ Compliance
- ❏ Computer-integrated manufacturing
- ❏ Cost-reduction programs
- ❏ Cost/return analysis
- ❏ Costing
- ❏ Customer needs assessment
- ❏ Customer order tracking systems development
- ❏ Customer satisfaction
- ❏ Distribution
- ❏ Distribution management
- ❏ Electromechanical equipment
- ❏ Electronic production schedules
- ❏ Engineering
- ❏ Equipment maintenance and repair
- ❏ Equipment operation
- ❏ Equipment validation
- ❏ Fabricating
- ❏ Finished goods
- ❏ Fulfillment
- ❏ Inventory control
- ❏ Inventory control management
- ❏ Labeling
- ❏ Logistics
- ❏ Low incident rates
- ❏ Machines set-up
- ❏ Manpower coverage
- ❏ Manufacturing procedures evaluations
- ❏ Manufacturing scale processes
- ❏ Materials management
- ❏ Materials scheduling
- ❏ Merchandise pricing
- ❏ Methods development
- ❏ On-time delivery improvement
- ❏ Order processing
- ❏ Packaging
- ❏ Packing materials inspections
- ❏ Pilot manufacturing
- ❏ Pilot scale processes
- ❏ P&L responsibilities
- ❏ Plant operations management
- ❏ Precision measuring instruments
- ❏ Process validation
- ❏ Product batch record documentation
- ❏ Product development
- ❏ Product implementation
- ❏ Product release tracking
- ❏ Product testing
- ❏ Product validation
- ❏ Production gains
- ❏ Production scheduling
- ❏ Productivity improvement
- ❏ Productivity monitoring
- ❏ Productivity monitoring systems development
- ❏ Prototype assembly
- ❏ Purchasing cost reductions
- ❏ Quality assurance
- ❏ Quality control
- ❏ Quality workmanship
- ❏ Raw materials purchasing
- ❏ Safety performance
- ❏ Shipping initiatives
- ❏ Specification documentation
- ❏ Stability testing
- ❏ Systems validation
- ❏ Technical support
- ❏ Trackable work order systems development
- ❏ Visual inspections
- ❏ Warehouse management
- ❏ Warehousing
- ❏ Workload forecasting

(continued)

KEYWORDS/AREAS OF EXPERTISE (continued)
Information Technology Management

- ❑ Account management
- ❑ Automated solutions direction
- ❑ Business case development
- ❑ Business start-ups
- ❑ Business strategizing
- ❑ Capacity planning
- ❑ Capital equipment budgets
- ❑ Communication technology management
- ❑ Competitive edge in technology
- ❑ Contract negotiations
- ❑ Data management
- ❑ Database management systems
- ❑ Diversified services
- ❑ Forecasting
- ❑ Global IT services
- ❑ Hardware acquisitions
- ❑ Information delivery systems direction

- ❑ Information resources policies and procedures
- ❑ Information systems management
- ❑ IT direction
- ❑ IT initiatives
- ❑ Local area network (LAN) management
- ❑ Long-term IT planning
- ❑ Market strategy
- ❑ Multimillion-dollar P&L direction
- ❑ Multiple technology areas management
- ❑ National IT services
- ❑ New market identification
- ❑ New product lines
- ❑ Policy formulation
- ❑ Project management
- ❑ Risk management

- ❑ Satellite/wideband communications direction
- ❑ Strategic IT vision
- ❑ System requirements establishment
- ❑ Technology planning and direction
- ❑ Technology standards development
- ❑ Telecommunications systems management
- ❑ Training direction
- ❑ Visionary strategies
- ❑ Voice and data communications management
- ❑ Web site presence
- ❑ Wide area network (WAN) management
- ❑ Wireless network management

Marketing and Public Relations

- ❑ Campaign management
- ❑ Community relations
- ❑ Competitive analysis
- ❑ Competitive product positioning
- ❑ Data collection
- ❑ Demographic/psychographic analysis
- ❑ Direct-mail marketing
- ❑ Direct-response marketing
- ❑ Drafting speeches
- ❑ e-commerce
- ❑ Economic trends
- ❑ Editorials
- ❑ Fund-raising benefits
- ❑ Incentive planning
- ❑ Internet marketing and research
- ❑ Market analysis and assessment
- ❑ Market development
- ❑ Market identification
- ❑ Market launch

- ❑ Market positioning
- ❑ Market research
- ❑ Market share ratings
- ❑ Market surveys
- ❑ Market trend forecasting
- ❑ Marketing strategy
- ❑ Media analysis
- ❑ Media-friendly materials
- ❑ Media packets
- ❑ Media relations
- ❑ Media sources
- ❑ New market identification
- ❑ News coverage
- ❑ Political trends
- ❑ Press releases
- ❑ Product analysis
- ❑ Product development
- ❑ Product launch
- ❑ Product lifecycle management
- ❑ Product positioning

- ❑ Product presentations
- ❑ Product testing
- ❑ Promotions and campaigns
- ❑ Public contacts
- ❑ Public relations strategies
- ❑ Public speaking
- ❑ Publicity programs
- ❑ Script development
- ❑ Social trends
- ❑ Special events coordination
- ❑ Special-interest groups
- ❑ Spokesperson
- ❑ Sports reporting
- ❑ Strategizing client needs
- ❑ Trade shows
- ❑ Trend analysis
- ❑ Trends forecasting
- ❑ Working with the press/media

Purchasing

- ❏ Acquisition Management
- ❏ Adjustments
- ❏ Barter arrangements
- ❏ Bidding
- ❏ Blanket orders
- ❏ Capital equipment acquisition
- ❏ Client interface
- ❏ Client and vendor records maintenance
- ❏ Comparative cost analyses
- ❏ Competitive bidding
- ❏ Computer equipment
- ❏ Contract change orders
- ❏ Contract terms and negotiations
- ❏ Delivery scheduling
- ❏ Distribution management
- ❏ Expediting
- ❏ High-volume processing

- ❏ International trade
- ❏ Inventory control/management
- ❏ Leasing
- ❏ Logistics management
- ❏ Materials management
- ❏ Materials replenishment ordering (MRO)
- ❏ Merchandise components pricing and purchasing
- ❏ Merchandise sales projections
- ❏ Merchandising
- ❏ Negotiations
- ❏ Office machinery
- ❏ Office supplies
- ❏ Order processing
- ❏ Overseas importing
- ❏ Phone systems
- ❏ Pricing negotiations

- ❏ Procurement
- ❏ Production materials
- ❏ Production schedule monitoring
- ❏ Production scheduling
- ❏ Promotional items
- ❏ Purchase orders
- ❏ Purchasing
- ❏ Requests for proposals (RFPs)
- ❏ Requests for quotations (RFQs)
- ❏ Strong follow-up
- ❏ Supplier management
- ❏ Trade shows
- ❏ Vendor bids
- ❏ Vendor partnerships
- ❏ Vendor relations
- ❏ Warehouse management
- ❏ Warehousing

Sales

- ❏ Account development
- ❏ Account management
- ❏ Account retention
- ❏ Account servicing
- ❏ Brand management
- ❏ Brand share
- ❏ Business development
- ❏ Client relations
- ❏ Competitive analysis
- ❏ Competitive profiles
- ❏ Consultative sales
- ❏ Consumer values
- ❏ Contract negotiations
- ❏ Conversion of customer desires into needs
- ❏ Costing and budgeting
- ❏ Creative sales techniques
- ❏ Cross-selling
- ❏ Customer-focused service
- ❏ Customer needs assessment
- ❏ Customer retention
- ❏ Customer satisfaction
- ❏ Customer service
- ❏ Demand forecasting
- ❏ Demographic analysis
- ❏ Direct sales
- ❏ Distributor networks

- ❏ Field sales management
- ❏ Fiscal controls
- ❏ Forecasting marketplace trends
- ❏ Fulfillment
- ❏ Global markets/sales
- ❏ Growth strategies
- ❏ High referral base
- ❏ Indirect sales
- ❏ Key account management
- ❏ Lead development and generation
- ❏ Maintaining account base
- ❏ Market expansion
- ❏ National account management
- ❏ National sales
- ❏ Negotiations
- ❏ Network development
- ❏ New business development
- ❏ New product introductions
- ❏ Niche markets
- ❏ Post-sales support
- ❏ Presentations
- ❏ Pricing and sales analysis
- ❏ Profit and loss (P&L) management
- ❏ Profit maximization
- ❏ Prospecting/cold calling

- ❏ Relationship building
- ❏ Repeat business
- ❏ Resolving client concerns
- ❏ Retail management
- ❏ Revenue growth
- ❏ Revenue stream
- ❏ Sales cycle management
- ❏ Sales forecasting
- ❏ Sales incentive programs
- ❏ Sales management
- ❏ Sales strategies
- ❏ Sales team management
- ❏ Sales training
- ❏ Solution selling
- ❏ Strategic alliances
- ❏ Strategic planning
- ❏ Strategizing customer needs
- ❏ Strong closer
- ❏ Strong follow-up
- ❏ Telemarketing
- ❏ Territory development
- ❏ Territory management
- ❏ Top producer
- ❏ Trade shows
- ❏ Value-added sales
- ❏ Warehouse management

(continued)

KEYWORDS/AREAS OF EXPERTISE *(continued)*
Secretarial/Office Support

- Activity coordination
- Administrative functions
- Appointment scheduling
- Assignment oversight
- Billing
- Bookkeeping
- Budget monitoring
- Complex information interpretation
- Complex tasks
- Conference coordination
- Confidential matters
- Correspondence writing
- Customer complaint handling
- Customer service and support
- Dictation and transcription
- Document processing
- E-mail generation

- Event coordination
- Exercising discretion
- Filing
- Financial recordkeeping
- Financial transactions
- Greeting visitors
- Handling multiple projects
- Independent judgment
- Keyboarding
- Legal secretarial support
- Letter composition
- Management liaison
- Medical secretarial support
- Medical terminology
- Meeting scheduling
- Memoranda
- Minutes of meetings

- Nonroutine secretarial functions
- Office management
- Office support
- Problem resolution
- Procedure development
- Public relations contacts
- Recordkeeping
- Report generation
- Report preparation
- Research and analysis
- Sales contracts
- Screening callers and visitors
- Shorthand
- Spreadsheets
- Support staff supervision
- Telephone answering
- Word processing

Training and Development

- Adjunct training materials
- Budget development and management
- Career development activities
- Compliance
- Computer-assisted training courses
- Consultation
- Course materials
- Coursework development
- Employee assistance
- Employee counseling
- Implementation
- Instructor training seminars
- Long-range strategizing
- Management consultation

- Management practices
- Management trainee programs
- Management training and development
- Maximizing employee potential
- Monitoring training
- New hire training centers
- On-the-job training programs
- Organizational development
- Orientation sessions
- Planning
- Program compliance
- Program development
- Program scheduling
- Specialized training courses

- Staff training and development
- Strategic planning
- Train-the-trainer programs
- Training classes
- Training concepts, practices, and theories
- Training coordination
- Training and development programs
- Training direction
- Training needs assessments
- Video instructional courses
- Workshops

COMPUTER SKILLS

Hardware/Operating System Platforms

- ❏ PC
- ❏ Macintosh
- ❏ Amdahl Mainframe
- ❏ Cabling
- ❏ CD writers
- ❏ Ethernet devices
- ❏ Expansion boards
- ❏ Firewalls
- ❏ Hard drives
- ❏ Handheld devices
- ❏ Hardware upgrades

- ❏ HP-UX
- ❏ Hubs
- ❏ IBM AS/400
- ❏ IBM desktops
- ❏ IBM mainframe
- ❏ IBM RS/6000
- ❏ KVM switches
- ❏ LANs
- ❏ Laptops
- ❏ Modems
- ❏ Motherboards

- ❏ MVS
- ❏ Network configurations
- ❏ Network interfaces
- ❏ NIC cards
- ❏ PC hardware configuration
- ❏ Peripheral hookups
- ❏ Printers
- ❏ Rack systems

- ❏ Random Access Memory (RAM)
- ❏ Routers
- ❏ Scanners/imaging devices
- ❏ Servers
- ❏ SUN Solaris
- ❏ Tandem
- ❏ Unisys mainframe
- ❏ USB ports

Operating Systems

- ❏ Windows
- ❏ Apple Macintosh OS
- ❏ Microsoft Proxy Server
- ❏ Linux

- ❏ Novell OS
- ❏ PSOS
- ❏ Solaris
- ❏ TCL

- ❏ UNIX OS
- ❏ VXWorks
- ❏ Installation
- ❏ Upgrading

- ❏ Troubleshooting
- ❏ Conflict resolution
- ❏ Monitor calibration

Word Processing/Presentation/Database Programs

- ❏ Microsoft Access
- ❏ Microsoft Office Suite
- ❏ Microsoft PowerPoint

- ❏ Microsoft Word
- ❏ Microsoft Works
- ❏ Lotus WordPro

- ❏ Corel WordPerfect
- ❏ Foxbase+
- ❏ Filemaker Pro

Accounting/Spreadsheet/Legal Programs

- ❏ LexisNexis
- ❏ Lotus 1-2-3
- ❏ Lotus SmartSuite
- ❏ Microsoft Excel

- ❏ MYOB Account Edge
- ❏ QuickBooks Pro
- ❏ Quicken
- ❏ Real World

- ❏ Skyline Property Management
- ❏ TurboTax Deluxe
- ❏ Westlaw

Graphic Design/Digital Imaging Programs

- ❏ Adobe Illustrator
- ❏ Adobe InDesign
- ❏ Adobe Pagemaker
- ❏ Adobe Photoshop

- ❏ Computer-aided design and drafting (CADD)
- ❏ Extensis QX-Tools Pro
- ❏ Fractal Design Painter
- ❏ Microsoft Publisher

- ❏ Multi-Ad Creator
- ❏ PhotoVista
- ❏ Photoshop Plug-ins
- ❏ Quark Publishing System
- ❏ QuarkXPress

Programming

- ❏ ABAP
- ❏ ActionScript
- ❏ C
- ❏ C++
- ❏ Delphi
- ❏ Go
- ❏ Java

- ❏ JavaScript
- ❏ Logo
- ❏ Lua
- ❏ MATLAB
- ❏ Objective-C
- ❏ Pascal
- ❏ Perl

- ❏ PHP
- ❏ PL/SQL
- ❏ Ruby
- ❏ SAS
- ❏ VisualBasic.NET
- ❏ XML

Step 1

PROFESSION-SPECIFIC KEYWORDS

Just as your management, supervisory, and business skills are important, if you are in a field other than those included on the preceding pages, it is important to identify all of your skills in that area. In the following spaces, list all of your areas of expertise in your industry.

- ❏ _____
- ❏ _____
- ❏ _____
- ❏ _____
- ❏ _____
- ❏ _____
- ❏ _____
- ❏ _____
- ❏ _____
- ❏ _____
- ❏ _____
- ❏ _____
- ❏ _____
- ❏ _____

- ❏ _____
- ❏ _____
- ❏ _____
- ❏ _____
- ❏ _____
- ❏ _____
- ❏ _____
- ❏ _____
- ❏ _____
- ❏ _____
- ❏ _____
- ❏ _____
- ❏ _____
- ❏ _____

- ❏ _____
- ❏ _____
- ❏ _____
- ❏ _____
- ❏ _____
- ❏ _____
- ❏ _____
- ❏ _____
- ❏ _____
- ❏ _____
- ❏ _____
- ❏ _____
- ❏ _____
- ❏ _____

You can obtain the profession-specific keywords for your specific industry from Evelyn Salvador's book on CD, 12,000+ Keywords by Profession (Creative Image Builders), by using the order form at the end of this book.

COMPILE YOUR CUSTOMIZED AREAS OF EXPERTISE

Now that you have completed the skills assessment exercise, here's the good news: Your final Areas of Expertise section needs to contain only about 12 to 20 items. If you have many more, that's fine, too, but first check each to be sure that the ones you include are targeted to and required in the position you seek. Omit any irrelevant, less important, or redundant skills.

Follow these instructions to pull together the "Areas of Expertise" section of your resume. (Please read all steps first before proceeding.)

1. Transfer all your primary (underlined) attributes from pages 6–7 into the Areas of Expertise section on the next page. When you start to compile your first draft (in Step 5), you will put this information directly into your resume. (You will use some of the other items you checked in your Professional Experience section, which you will build in Step 4.)

2. If you find that your list is long (more than 20 items), first eliminate any of the more mundane or understood items, especially those that might fall within the realm of another profession. For example, an attorney might have checked off "Presenting of evidence" and "Defense litigation." Because in order to litigate, one must present evidence, "Presenting of evidence" is redundant and can be eliminated. (On the other hand, if you are new to the profession and have few skills, leaving in the additional one or two would be beneficial.)

   Then, consider breaking up your expertise into two or more areas and categorizing them, giving them titles such as "Social Work Areas of Expertise," "Counseling Strengths," and "Technical Proficiencies."

3. Number the remaining items according to their importance in your field—that is, the order in which you will later list them in your resume draft (but without numbers)—under your Areas of Expertise section.

4. If your profession is very technical in nature (such as Information Technology Specialist or Scientist), it is also acceptable to list all of your skill proficiencies on a separate (last) page of your resume and include only the primary ones in your main Areas of Expertise and Professional Summary sections on page 1 of your resume. (Professional Summaries are covered in Step 5.)

5. If you are a management professional, you may not want to include every skill you checked. Obviously, you will have many. Instead, cross off the ones that will be understood to be within your realm of responsibility (for example, skills or functions your subordinates would be required to fulfill, unless, of course, it is important to note your hands-on abilities as well).

6. You will also include your primary skills in your cover letter (addressed in Step 7).

7. If you have many items, another way to portray your expertise is to select three or four of your main skill areas and center them across one line under your contact information. For example, a sales executive might use this format:

Sales • Marketing • New Business Development

That's it for the Areas of Expertise section. Be sure to keep all of your targeted skills in mind as you develop your resume, as well as during the interview phase of your job search.

YOUR CUSTOMIZED AREAS OF EXPERTISE

Areas of Expertise

Include all of your profession-specific keywords first.

❏ _____   ❏ _____   ❏ _____
❏ _____   ❏ _____   ❏ _____
❏ _____   ❏ _____   ❏ _____
❏ _____   ❏ _____   ❏ _____
❏ _____   ❏ _____   ❏ _____
❏ _____   ❏ _____   ❏ _____
❏ _____   ❏ _____   ❏ _____
❏ _____   ❏ _____   ❏ _____

Management/Supervisory Expertise

❏ _____   ❏ _____   ❏ _____
❏ _____   ❏ _____   ❏ _____
❏ _____   ❏ _____   ❏ _____
❏ _____   ❏ _____   ❏ _____
❏ _____   ❏ _____   ❏ _____

Technical Proficiency

❏ _____   ❏ _____   ❏ _____
❏ _____   ❏ _____   ❏ _____
❏ _____   ❏ _____   ❏ _____
❏ _____   ❏ _____   ❏ _____
❏ _____   ❏ _____   ❏ _____

Other Areas of Strength: _____

(List the appropriate category.)

❏ _____   ❏ _____   ❏ _____
❏ _____   ❏ _____   ❏ _____
❏ _____   ❏ _____   ❏ _____
❏ _____   ❏ _____   ❏ _____
❏ _____   ❏ _____   ❏ _____
❏ _____   ❏ _____   ❏ _____
❏ _____   ❏ _____   ❏ _____
❏ _____   ❏ _____   ❏ _____

step 2

Set Your Resume Strategy

- Decide What to Include
- Outline Your Work History
- Select Your Relevant Experience
- Select Your Resume Format
  - Reverse-Chronological
  - Functional
  - Combination
  - Curriculum Vitae (CV)

DECIDE WHAT TO INCLUDE

The first step in the preparation of your resume is to strategize and determine what information to include, what to exclude, and what format you will use in the final resume. Although this step can be a little tricky because it is thought-provoking, it is the most critical because it will become the foundation of your resume. Just like a home might be beautiful to the eye, if the foundation is not solid, it will not stand up on its own. So review the components of this step carefully and thoroughly.

Strategizing is an all-important first action because if you muddy up your resume with too much experience, show several jobs that were for short periods of time, or include jobs that are not in sync with your target job, this is a red flag for prospective employers. Your resume might be screened out rather than screened in. The first step employers take when reviewing resumes is to determine which ones to "screen out." You want to be sure you pass that stage with flying colors. And at the same time, you need to be factual about all of your information in order to create the right fit between you and the employer. (Also keep in mind that obtaining a position with falsified information is grounds for dismissal at many firms.)

How many positions should you include? This may seem like an odd question at first. You might think you have what experience you have and that is what you should include. Not so.

Employers often size up applicants based on what they see on the resume. If they see too few positions or the resume looks scant or lean, they might at first glance think the applicant is not qualified. And if you include too many positions (especially in different fields), it can lead the employer to look at you as a job hopper or one who isn't in touch with what he or she is seeking—and your resume might be screened out.

Experience has shown that a successful resume includes from two to five positions, which are described to their fullest (in a concise fashion) in your resume. If you have more or fewer jobs than the two-to-five range, you will want to adjust the way the information "looks" (that is, is notated and grouped) on your resume. You want to include what is targeted to your job objective and omit or move (perhaps to a later section of your resume) what is not.

Here are some examples:

✔ If you are entry level and have only one part-time position, you can include everything you have done that is related to your targeted profession—that is, volunteer work, personal interests, intern-ships, and so on. You can write them up as fully as you would a full-time position.

✔ If you have more than five positions, I suggest grouping or organizing the information so that it looks like no more than five positions (more on that later in this step). The way the information is presented determines how compelling you may or may not look to the employer.

OUTLINE YOUR WORK HISTORY

The way you determine what to include is by first outlining all of your job history. Do that now. In the worksheet that follows, list every place you have worked (including internships, part-time work, freelance jobs, volunteer work, and other activities where you have gained experience), along with the years you were there and your job titles.

Examples: An auto mechanic might never have worked at a car-repair shop; however, he or she might have worked on many of his own, his friends', or his family's cars. That is credible experience, especially when you're showcasing what you are able to tackle.

Similarly, a homemaker might have performed volunteer work for the PTA or other organizations. His or her household expertise could be beneficial in several positions, such as organization skills for an administrative job, creative menu selections for an entry-level catering position, bill paying for a bookkeeping position, supervisory skills for managing teenagers, and so on.

A teacher might have performed internship work to get his or her degree and might have had experience working with students, assisting teachers, and even developing lesson plans or thematic units, for example. He or she might also have instructed others in the corporate world, worked as a counselor at a summer camp, babysat using creative discipline methods that worked, and so on. Those feats are indeed credible experience.

YOUR WORK HISTORY
Paid Positions and Internships

❏ _____ – _____   Job Title:_____

Organization:_____

Primary Functions:_____

❏ _____ – _____   Job Title:_____

Organization:_____

Primary Functions:_____

❏ _____ – _____   Job Title:_____

Organization:_____

Primary Functions:_____

❏ _____ – _____   Job Title:_____

Organization:_____

Primary Functions:_____

❏ _____ – _____   Job Title:_____

Organization:_____

Primary Functions:_____

❏ _____ – _____   Job Title:_____

Organization:_____

Primary Functions:_____

(continued)

(continued)

❑ _____–_____   Job Title:_____

Organization:_____

Primary Functions:_____

❑ _____–_____   Job Title:_____

Organization:_____

Primary Functions:_____

❑ _____–_____   Job Title:_____

Organization:_____

Primary Functions:_____

Volunteer Work

❑ _____–_____   Function:_____

Organization:_____

❑ _____–_____   Function:_____

Organization:_____

❑ _____–_____   Function:_____

Organization:_____

❑ _____–_____   Function:_____

Organization:_____

Other Activities Where You Have Gained Experience

❑ _____

❑ _____

❑ _____

❑ _____

❑ _____

❑ _____

❑ _____

❑ _____

❑ _____

❑ _____

❑ _____

❑ _____

❑ _____

❑ _____

SELECT YOUR RELEVANT EXPERIENCE

Now you need to determine which positions to include in your resume and which ones to exclude and how you will group and present that information. Each step is important to your resume foundation, so do not omit any of them!

1. **Check off targeted positions.** Take a look at each of the positions you listed on pages 23–24 and check all that are applicable to your targeted profession. You will probably include almost all of these.

2. **Check for gaps.** If you included only the targeted positions and excluded other unrelated jobs where you worked less than a year, does your work chronology show gaps? If not, delete the unrelated position(s).

    note If you are asked during an interview whether you have had any other positions that are not on your resume, it should be acceptable to state that you took a temporary position between others that was not applicable to your job target and, therefore, not appropriate to include on your resume.

   For example, if you worked at one place from 2000 to 2002, at another in 2002, and at a third from 2003 to 2010, if the short job in 2002 was left out, your resume would not show a gap because resumes are generally written to show years only. If no gap will show, you can cross the unrelated job off of your list.

3. **Determine targeted functions in unrelated jobs.** If deleting the unrelated job would have caused a gap and you included it, are there any functions whatsoever that you performed in that position that can be related somehow to the position you are now targeting—even just a small percentage of your work? If so, leave it in and address mainly the targeted functions and achievements you performed.

   note Being at a position for one or two years is no longer considered job hopping. In fact, because of the nature of the job market now, sometimes in certain professions (such as sales), being at a company for a long period of time (a decade, for example), makes employers tend to wonder why you stayed so long.

4. **Look at any other positions you were at for less than a year** (not including internships if you are entry level). If you did a lot of job hopping, you'll want to leave out any short-term positions if you can still substantiate your experience in the field and not create gaps. In other words, if you left the job out, would you have sufficient other experience to showcase your qualifications?

5. **Look at your remaining job history.** Generally, it is not necessary to go back more than 10 to 15 years. To determine just how far back to go, consider the following:

   A. If in the past 10 years you have had enough experience to substantiate the position you are targeting and to show career progression, you need not go further back (unless you have a specific need to do so).

   B. If you do not have current relevant experience but you do have related experience in prior years, include positions going back 15 years.

   C. Age discrimination is illegal. However, employers do tend to try to determine your age from your resume information. If you are attempting to look older than you are, going back 15 years will help. If you want to appear younger, going back fewer years can lend that appearance. Either way, once you get your foot in the door for an interview, you can sell yourself on your qualifications. Cross off any older positions you do not want to include now.

6. **Include internships.** If you are entry level, definitely include all internship positions related to your targeted profession. You will develop those entries as you would for any other position. Showing what you learned and achieved is excellent resume material. If you didn't already include internships, add them to your work history now.

7. **Review earlier experience.** If you have a lot of other or earlier experience that is not related to your job target, you can do one of three things:

A. Omit it altogether if you have enough targeted experience and it doesn't cause a gap.

B. Put the unrelated positions after your Professional Experience section in its own separate section entitled Earlier Career Development.

C. Use a functional or combination resume format (explained on pages 31–32) if you have more current unrelated experience than targeted (related) positions.

8. **Categorize positons.** Now look at the remaining positions on your list. Do you have more than five? If so, can you categorize the positions in some way? For example, say you have seven positions. You were a scientist at three of them and a chemist at four of them. One way to handle this is to include the position titles together and identify your job responsibilities and achievements once for the whole group. Here's an example of this format:

SCIENTIST: **Company Name,** Town, State (0000–0000)

              Company Name, Town, State (0000–0000)

              Company Name, Town, State (0000–0000)

- xxxxxxxxxxxxxxxxxxxxxxxxxxxxxxxxxxxxxxxxxxxxxxxxxxxxxxxxxxxxxxxxxxxxxxxxxxxxx
- xxxxxxxxxxxxxxxxxxxxxxxxxxxxxxxxxxxxxxxxxxxxxxxxxxxxxxxxxxxxxxxxxxxxxxxxxxxxx
- xxxxxxxxxxxxxxxxxxxxxxxxxxxxxxxxxxxxxxxxxxxxxxxxxxxxxxxxxxxxxxxxxxxxxxxxx, etc.

CHEMIST: **Company Name,** Town, State (0000–0000)

              Company Name, Town, State (0000–0000)

              Company Name, Town, State (0000–0000)

              Company Name, Town, State (0000–0000)

- xxxxxxxxxxxxxxxxxxxxxxxxxxxxxxxxxxxxxxxxxxxxxxxxxxxxxxxxxxxxxxxxxxxxxxxxxxxxx
- xxxxxxxxxxxxxxxxxxxxxxxxxxxxxxxxxxxxxxxxxxxxxxxxxxxxxxxxxxxxxxxxxxxxxxxxxxxxx
- xxxxxxxxxxxxxxxxxxxxxxxxxxxxxxxxxxxxxxxxxxxxxxxxxxxxxxxxxxxxxxxxxxxxxxxxx, etc.

Or if the past three positions as scientist are more targeted to what you are seeking, you can add detail about those three and then categorize the earlier chemist positions together. Your resume will look less like job hopping. At the same time, it will be easier and less cumbersome reading for the employer because he or she will not have to read through much of the same information more than once—especially for positions of less importance. The following is an example of this format:

0000–0000:   **SCIENTIST**

             Company Name, Town, State

- xxxxxxxxxxxxxxxxxxxxxxxxxxxxxxxxxxxxxxxxxxxxxxxxxxxxxxxxxxxxxxxxxxxxxxxxxxxxx
- xxxxxxxxxxxxxxxxxxxxxxxxxxxxxxxxxxxxxxxxxxxxxxxxxxxxxxxxxxxxxxxxxxxxxxxxx, etc.

0000–0000:   **SCIENTIST**

             Company Name, Town, State

- xxxxxxxxxxxxxxxxxxxxxxxxxxxxxxxxxxxxxxxxxxxxxxxxxxxxxxxxxxxxxxxxxxxxxxxxxxxxx
- xxxxxxxxxxxxxxxxxxxxxxxxxxxxxxxxxxxxxxxxxxxxxxxxxxxxxxxxxxxxxxxxxxxxxxxxx, etc.

0000–0000:   **SCIENTIST**

             Company Name, Town, State

- xxxxxxxxxxxxxxxxxxxxxxxxxxxxxxxxxxxxxxxxxxxxxxxxxxxxxxxxxxxxxxxxxxxxxxxxxxxxx
- xxxxxxxxxxxxxxxxxxxxxxxxxxxxxxxxxxxxxxxxxxxxxxxxxxxxxxxxxxxxxxxxxxxxxxxxx, etc.

Step 2

0000–0000:   **CHEMIST:**

Company Name, Town, State (0000–0000)

Company Name, Town, State (0000–0000)

Company Name, Town, State (0000–0000)

Company Name, Town, State (0000–0000)

- xxxxxxxxxxxxxxxxxxxxxxxxxxxxxxxxxxxxxxxxxxxxxxxxxxxxxxxxxxxxxxxxxxxxx
- xxxxxxxxxxxxxxxxxxxxxxxxxxxxxxxxxxxxxxxxxxxxxxxxxxxxxxxxxxxxxxxxxxxx, etc.

9. **Highlight your promotions.** If you have had a number of employers and have held several positions in the same company, you can write up those positions as follows, listing the most current first (note how the dates are documented). You would describe primarily the functions from your most current position and include achievements from each of the other positions as follows:

> **note** You'll learn more about how to highlight your promotions in Step 3.

0000–0000:   **Company Name,** Town, State

JOB TITLE (0000–0000)

JOB TITLE (0000–0000)

JOB TITLE (0000–0000)

- xxxxxxxxxxxxxxxxxxxxxxxxxxxxxxxxxxxxxxxxxxxxxxxxxxxxxxxxxxxxxxxxxxxxx
- xxxxxxxxxxxxxxxxxxxxxxxxxxxxxxxxxxxxxxxxxxxxxxxxxxxxxxxxxxxxxxxxxxx, etc.

If the promotions within the company are important progression steps to showcase in your resume (especially if that company is your most current employer) and you have only one or two employers, you can write up each as a separate position. Here's an example:

0000–0000:   **Company Name,** Town, State

JOB TITLE (0000–0000)

- xxxxxxxxxxxxxxxxxxxxxxxxxxxxxxxxxxxxxxxxxxxxxxxxxxxxxxxxxxxxxxxxxxxxx
- xxxxxxxxxxxxxxxxxxxxxxxxxxxxxxxxxxxxxxxxxxxxxxxxxxxxxxxxxxxxxxxxxxx, etc.

JOB TITLE (0000–0000)

- xxxxxxxxxxxxxxxxxxxxxxxxxxxxxxxxxxxxxxxxxxxxxxxxxxxxxxxxxxxxxxxxxxxxx
- xxxxxxxxxxxxxxxxxxxxxxxxxxxxxxxxxxxxxxxxxxxxxxxxxxxxxxxxxxxxxxxxxxx, etc.

JOB TITLE (0000–0000)

- xxxxxxxxxxxxxxxxxxxxxxxxxxxxxxxxxxxxxxxxxxxxxxxxxxxxxxxxxxxxxxxxxxxxx
- xxxxxxxxxxxxxxxxxxxxxxxxxxxxxxxxxxxxxxxxxxxxxxxxxxxxxxxxxxxxxxxxxxx, etc.

10. **Does your list now include from two to five positions or groups of positions?** If so, you're in good shape. If not and you are entry level, you can write up college achievements or theses to show your knowledge in the field. (Complete the Entry-Level/New Graduate Achievements worksheet on page 89.) If you still have six or more positions, you can consider preparing a combination resume (more on this in a moment).

11. **Now look at all of the job titles you have listed.** Are any of your actual titles different from your functional titles? (That is, do the position titles your employers gave you differ from your actual job functions?) Or is your job title different than one that would be better known in the industry? If so, either use your functional title or state your actual title followed by a slash and then your functional title.

    Example: One of my clients was a teacher who wanted to work for the public school system. This particular client had worked for various schools for the deaf for the past eight years. So she included in her self-prepared resume her title, Teacher for the Deaf (or Hearing-Impaired), on each of her positions, and then listed the school names, which all included the word "deaf" or "hearing-impaired." She got no responses on her resume. Ever.

    By using the words "deaf" and "hearing-impaired" all over her resume, it immediately showed school districts that her specialty was too specific for the industry; it pigeonholed her. She was screened out before she ever had a chance. Once I rewrote her resume and used her functional title of Teacher (which was not inaccurate) and eliminated the words "deaf" and "hearing-impaired" wherever possible (and, of course, wrote her positions carefully), she was immediately called for interviews.

12. **Transfer your final list of jobs.** Once you have a final targeted list of jobs, transfer them over to pages 29–30 and fill in the related company information along with your primary job functions. You will be using this information in Step 3.

    If you still have a gap of more than a year between jobs and have an explanation of why you were not working (it is better to address a red flag, if you have some good information to provide, than to let prospective employers come up with the answers themselves), you can note this between jobs, as follows:

2004–Present: **JOB TITLE**

Company Name, Town, State

- xxxxxxxxxxxxxxxxxxxxxxxxxxxxxxxxxxxxxxxxxxxxxxxxxxxxxxxxxxxxxxxxxxxxxxxxxx
- xxxxxxxxxxxxxxxxxxxxxxxxxxxxxxxxxxxxxxxxxxxxxxxxxxxxxxxxxxxxxxxxxxxxxx, etc.

2001–2004: **JOB TITLE**

Company Name, Town, State

- xxxxxxxxxxxxxxxxxxxxxxxxxxxxxxxxxxxxxxxxxxxxxxxxxxxxxxxxxxxxxxxxxxxxxxxxxx
- xxxxxxxxxxxxxxxxxxxxxxxxxxxxxxxxxxxxxxxxxxxxxxxxxxxxxxxxxxxxxxxxxxxxxx, etc.

1997–2001: Attending College to obtain Bachelor's Degree*

1995–1997: **JOB TITLE**

Company Name, Town, State

- xxxxxxxxxxxxxxxxxxxxxxxxxxxxxxxxxxxxxxxxxxxxxxxxxxxxxxxxxxxxxxxxxxxxxxxxxx
- xxxxxxxxxxxxxxxxxxxxxxxxxxxxxxxxxxxxxxxxxxxxxxxxxxxxxxxxxxxxxxxxxxxxxx, etc.

---

*OR	Raising Young Children/PTA Volunteer
	Independent Study
	Traveling Abroad (to learn cultures of _____)
	Home Care Provider for (elderly parent)
	Family or Home Management
	Other Activities (try to make them position-related)

13. **Title your employment section.** If your Work History section includes volunteer work or other unpaid experience, title the section Experience or Work History as opposed to Employment or Professional Experience. Then it's not necessary to highlight your work as "volunteer work."

14. **Determine placement of job years.** If your years at each job reveal gaps and there is no explanation to provide, do not highlight them in the front (as on the preceding page). Rather, tuck the dates at the end so that they are not as obvious. In this way, your most important information is your job title.

JOB TITLE (2002–Present)

Company Name, Town, State

- xxxxxxxxxxxxxxxxxxxxxxxxxxxxxxxxxxxxxxxxxxxxxxxxxxxxxxxxxxxxxxxxxxxxxxxxx
- xxxxxxxxxxxxxxxxxxxxxxxxxxxxxxxxxxxxxxxxxxxxxxxxxxxxxxxxxxxxxxxxxxx, etc.

JOB TITLE (1999–2000)

Company Name, Town, State

- xxxxxxxxxxxxxxxxxxxxxxxxxxxxxxxxxxxxxxxxxxxxxxxxxxxxxxxxxxxxxxxxxxxxxxxxx
- xxxxxxxxxxxxxxxxxxxxxxxxxxxxxxxxxxxxxxxxxxxxxxxxxxxxxxxxxxxxxxxxxxx, etc.

JOB TITLE (1997)

Company Name, Town, State

- xxxxxxxxxxxxxxxxxxxxxxxxxxxxxxxxxxxxxxxxxxxxxxxxxxxxxxxxxxxxxxxxxxxxxxxxx
- xxxxxxxxxxxxxxxxxxxxxxxxxxxxxxxxxxxxxxxxxxxxxxxxxxxxxxxxxxxxxxxxxxx, etc.

YOUR RESUME FOUNDATION

Job Number	Details
1	_____ – _____: Job title: _____
	Company name: _____
	Town and state: _____
	Type of firm: _____
	Company's target market: _____
	Annual revenue: _____ Number of locations: _____
	Total number of employees: _____
	Number you manage/supervise directly: _____ Indirectly: _____
	Your primary functions: _____

(continued)

YOUR RESUME FOUNDATION *(continued)*

Job Number	Details

2

_____ – _____: Job title: _____

Company name: _____

Town and state: _____

Type of firm: _____

Company's target market: _____

Annual revenue: _____   Number of locations: _____

Total number of employees: _____

Number you manage/supervise directly: _____   Indirectly: _____

Your primary functions: _____

_____

3

_____ – _____: Job title: _____

Company name: _____

Town and state: _____

Type of firm: _____

Company's target market: _____

Annual revenue: _____   Number of locations: _____

Total number of employees: _____

Number you manage/supervise directly: _____   Indirectly: _____

Your primary functions: _____

_____

4

_____ – _____: Job title: _____

Company name: _____

Town and state: _____

Type of firm: _____

Company's target market: _____

Annual revenue: _____   Number of locations: _____

Total number of employees: _____

Number you manage/supervise directly: _____   Indirectly: _____

Your primary functions: _____

_____

5

_____ – _____: Job title: _____

Company name: _____

Town and state: _____

Type of firm: _____

Company's target market: _____

Annual revenue: _____   Number of locations: _____

Total number of employees: _____

Number you manage/supervise directly: _____   Indirectly: _____

Your primary functions: _____

_____

SELECT YOUR RESUME FORMAT

Now you will select the resume format that works best for your situation. There are four basic resume formats: reverse-chronological, functional, combination, and Curriculum Vitae. Take a look at your resume foundation and the criteria following each of the formats to select the resume format that's right for you. Then place a checkmark in the box next to the format you will be using. Templates and samples for all formats are included on the CD-ROM at the back of the book.

❏ Reverse-Chronological

The reverse-chronological format is the one that human resource professionals prefer and are most familiar with. If you have successive targeted employment, this is the format you should use (unless you are a doctor or lawyer, for example, and a CV is required). It is the most traditional resume format, identifying each of your position titles, companies, years of employment, and respective responsibilities and achievements with your most current position first (hence, *reverse*-chronological).

Use the reverse-chronological format if one or more of the following is true:

- ✔ Your employment history shows career growth and advancement.
- ✔ The years of your employment history flow from one job to the next.
- ✔ There are few or no employment gaps.
- ✔ You have not made frequent job changes.
- ✔ The position you are targeting is in the same field as your experience.
- ✔ Your most recent positions can be targeted in some way to your job goal.

❏ Functional

The functional format concentrates on your skills and strengths as they relate to your specific job target, as opposed to focusing on your actual employment history. It presents your qualifications and accomplishments up front under skills headings, and lists your employment at the end of the resume. Because job seekers generally use this format to deemphasize employment gaps or an irrelevant career history, it is the format employers prefer least because it is perceived that the applicant is hiding something. You should use it only if the other formats will not work for you.

Use the functional format if one or more of the following is true:

- ✔ Your employment gaps are significant and cannot be explained in a positive way.
- ✔ You are entry level and do not have any work history, internships, volunteer work, or other activities related to your targeted position.
- ✔ You are changing careers and cannot substantiate any experience in the field through targeted responsibilities in recent jobs.
- ✔ You are reentering the job market after an extended period of time.
- ✔ You have held many positions within a short period of time.
- ✔ You are seeking consulting or subcontracting work.
- ✔ Your targeted job is one you performed many years ago and your current work is not related to your objective in any way (that is, you need to highlight skills from earlier career development).

❑ Combination

The combination format combines the best of the reverse-chronological and functional formats and show-cases both your transferable skills (noted first) and supportive employment history (included last). It is human resource professionals' second most preferred format.

Use the combination format if one or more of the following is true:

✔ Promoting your qualifications, knowledge, attributes, and achievements is more significant and will have more impact than showcasing your employment history first.

✔ Your employment information can support your qualifications.

✔ You can highlight some experience that matches your targeted profession.

✔ You have some gaps in employment that cannot be explained using the reverse-chronological format.

❑ Curriculum Vitae (CV)

Use a curriculum vitae format if one or both of the following is true:

✔ You are a doctor, lawyer, pilot, professor, actor, or other professional where the mere nature of stating your credentials speaks for itself.

✔ It is the standard in your industry to use a CV.

Now you know which format you will be using. You will use that information in Step 5 when you prepare your first draft. Templates, or foundations, for each format are also supplied in Step 5.

step 3

List Your General Information and Job Responsibilities

- List Your General Information
- Write Your Job Responsibilities Bullets
  - Bullet Starters: Action Verbs
  - "Implied" Information
  - Quantify Your Job Functions
  - Gather Material for Your First Responsibility Bullets
  - Write Your First Resume Bullet for Each Position
  - Document Your First Bullets
  - Promotions: Your Second Resume Bullet
  - Write Your Second Bullet
- Use Action Verbs to Start Each of Your Bullets
  - About Resume Action Verbs
  - Instructions to Check Off Your Action Verbs
  - Getting Creative with Powerful Action Verbs
  - Double-Playing Action Verbs
- Start Your First Draft

LIST YOUR GENERAL INFORMATION

When I told you in the Introduction not to worry about your writing skills and that I'd help you write the resume, I meant it. This section will show you exactly what I mean.

In this step, you will list your general information (such as contact information and education) and job responsibilities. You will use several worksheets—including the General Worksheet, Job Responsibilities worksheets, and Action Verbs lists—to catalog the details. By the end of this step, you will have the beginning of your first draft.

Don't worry too much about wording at this point. You will edit everything later. Be as specific as possible to explain fully everything you do—especially that which is relative to your job target. It is not unusual for clients who are given worksheets by professional resume writers to not answer all questions fully on the first go-round. It will take some thinking, so work on it when your mind is sharpest and you have some unrushed time to spend. And remember, this process is excellent interview preparation.

> **tip**
>
> Using job descriptions, performance evaluations, job postings, and company Web sites is very helpful for extracting pertinent information, especially for your responsibilities information.
> If you can get your hands on any of these documents, include the relative job functions from them in this step, and then adjust the text so that it reflects the functions you actually performed.

In Step 5, you will transfer all of the information you complete in this step into your resume draft. This is the exact process professional resume writers use when we create customized resumes for our clients.

Ready to get started? Complete the first General Worksheet on the next page.

GENERAL WORKSHEET

Contact Information

Name: _____

Street address: _____

Town: _____ State: _____ ZIP: _____

Phone: _____ Fax: _____

Cell: _____ E-mail address: _____

If you have more than one e-mail address, choose the one that sounds the most professional. If yours does not, consider selecting a new one with a professional ring to it. Do not use a business phone number on your resume. Also, be sure any phone number you use is one that is always answered professionally—in person or on voice mail. You may also choose to include the URL of an online portfolio or professional profile.

Professional Summary Information

What position(s) are you targeting? List all that might apply. Pick up this information from page 2 of Step 1.

_____

_____

How many years of experience do you have in this field?

_____

What can you offer employers that would be an asset to them? Explain your best-selling qualifications for this line of work.

_____

_____

_____

_____

Why should employers consider you over others applying for the same position?

_____

_____

_____

_____

What else would you like employers to know about you? Think about ways you can help a company or its clients.

_____

_____

_____

_____

Present/most recent salary: $_____/Salary goal: $_____

Keep your salary goal in mind when you are completing your resume. In other words, if the salary you seek is a lot higher than your most recent salary, look at the functions your supervisors performed and be sure to include any higher-level functions you might have performed (such as when you acted on behalf of your supervisors in their absence or performed functions on their behalf). Do not include salary information on your resume.

(continued)

GENERAL WORKSHEET *(continued)*
Education

If you hold bachelor's and master's degrees, include both. If you have bachelor's and associate degrees, include only the bachelor's. If you earned your degree more than 15 years ago, you can leave out the year. If your GPA in your major is higher than your overall GPA, you can include that instead (indicate "GPA in Major:").

College: _____ Town: _____ State: _____

Type of degree received or related coursework: _____

_____

Year degree received or years attended: _____ GPA: _____

Honors/Achievements: _____

_____

College: _____ Town: _____ State: _____

Type of degree received or related coursework: _____

_____

Year degree received or years attended: _____ GPA: _____

Honors/Achievements: _____

_____

Certifications/Licenses

List all certifications or licenses and their numbers.

_____

_____

Seminars and Additional Training

List all training courses you have taken that are relevant to the position you are targeting.

_____

_____

Computer Expertise

Operating systems, hardware, software. (See page 17 in Step 1.)

_____

_____

Volunteer Work

Places, years, and functions.

_____

_____

Professional Affiliations/Memberships

_____

_____

Related Interests and Activities

_____

_____

WRITE YOUR JOB RESPONSIBILITIES BULLETS

The instructions for the Professional Experience section of your resume are divided into two steps, your "Responsibilities" (Step 3) and your "Achievements" (Step 4). This step deals with your responsibilities only.

The difference between listing your job responsibilities (the functions you performed) and identifying your achievements (the accomplishments you attained) is the difference between whether your resume will result in a few or a significant number of interviews. Ninety-eight percent of the general public lists responsibilities when they write their own resumes: They write a task-oriented resume. Writing an achievement-based resume will get you into your new position much faster.

In this step, you will write your job responsibilities and convert those to achievement-based bullets.

Bullet Starters: Action Verbs

When you complete the Professional Experience section of your resume, each bullet must start with an action verb, such as "Built" or "Supervised." This is the standard format for resume bullets. (The word "I" in front of the action verb is assumed and not required.) Later in this step, you will choose your action verbs from a complete list of more than 350 powerful verbs. I will show you precisely how to use your action verbs to write your responsibility sentences.

"Implied" Information

Forget "implied information." This is your resume, and you know everything you do; that doesn't mean everyone else does. If it is important, targeted information, it belongs in your resume. (Like anything else, there are exceptions, such as it is not necessary to list every last detail of functions that everyone in your field knows.) But for now, you should be more concerned about getting down the important facts. You can always edit it later.

Quantify Your Job Functions

Quantifying your information as much as possible is the key to writing a winning resume that gets results. By "quantifying," I mean including how many, how much, how big, how fast, how well, how often, how difficult, percentages, dollar amounts, time frames, and so on. Just like a picture is worth a thousand words, quantifying by using numbers in your resume has a huge impact.

When thinking in terms of quantifying your experience, consider this:

> Bookkeeper A works for a small auto dealership with four salespeople for whom she prepares payroll and handles payables and receivables.

> Bookkeeper B works for a large worldwide automobile leasing firm with more than 1,000 salespeople for whom she must manage payroll and handle payables and receivables.

Both bookkeepers would be accurate if they portrayed their bookkeeping experience like this:

- Handle Accounts Payable, Accounts Receivable, and Payroll.

Pretty bland, huh? It doesn't say much about the realm of responsibility of bookkeeper B. Now try this:

- Manage Accounts Payable, Accounts Receivable, and Payroll for <u>more than 1,000 employees</u> of a <u>multimillion-dollar worldwide</u> automobile leasing firm with <u>150 locations</u> and <u>more than 75,000 patrons served annually.</u>

Now that's impressive. See the difference quantifying makes? And prospective employers will see it, too!

What happens if you are bookkeeper A and the numbers concerning the size of your payables and receivables, your firm, its number of locations, and its number of patrons do not shout out "I am super-qualified for this position!"? How then do you quantify your responsibilities in the form of an achievement statement? And more so, how do you compete against a bookkeeper B applicant for the same position?

Well, let's examine this. How else is your position challenged? Do you have a completely automated system like bookkeeper B must have, or do you have to prepare everything yourself? Do you have all the time in the world to handle your functions, or are you bogged down with work and tight deadlines? Do you multitask many other functions simultaneously yet accurately? What else do you do that bookkeeper B might not?

Try using a bullet like this:

- Accurately perform all dealership Accounts Payable, Accounts Receivable, and Payroll functions on QuickBooks while simultaneously managing the office, supporting four sales agents, and processing sales contracts as their immediate customer needs dictate.

Can you visualize this person multitasking and holding it all together? Here the how many, how much, and so on is a little more obscure; but the bullet does address quantifying information: How much? All (the whole enchilada). Multiple functions. How well? Accurately. Simultaneously. How fast? Immediately. How many? Supports four sales agents.

 tip Use this rule of thumb: If the numbers shout, use them. If the numbers don't shout, find other numbers (or something else) and make them shout.

If you had said just "Handle Accounts Payable, Accounts Receivable, and Payroll," a prospective employer in a larger firm might have otherwise thought, "Small firm. Small numbers. Lots of time. Not a lot of work. No big deal. Not qualified."

Quantifying is the key to letting prospective employers visualize you functioning exceptionally well in a similar position for their firm. It is also the difference between a task-oriented resume and an achievement-based resume—one that gets calls for interviews! And that's where your resume will stand out from the other 98 percent of the general public who prepare their own resumes.

Gather Material for Your First Responsibility Bullets

On the next page, you will start to write up your job functions, beginning with the first bullet under each of your positions. Then you'll expand each bullet to quantify the type of work you do. For example, tell how many employees you supervise or how many clients you handle, how big the firm is (in terms of dollar amount, number of locations, square footage if that is important to your position, or the number of customers your company has or you serve), the dollar amount of the budget you oversee, and so on.

Following are some fill-in-the-blank bullet examples (you will find more of these in Step 6). Try a few of the bullets to see which ones work best for you. Then, on the page that follows the examples, write your own first bullet for each of your positions. When you perform this activity, also check the targeted qualifications you noted in Step 1 (pages 6–7) to be sure that you incorporate those that are required in the position you seek.

QUANTIFY YOUR JOB INFORMATION

Following are a number of thoughts and questions that could relate to just about any facet of your position or your employer. Think in terms of quantifying. When you read the questions, what is the first thing that comes to mind that might relate to your work, your firm, the people it services, the products it sells, the goals you must meet, the challenges you face, and so on? Brainstorm and jot down your thoughts as they come to you, starting with your most recent position. Make your numbers count; compare them with the numbers an average person would accomplish in the same position. If your numbers meet or exceed the norm, they belong in your resume! This worksheet has space for three jobs. If you are including more jobs than this, you can use additional pages.

Job 1

How many? _____

    Relates to the number of (what?): _____

How much? _____

    Relates to the quantity or cost of (what?): _____

How big? _____

    Relates to the size of (what?): _____

How fast? _____

    Relates to how quickly you do (what functions?): _____

How well? _____

    Relates to how well you do (what functions?): _____

How often? _____

    Relates to how often you do (what functions?): _____

How difficult? _____

    Relates to (what challenge you face?): _____

Percentages: _____

    Of (what?): _____

Dollar amounts: _____

    Of (what?): _____

Time frames: _____

    Of (what?): _____

Job 2

How many? _____

    Relates to the number of (what?): _____

How much? _____

    Relates to the quantity or cost of (what?): _____

How big? _____

    Relates to the size of (what?): _____

(continued)

QUANTIFY YOUR JOB INFORMATION *(continued)*

How fast? _____

   Relates to how quickly you do (what functions?): _____

How well? _____

   Relates to how well you do (what functions?): _____

How often? _____

   Relates to how often you do (what functions?): _____

How difficult? _____

   Relates to (what challenge you face?): _____

Percentages: _____

   Of (what?): _____

Dollar amounts: _____

   Of (what?): _____

Time frames: _____

   Of (what?): _____

Job 3

How many? _____

   Relates to the number of (what?): _____

How much? _____

   Relates to the quantity or cost of (what?): _____

How big? _____

   Relates to the size of (what?): _____

How fast? _____

   Relates to how quickly you do (what functions?): _____

How well? _____

   Relates to how well you do (what functions?): _____

How often? _____

   Relates to how often you do (what functions?): _____

How difficult? _____

   Relates to (what challenge you face?): _____

Percentages: _____

   Of (what?): _____

Dollar amounts: _____

   Of (what?): _____

Time frames: _____

   Of (what?): _____

Write Your First Resume Bullet for Each Position

Now that you've identified some quantifying information that might be helpful to include in your resume, you can start to jot down some thoughts for your first resume bullet for each of your positions. At this point, write just those important pieces of information you definitely want to include. You will piece it all together momentarily.

Your first resume bullet under each employer should state the primary functions that relate to your targeted goal in a nutshell so that the reader will instantly know the scope of your job (what you do) by reading just that first sentence. The bullets that follow will explain your functions in more detail and include your significant accomplishments thereafter.

For example, if you are a manager or supervisor, you might start with the words *manage, oversee, supervise, direct, head, design, develop,* or *lead.* Indicate what you do this for—is it people, projects, a particular function, a division? Be sure to include your quantifying information as it relates to your firm, its customers, your functions, and so on.

Step 3

THOUGHTS TO INCLUDE IN YOUR FIRST BULLETS FOR EACH POSITION

Position 1 _____

_____

_____

_____

_____

Position 2 _____

_____

_____

_____

_____

Position 3 _____

_____

_____

_____

Position 4 _____

_____

_____

_____

Position 5 _____

_____

_____

_____

_____

Here are some first bullet examples for management, supervisory, and other positions that you can use to alter what you previously jotted down, use as-is by filling in the blanks, or modify to meet your specific needs.

> **note**   Throughout this book, the lines and optional answers are for your fill-in or selection. By filling in each blank and choosing the best wording for your situation, you will take the foundations provided in this book and create a resume that is absolutely unique and tailored to you.

First Bullet Examples for Management

Step 3

❏ Manage and oversee all _____ [type of] functions and programs of this $_____ [firm size] _____ [type of] firm, which [develops/manufactures/distributes/other: _____] _____ [type of] products to _____ [what market?].

❏ Direct, manage, and coordinate all aspects of [daily operations/production/sales/marketing/customer service/other: _____] for this [$_____/multimillion-dollar] _____ [type of] firm.

❏ Direct day-to-day [corporate affairs/operations/other: _____] overseeing _____ [#] employees in _____ [#] states of this [nationally/globally] distributed _____ [type of] firm coordinating activities with _____ [#] senior managers.

❏ Head the [Sales and Marketing/New Business Development/Client Relations/New Program Development/other:_____] Division, including all [mergers and acquisitions/joint venture development/extensive support programs/ other: _____] for one of the top 10 industry leaders in [_____ what products or genre?].

❏ Direct [regional/national/global] sales of all _____ [type of] products, including _____, _____, and _____, for this [national/worldwide] leader in _____ [what?] with annual sales in excess of $_____.

❏ Manage [production/quality-control/compliance/other: _____] functions for the [manufacture/distribution/other: _____] of _____ [which?] products, including [internal audits/error investigations/release specifications/other: _____] and ensuring compliance with all [state/federal/other: _____] regulations.

❏ [Conceptualize/design/coordinate/schedule/implement/other: _____] _____ [type of] [projects/products/programs/campaigns/employees/special events/other: _____] from concept to completion, including _____, _____, _____, and _____.

❏ Design and develop _____ [what?] for _____ [type of] [clients/users] using _____ [type of] [programs/scripting/other: _____].

❏ [Manage/Direct/Oversee/Supervise] _____ [which?] operations of this _____ [type of] firm, which sells _____ [what?] to _____ [whom?] by _____ [doing what?].

❏ _____
   _____
   _____
   _____

FIRST BULLET EXAMPLES FOR SUPERVISORY PERSONNEL

❏ Supervise the daily activities and oversee [administrative/customer service/production/retail sales/other: _____]
operations of _____ [#] employees for this [worldwide/nationwide/other: _____] [retailer for/manufacturer
of/industry leader in/distributor of/other: _____] _____ [what genre?].

❏ Supervise a [retail/office support/production/administrative/other: _____] staff of _____[#];
and coordinate and schedule _____, _____, and _____ [type of]
functions for this [$_____/multimillion-dollar] _____ [type of] firm with _____ [#]
[locations/branches/employees/customers/other: _____].

❏ Coordinate, oversee, and monitor the _____, _____, and _____
functions of a(n) [office support/production/administrative/other: _____] staff of _____ [#] for this
_____ [type of] firm.

❏ Supervise diversified office activities, including [correspondence/bookkeeping/billing/travel arrangements/insurance/dispatch/timekeeping/
job inquiries/payroll reports/other:_____].

❏ Supervise and oversee the manufacture of _____ [type of] products for this $_____ [size]
_____ [type of] [manufacturer/facility/distributor/firm] with _____ [#] locations [state/nation/world] -wide.

❏ Perform production supervision and coordination of the manufacturing of all product lines, including _____,
_____, and _____ in compliance with all regulations for this _____
[type of] firm with annual sales over $_____.

❏ Train, develop, and coach _____ [#] subordinates in the [areas/topics] of _____, _____,
_____, and _____ and ensure staff compliance in all [areas/regulations/policies and proce-
dures/other: _____].

❏ Supervise, energize, and motivate a _____ [type of] staff of _____ [#] to [produce high-quality products/
meet high levels of customer service/meet difficult deadlines/meet and exceed sales goals/other: _____].

❏ Recruit, schedule, train, and develop a staff of _____ [#] _____ [job titles] for this
_____ [type of] firm with annual sales over $_____.

❏ _____
_____
_____

FIRST BULLET EXAMPLES FOR OTHERS

❏ Perform _____ [what functions?] for this $_____ [revenues] _____
_____ [type of] firm with _____ [#] [employees/locations], which offers _____ [type
of] [products/services] to the _____ market.

❏ Provide _____ [type of] [pre- and post-sales support/technical support/expertise/consultation/other: _____
_____] to [customers/clients/end users/other: _____] for _____
[purpose?], in the areas of _____, _____, and _____.

❏ Research, analyze, and coordinate _____ [what functions?] for this _____ [type of]
firm, which [sells/offers/produces/distributes/other: _____] _____ [type of]
[products/services] for the _____ market.

❏ Involved in development through implementation phases of all _____, _____, and
_____ [products/stages] for the _____ [division/department] of this $_____
_____ [type of] firm.

(continued)

(continued)

❏ Develop quality _____ [type of] systems for _____
_____ [what purpose?] and oversee personnel training for _____ [#] employees to ensure all procedures are followed.

❏ Perform various office and administrative functions, including [keyboarding/switchboard operations/client correspondence/legal document processing/mailings/bookkeeping/collections/filing/copying/faxing/other: _____] for this _____ [type of] firm.

❏ Handle all [keyboarding/legal document processing/client correspondence preparation/other: _____ _____] for [the firm/my superior/the department/clients/customers/end users/other: _____ _____].

❏ Provide support to the _____ [which?] departments, handling all [correspondence/memoranda/faxes/advertising/ mailings/other: _____] in a timely and professional fashion.

❏ Service _____ [#] accounts by setting up _____ [#] [daily/weekly] [delivery routes/account or product servicing/ follow-up/sales support/other: _____] and providing _____, _____, and _____ [what?].

❏ _____
_____
_____

Document Your First Bullets

Review the bullets you worked up in the preceding section and check off the ones that work best for you. Rework each bullet as applicable to your specific situation and make them "true statements," or prepare your own based on the examples. Then select the best for use in your resume.

Document the first bullet for each of your positions in the following worksheet. When you complete this activity, you will have the all-important first bullet for each of your employers under the Professional Experience (or Employment) section of your resume. For this step, use the company information you completed in your "Resume Foundation" in Step 2. Also be sure to mention the primary functions of your targeted goal, which you identified in Step 1, if applicable.

YOUR FINAL FIRST BULLETS FOR EACH POSITION

Position 1

_____

_____

_____

_____

Position 2

_____

_____

_____

_____

Position 3

_____

_____

_____

_____

Position 4

_____

_____

_____

_____

Position 5

_____

_____

_____

_____

Step 3

Congratulations! You just completed what is probably your most difficult responsibility bullet. Now let's move on to your second bullet.

Promotions: Your Second Resume Bullet

Always address promotions you have earned within a company. There are three ways to do this. This step coincides somewhat with the strategizing you did in Step 2, but provides more specific strategies regarding highlighting your promotions.

METHOD 1: LIST YOUR PROMOTIONS IN AN ACHIEVEMENT-BASED BULLET

The first method is to just list your promotions in an achievement-based bullet under the applicable employers. Making this your second bullet right after stating your overall responsibilities in your current title works well. Or you can incorporate it within your first bullet.

Examples:

❑ Promoted through a series of progressively responsible positions from _____ [your starting position] to _____ [first promoted position], _____ [second promoted position], and _____ [your final position].

❑ Promoted from _____ to _____ within _____ [time period] by _____ [state how you accomplished this so quickly].

❑ Received various promotions within this _____ [type of] firm specializing in _____ _____, including _____, _____, and _____ [list positions].

State your promotions within one bullet when one or more of the following is true:

✔ The functions in each position are for the most part greatly the same and it would be redundant to repeat them. That is, you will have one set of responsibility and achievement bullets under the particular employer, regardless of how many different job titles you had there.

✔ You have had quite a few jobs and breaking out each of the positions for each employer would make your resume lengthy and too overwhelming for a recruiter to read. (For example, if you have worked for four companies and held three positions in one, two in another, and one in the last two, that would mean you would be writing up seven positions—far too many!)

When you list the promotions within your responsibilities information, separate out the dates (years only are necessary) of the various positions in a way that readily shows each position within the realm of the total number of years at the job. For example, use this:

1999-present: **ABC Company, Anytown, NY**
VICE PRESIDENT *(2009–present)*
DIRECTOR OF SALES *(2004–2009)*
REGIONAL SALES MANAGER *(2002–2004)*
SALES MANAGER *(1999–2002)*
- xxxxxxxxxxxxxx [your first bullet] xxxxxxxxxxxxxxxxxxxxxxxxxxxxxxxxxxxxxxxxxxxxx
- xxxxxxxxxxxx [your promotional bullet] xxxxxxxxxxxxxxxxxxxx xxxxxxxxxxxxxxxxxxxxxxxx
- xxxxxx [most remaining bullets re: VP position] xxxxxxxxxxxxxxxxxxxxxxxxxxxxxxxxxxxx
- xxxxxxxxxxxxxxxxxxxxxxxxxxxxxxxxxxxxxxxxxxxxxxxxxxxxxxxxxxxxxxxxxxxxxxxxxxxxxxxx
- xxxxxxxxxxxxxxxxxxxxxxxxxxxxxxxxxxxxxxxxxxxxxxxxxxxxxxxxxxxxxxxxxxxxxxxxxxxx, etc.
- xxxx [additional achievements in other positions] xxxxxxxxxxxxxxxxxxxxxxxxxxxxxxxxxx
- xxxxxxxxxxxxxxxxxxxxxxxxxxxxxxxxxxxxxxxxxxxxxxxxxxxxxxxxxxxxxxxxxxxxxxxxxxx, etc.

Instead of this:

2009–present:	**VICE PRESIDENT—ABC Company, Anytown, State**
	• xxxxxxxxxxxxxxxxxxxxxxxxxxxxxxxxxxxxxxxxxxxxxxxxxxxxxxxxxxxxxxxxxxxxxxxxxxxxxxxxxx
	• xxxxxxxxxxxxxxxxxxxxxxxxxxxxxxxxxxxxxxxxxxxxxxxxxxxxxxxxxxxxxxxxxxxxxxxxxxxxxx, etc.
2004–2009:	**DIRECTOR OF SALES—ABC Company, Anytown, State**
	• xxxxxxxxxxxxxxxxxxxxxxxxxxxxxxxxxxxxxxxxxxxxxxxxxxxxxxxxxxxxxxxxxxxxxxxxxxxxxxxxxx
	• xxxxxxxxxxxxxxxxxxxxxxxxxxxxxxxxxxxxxxxxxxxxxxxxxxxxxxxxxxxxxxxxxxxxxxxxxxxxxx, etc.
2002–2004:	**REGIONAL SALES MANAGER—ABC Company, Anytown, State**
	• xxxxxxxxxxxxxxxxxxxxxxxxxxxxxxxxxxxxxxxxxxxxxxxxxxxxxxxxxxxxxxxxxxxxxxxxxxxxxxxxxx
	• xxxxxxxxxxxxxxxxxxxxxxxxxxxxxxxxxxxxxxxxxxxxxxxxxxxxxxxxxxxxxxxxxxxxxxxxxxxxxx, etc.
1999–2002:	**SALES MANAGER—ABC Company, Anytown, State**
	• xxxxxxxxxxxxxxxxxxxxxxxxxxxxxxxxxxxxxxxxxxxxxxxxxxxxxxxxxxxxxxxxxxxxxxxxxxxxxxxxxx
	• xxxxxxxxxxxxxxxxxxxxxxxxxxxxxxxxxxxxxxxxxxxxxxxxxxxxxxxxxxxxxxxxxxxxxxxxxxxxxx, etc.

Think about each job you will be including in your resume. Does this method work for you? If not (or before you make your final decision), review the next two methods.

METHOD 2: WRITE UP EACH POSITION SEPARATELY

The second way to document your promotions is to work up each of these positions separately, showing your responsibilities and achievements for each. Each would look like a separate position.

Use the second method (work up each position) when one or more of the following is true:

- ✔ You have been employed by only one or two companies and your resume would be lean without working up each position.

- ✔ Working up each position would show appropriate progression in your field. (If you have a number of positions, you might want to do this with only the first and second firms.)

- ✔ Each of the positions is important to your targeted profession, and showcasing your achievements in each position would be beneficial. For example, if you are a manager and you started in a technical position, it would be important to showcase your hands-on technical knowledge as well.

- ✔ The differences in the functions you performed within each of the positions vary enough to document them separately, and each is (or most are) important to your targeted profession.

- ✔ You are a manager or other professional who by nature of your work has a lot of achievements, and separating the positions out from each other would make your resume more readable and less "run-on." See the following example. (In this situation, you could also use the third method, which is detailed on the next page.)

For example:

2006–present:	**ABC Company, Anytown, NY**
	VICE PRESIDENT (2009–present)
	• xxxxxxxxxxxxxx [your first bullet] xxxxxxxxxxxxxxxxxxxxxxxxxxxxxxxxxxxxxxxxxxxxxxxxxx
	• xxxxxxxxx [significant core responsibility bullet] xxxxxxxxxxxxxxxxxxxxxxxxxxxxxxxxxxx
	• xxxxxxxxx [significant core responsibility bullet] xxxxxxxxxxxxxxxxxxxxxxxxxxxxxxxx, etc.
	• xxxxxxxxxx [other primary targeted function] xxxxxxxxxxxxxxxxxxxxxxxxxxxxxxxxxxx, etc.
	• xxxxxxxxxxxxx [achievement bullet] xxxxxxxxxxxxxxxxxxxxxxxxxxxxxxxxxxxxxxxxxxxxxx
	• xxxxxxxxxxxxx [achievement bullet] xxxxxxxxxxxxxxxxxxxxxxxxxxxxxxxxxxxxxxxxxxxxx
	• xxxxxxxxxxxxx [achievement bullet] xxxxxxxxxxxxxxxxxxxxxxxxxxxxxxxxxxxxxxxxxxxx, etc.

(continued)

(continued)

DIRECTOR OF SALES (2004–2009)
- xxxxxxxxxxxxxx [your first bullet] xxxxxxxxxxxxxxxxxxxxxxxxxxxxxxxxxxxxxxxxxxxxxxxxxx
- xxxxxxx [significant core responsibility bullet] xxxxxxxxxxxxxxxxxxxxxxxxxxxxxxxxxxxxx
- xxxxxx [significant core responsibility bullet] xxxxxxxxxxxxxxxxxxxxxxxxxxxxxxxxxxx, etc.
- xxxxxxxxx [other primary targeted functions] xxxxxxxxxxxxxxxxxxxxxxxxxxxxxxxxxxxxx, etc.
- xxxxxxxxxxxxxx [achievement bullet] xxxxxxxxxxxxxxxxxxxxxxxxxxxxxxxxxxxxxxxxxxxxxxxxx
- xxxxxxxxxxxxxx [achievement bullet] xxxxxxxxxxxxxxxxxxxxxxxxxxxxxxxxxxxxxxxxxxxxxxxxx
- xxxxxxxxxxxxxx [achievement bullet] xxxxxxxxxxxxxxxxxxxxxxxxxxxxxxxxxxxxxxxxxxxxx, etc.

REGIONAL SALES MANAGER (2002–2004)
- xxxxxxxxxxxxxx [your first bullet] xxxxxxxxxxxxxxxxxxxxxxxxxxxxxxxxxxxxxxxxxxxxxxxxxx
- xxxxxxx [significant core responsibility bullet] xxxxxxxxxxxxxxxxxxxxxxxxxxxxxxxxxxx, etc.
- xxxxxxxxx [other primary targeted functions] xxxxxxxxxxxxxxxxxxxxxxxxxxxxxxxxxxxxx, etc.
- xxxxxxxxxxxxxx [achievement bullet] xxxxxxxxxxxxxxxxxxxxxxxxxxxxxxxxxxxxxxxxxxxxxxxxx
- xxxxxxxxxxxxxx [achievement bullet] xxxxxxxxxxxxxxxxxxxxxxxxxxxxxxxxxxxxxxxxxxxxx, etc.

SALES MANAGER (1999–2002)
- xxxxxxxxxxxxxx [your first bullet] xxxxxxxxxxxxxxxxxxxxxxxxxxxxxxxxxxxxxxxxxxxxxxxxxx
- xxxxxxx [significant core responsibility bullet] xxxxxxxxxxxxxxxxxxxxxxxxxxxxxxxxxxx, etc.
- xxxxxxxxxxxxxx [achievement bullet] xxxxxxxxxxxxxxxxxxxxxxxxxxxxxxxxxxxxxxxxxxxxx, etc.

Note also in the preceding examples that as you document each position, the first (most recent) position includes much more detailed information. As you go back to older and less important positions, the information you include decreases.

METHOD 3: COMBINATION

The third method is a combination of the two preceding methods. You include one heavy-hitter significant core responsibility bullet for each of the positions you held; thereafter, you include only the main achievements you accomplished for each. In this way, all of your significant functions and achievements are highlighted and you won't bore your reader.

Use the third (combination) method when one or more of the following is true:

✔ You have held a number of positions and each of them is very important to your targeted profession.

✔ You accomplished many achievements in each of the positions that are important to note, and a more concise method of presenting your job functions would have more impact and allow you to put more emphasis on your accomplishments. This method works especially well for managers and technical professionals, where there are many goals to meet and exceed, as well as project success stories to identify.

✔ You are an executive or manager and your specific responsibility functions are well known in the industry and might be redundant to include. Therefore, your achievements are the most important things to highlight.

Example:

1999–present: ABC Company, Anytown, NY
VICE PRESIDENT, SALES (2009–present)
- xxxxxx [one significant core responsibility bullet] xxxxxxxxxxxxxxxxxxxxxxxxxxxxxxxxxxxxxxxxx
- xxxxxxxxxxxxxx [achievement bullet] xxxxxxxxxxxxxxxxxxxxxxxxxxxxxxxxxxxxxxxxxxxxxxxxx
- xxxxxxxxxxxxxx [achievement bullet] xxxxxxxxxxxxxxxxxxxxxxxxxxxxxxxxxxxxxxxxxxxxxxxxx
- xxxxxxxxxxxxxx [achievement bullet] xxxxxxxxxxxxxxxxxxxxxxxxxxxxxxxxxxxxxxxxxxxxxxxxx
- xxxxxxxxxxxxxx [achievement bullet] xxxxxxxxxxxxxxxxxxxxxxxxxxxxxxxxxxxxxxxxxxxxx, etc.

DIRECTOR OF SALES (2004–2009)
- xxxxxx [one significant core responsibility bullet] xxxxxxxxxxxxxxxxxxxxxxxxxxxxxxxxxxxxxxxx
- xxxxxxxxxxxxxx [achievement bullet] xxxxxxxxxxxxxxxxxxxxxxxxxxxxxxxxxxxxxxxxxxxxxxxxxx
- xxxxxxxxxxxxxx [achievement bullet] xxxxxxxxxxxxxxxxxxxxxxxxxxxxxxxxxxxxxxxxxxxxxxxxxx
- xxxxxxxxxxxxxx [achievement bullet] xxxxxxxxxxxxxxxxxxxxxxxxxxxxxxxxxxxxxxxxxxxxxxxxxx
- xxxxxxxxxxxxxx [achievement bullet] xxxxxxxxxxxxxxxxxxxxxxxxxxxxxxxxxxxxxxxxxxxxxxx, etc.

REGIONAL SALES MANAGER (2002–2004)
- xxxxxx [one significant core responsibility bullet] xxxxxxxxxxxxxxxxxxxxxxxxxxxxxxxxxxxxxxxx
- xxxxxxxxxxxxxx [achievement bullet] xxxxxxxxxxxxxxxxxxxxxxxxxxxxxxxxxxxxxxxxxxxxxxxxxx
- xxxxxxxxxxxxxx [achievement bullet] xxxxxxxxxxxxxxxxxxxxxxxxxxxxxxxxxxxxxxxxxxxxxxx, etc.

SALES MANAGER (1999–2002)
- xxxxxx [one significant core responsibility bullet] xxxxxxxxxxxxxxxxxxxxxxxxxxxxxxxxxxxxxxxx
- xxxxxxxxxxxxxx [achievement bullet] xxxxxxxxxxxxxxxxxxxxxxxxxxxxxxxxxxxxxxxxxxxxxxxxxx
- xxxxxxxxxxxxxx [achievement bullet] xxxxxxxxxxxxxxxxxxxxxxxxxxxxxxxxxxxxxxxxxxxxxxx, etc.

Or you could break out your most current position by including all of the bullets in the preceding example for only your most recent employer (if that position is the primary focus of your resume). Then you can group together all of the remaining positions, which would deemphasize those by putting greater emphasis on the detailed current position, as in the following example:

2006–2009: **SCIENTIST**
Company Name, Town, State
- xxxxxxxxxxxxxxxxxxxxxxxx [your first bullet] xxxxxxxxxxxxxxxxxxxxxxxxxxxxxxxxxxxxxxxxxxxxxxxx
- xxxxxxxxxxxxxx [significant core responsibility bullet] xxxxxxxxxxxxxxxxxxxxxxxxxxxxxxxxxxxxxxxx
- xxxxxxxxxxxxxx [significant core responsibility bullet] xxxxxxxxxxxxxxxxxxxxxxxxxxxxxxxxxxxxx, etc.
- xxxxxxxxxxxxxx [other primary targeted functions] xxxxxxxxxxxxxxxxxxxxxxxxxxxxxxxxxxxxxxx, etc.
- xxxxxxxxxxxxxxxxxxxxxxx [achievement bullet] xxxxxxxxxxxxxxxxxxxxxxxxxxxxxxxxxxxxxxxxxxxxxx
- xxxxxxxxxxxxxxxxxxxxxxx [achievement bullet] xxxxxxxxxxxxxxxxxxxxxxxxxxxxxxxxxxxxxxxxxxxxxx
- xxxxxxxxxxxxxxxxxxxxxxx [achievement bullet] xxxxxxxxxxxxxxxxxxxxxxxxxxxxxxxxxxxxxxxxxxx, etc.

1998–2006: **CHEMIST**
Company Name, Town, State (2004–2006)
Company Name, Town, State (2001–2004)
Company Name, Town, State (2000–2001)
- xxxxxxxxxxxxxx [significant core responsibility bullet] xxxxxxxxxxxxxxxxxxxxxxxxxxxxxxxxxxxxxxxx
- xxxxxxxxxxxxxx [significant core responsibility bullet] xxxxxxxxxxxxxxxxxxxxxxxxxxxxxxxxxxxxxxxx
- xxxxxxxxxxxxxx [significant core responsibility bullet] xxxxxxxxxxxxxxxxxxxxxxxxxxxxxxxxxxxxx, etc.
- xxxxxxxxxxxxxx [other primary targeted functions] xxxxxxxxxxxxxxxxxxxxxxxxxxxxxxxxxxxxxxx, etc.
- xxxxxxxxxxxxxx [achievement bullet—indicate firm] xxxxxxxxxxxxxxxxxxxxxxxxxxxxxxxxxxxxxxxx
- xxxxxxxxxxxxxx [achievement bullet—indicate firm] xxxxxxxxxxxxxxxxxxxxxxxxxxxxxxxxxxxxxxxx
- xxxxxxxxxxxxxx [achievement bullet—indicate firm] xxxxxxxxxxxxxxxxxxxxxxxxxxxxxxxxxxxxx, etc.

Write Your Second Bullet

If you have decided to go with Method 1 (listing your promotions), use the following space to complete your second bullet for each of your positions where promotions were applicable. Leave the other employers blank. If you were promoted within several jobs, use a variation of the verbiage as provided in Method 1. If you are going to use Method 2 or 3, include them as separate positions under "Start Your First Draft," later in this step.

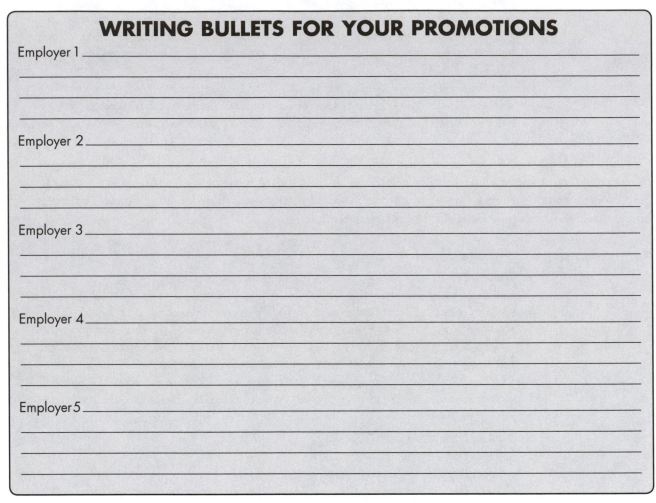

WRITING BULLETS FOR YOUR PROMOTIONS

Employer 1 _____

_____

_____

_____

Employer 2 _____

_____

_____

_____

Employer 3 _____

_____

_____

_____

Employer 4 _____

_____

_____

_____

Employer 5 _____

_____

_____

_____

Okay, you've tackled the first two bullets under each position. You will be transferring the information you just worked up into your resume draft shortly. Now let's move on to the meat of your resume: the remaining bullets of your Professional Experience section.

USE ACTION VERBS TO START EACH OF YOUR BULLETS

Now you're ready to move on to the next set of bullets—to complete the remaining job responsibilities (functions) you performed at each of your employers. You'll start by understanding and then using action verbs. From there, you will systematically develop your bullets, expand on these sentences with your functional responsibilities, and turn them into achievement-based sentences. Then you will have your full set of responsibility bullets under each employer completed.

 note You will complete the remaining achievement bullets in Steps 4 and 6.

About Resume Action Verbs

Each bullet in your Professional Experience (or Employment) section must start with an action verb. On the following pages, you will find the most complete list of resume action verbs anywhere—with approximately 2,800 action verbs for use by all professions. Starting your sentences with these words will also help to jog your memory during the resume writing process, as resume action verbs are actually job functions in their briefest form.

Instructions to Check Off Your Action Verbs

Review the lists of action verbs on the following pages and circle all of them that relate to your job functions and are the most important in your targeted profession. When you read each verb, let your mind explore your job functions to determine whether you performed any task that relates to that word. The words you select will become your bullet starters.

Here are some examples of action verbs that are particularly relevant to various positions:

note When you use action verbs for your current position, they must be in present tense (as shown here). Verbs for previous positions should always be written in past tense.

- ✔ **Executive/manager:** direct, manage, spearhead, establish, forecast, strategize, increase, orchestrate, initiate, negotiate, improve, reengineer, design, challenge, budget, augment, standardize, devise, project...

- ✔ **Supervisor:** supervise, oversee, delegate, implement, verify, assign, schedule, reschedule, ensure, instruct, comply with, develop, mentor, recruit, outsource, follow up...

- ✔ **Salesperson:** sell, cross-sell, upsell, close, demonstrate, present, launch, canvas, call, contact, entrench, increase, surpass, exceed, market, support, promote, service...

- ✔ **Scientist/chemist/lab technician:** research, analyze, evaluate, test, sample, cultivate, examine, decipher, classify, identify, interpret, translate, authenticate, detect, study, prepare, record, collect, formulate, cross-match, cross-type, sterilize...

- ✔ **Quality control/quality assurance manager:** ensure, validate, inspect, audit, verify, quantify, develop, systematize, generate, review, document, report...

- ✔ **Art director:** direct, manage, conceptualize, orchestrate, create, design, render, establish, forecast, strategize, increase, negotiate, synthesize, silhouette, meet with...

- ✔ **Software designer:** research, assess, design, code, script, test, develop, install, configure, program, troubleshoot, diagnose, debug, integrate, forecast, connect...

- ✔ **Interior decorator:** estimate, budget, bid, design, furnish, measure, cost, assess, renovate, oversee, monitor, tailor, assemble, drape...

ACTION VERBS FOR MANAGERS AND EXECUTIVES

This first list of action verbs is for managers and executives, and the second is applicable to all (and varied) professions.

Abolish	Calculate	Cooperate with	Divide	Maximize	Reinvent
Absorb	Calibrate	Coordinate	Document	Measure	Relocate
Abstract	Call	Correct	Draft	Merchandise	Render
Accelerate	Canvas	Correlate	Duplicate	Minimize	Reorder
Access	Capitalize on	Correspond with	Eliminate	Modify	Report
Acclaim	Carry out	Corroborate	Enhance	Mold	Represent
Acclimate	Catalog	Count	Ensure	Monitor	Reprocess
Accommodate	Categorize	Counteract	Enter	Motivate	Research
Accomplish	Cater to	Counterbalance	Equalize	Observe	Resell
Account for	Centralize	Couple	Eradicate	Obtain	Resolve
Accumulate	Change	Cover	Establish	Offer	Respond to
Achieve	Characterize	Create	Estimate	Open	Restructure
Acknowledge	Chart	Cross-check	Evaluate	Optimize	Retest
Acquire	Check	Cross-file	Examine	Order	Review
Activate	Circulate	Cross-index	Exceed	Organize	Run
Address	Cite	Cross-link	Exhibit	Outline	Safeguard
Adhere to	Claim	Cross-match	Expedite	Oversee	Sample
Adjust	Classify	Cross-reference	Explain	Package	Save
Administer	Cleanse	Cross-section	Explore	Participate in	Scale
Advance	Clear	Cross-sell	Facilitate	Patent	Search
Advise	Co-contribute	Cross-type	File	Penetrate	Sell
Affirm	Co-coordinate	Cultivate	Fill	Perform	Separate
Amend	Co-create	Cycle	Follow up on	Persuade	Serve (as)
Analyze	Code	Decide	Formulate	Plan	Service
Answer	Co-develop	Decipher	Gather	Plant	Set up
Apply	Co-direct	Declassify	Generate	Practice	Ship
Approach	Cohere	Decline	Greet	Prepare	Simplify
Appropriate	Co-invent	Decode	Grow	Present	Solicit
Archive	Collect	Decrease	Handle	Preserve	Sort
Arrange	Color code	Dedicate	Hasten	Prevent	Specialize in
Ascertain	Combine	Deduce	Help	Prioritize	Split
Assemble	Compare	Dehydrate	Hydrate	Problem-solve	Standardize
Assess	Compile	Delineate	Identify	Process	Streamline
Assist	Complete	Deliver	Illustrate	Produce	Substantiate
Attain	Comply with	Demagnetize	Implement	Project	Succeed
Attend	Composite	Demonstrate	Improve	Promote	Support
Audit	Compute	Demystify	Increase	Provide	Surpass
Augment	Concentrate on	Denote	Inform	Purchase	Survey
Automate	Conceptualize	Deposit	Initiate	Quantify	Tackle
Awarded	Conclude	Describe	Inspect	Question	Tailor
Backtrack	Condense	Design	Instruct	Reassess	Teach
Balance	Conduct	Detect	Integrate	Recalculate	Test
Begin	Confer with	Determine	Intensify	Receive	Track
Bid	Configure	Develop	Interface with	Recheck	Train
Bill	Confirm	Diagnose	Interpret	Recommend	Troubleshoot
Bind	Conform to	Discontinue	Introduce	Record	Upsell
Bisect	Connect	Discover	Invent	Recultivate	Use
Block	Conserve	Disinfect	Investigate	Redesign	Utilize
Brainstorm	Consolidate	Dispense	Join	Reduce	Validate
Brand	Construct	Display	Juggle	Reevaluate	Vaporize
Break down	Consult with	Dispute	Link	Re-examine	Verify
Breed	Contact	Dissect	Locate	Re-explore	Visit
Bridge	Contain	Dissipate	Magnetize	Refer	Work closely
Bring about	Contribute to	Dissolve	Maintain	Refill	with
Budget	Control	Distribute	Manufacture	Refute	Work out
Build	Converge	Diversify	Market	Regenerate	

ACTION VERBS FOR ALL PROFESSIONS

A

Abate
Abbreviate
Abide (by)
Abolish
Abridge
Absolve
Absorb
Abstract
Accelerate
Accentuate
Access
Acclaim
Acclimate
Accommodate
Accompany
Accomplish
Account for
Accredit
Accrue
Accumulate
Achieve
Acknowledge
Acquaint
Acquire
Act (as)
Activate
Actuate
Adapt (to)
Add
Address
Adhere to
Adjudge
Adjudicate
Adjust
Administer
Admit
Adopt
Advance
Advertise
Advise
Advocate
Aerate
Affect
Affiliate with
Affirm
Affix
Aid
Air
Air brush
Alert
Align
Alleviate
Allocate
Allot

Allow
Alter
Ambulate
Amend
Amplify
Analyze
Anchor
Anesthetize
Animate
Announce
Answer
Anticipate
Appeal
Appease
Apply
Appoint
Apportion
Appraise
Apprehend
Apprise
Approach
Appropriate
Approve
Approximate
Arbitrate
Archive
Arraign
Arrange
Arrest
Articulate
Ascertain
Ascribe
Ask
Aspire
Assemble
Assert
Assess
Assign
Assimilate
Assist
Assume
Assure
Attach
Attain
Attend
Attest
Attract
Auction
Audit
Augment
Authenticate
Author
Authorize
Automate
Avail
Averted

Avoid
Award

B

Backfill
Backtrack
Bag
Balance
Bargain
Batch
Bathe
Beat
Beautify
Beckon
Begin
Benchmark
Bend
Benefit
Bestow
Better
Bid
Bill
Bind
Bisect
Blend
Block
Board
Bolster
Book
Boost
Borrow
Brace
Brainstorm
Brand
Braze
Break down
Break up
Breed
Bridge
Brief
Briefen
Bring about
Broach
Broadcast
Broaden
Browse
Budget
Build
Bulk
Bump
Bundle
Buy

C

Calculate
Calibrate
Call
Campaign
Cancel
Canvas
Capitalize on
Captivate
Capture
Care for
Carry
Carry out
Carry over
Cart
Carve
Carve (out)
Cash
Cash in
Cash out
Cast
Catalog
Catalyze
Catapult
Catch
Categorize
Cater (to)
Cause
Caution
Cement
Centralize
Certify
Chair
Challenge
Champion
Change
Channel
Characterize
Charge
Charge off
Charm
Chart
Chauffeur
Check
Check in
Check out
Check up
Chisel
Choose
Chop
Chronicle
Circulate
Cite
Claim

Clarify
Classify
Clean
Cleanse
Clear
Clear out
Clear up
Climb
Clip
Clock
Close
Close out
Close up
Coach
Co-administer
Co-arrange
Coat
Co-author
Co-chair
Co-compose
Co-contribute
Co-coordinate
Co-create
Code
Co-defend
Co-design
Co-develop
Co-direct
Co-edit
Cofounded
Co-handle
Co-head
Cohere
Co-invent
Co-lead
Collaborate
Collate
Collect
Color code
Color correct
Co-manage
Combine
Command
Commence
Comment on
Commission
Commit to
Communicate with
Compare
Compensate
Compete with
Compile
Complement
Complete
Comply with

Compose
Compound
Compress
Compute
Computerize
Conceive
Concentrate on
Conceptualize
Conclude
Condense
Condition
Conduct
Confect
Confer with
Configure
Confirm
Confiscate
Conform to
Confront
Congregate
Conjure (up)
Connect
Consent to
Conserve
Consider
Consign
Console
Consolidate
Consort
Constrain
Constrict
Construct
Consult
Contact
Contain
Contemplate
Contest
Continue
Contract
Contrast
Contribute to
Contrive
Control
Convene
Converge
Converse
Convert
Convey
Convince
Cook
Cool (down)
Cooperate (with)
Coordinate
Co-partner

Co-present
Co-produce
Co-promote
Copy
Copy write
Copyright
Corral
Correct
Correlate
Correspond (with)
Corroborate
Cosign
Co-sponsor
Cost
Counsel
Count
Counteract
Counter-balance
Counterbid
Counter-demand
Counter-mand
Countersign
Couple
Cover
Co-write
Crack down on
Craft
Create
Credit
Critique
Crop
Cross-check
Cross-file
Cross-index
Cross-link
Cross-reference
Cross-section
Cross-sell
Cull
Cultivate
Culture
Cumulate
Curtail
Customize
Cut
Cut back
Cut down
Cycle

(continued)

ACTION VERBS FOR ALL PROFESSIONS *(continued)*

Step 3

D

Deactivate
Deal (with)
Debate
Debeak
Debit
Debrief
Debug
Decentralize
Decide
Decipher
Declare
Declassify
Decline
Decode
Decompress
Decorate
Decrease
Dedicate
Deduce
Deduct
Defeat
Defend
Defer
Define
Deflate
Deflect
Defray
Dehire
Dehydrate
Delay
Delegate
Delete
Deliberate
Delineate
Deliver
Demagnetize
Demise
Demolish
Demonstrate
Demount
Demystify
Denote
Densify
Deny
Deploy
Deport
Depose
Deposit
Depreciate
Depute
Deputize
Derive
Describe

Deselect
Design
Designate
Detach
Detail
Detain
Detect
Determine
Detoxify
Develop
Deviate
Devise
Devote
Diagnose
Diagram
Dictate
Differentiate
Diffuse
Dig
Digitize
Dilate
Diminish
Dine
Direct
Disable
Disallow
Disarm
Disassemble
Disband
Disburse
Discard
Disclaim
Disclose
Disconnect
Discontinue
Discount
Discover
Discuss
Disinfect
Dislocate
Dislodge
Dismantle
Dismiss
Dispatch
Dispense
Disperse
Displace
Display
Dispose of
Disprove
Dispute
Dissect
Dissemble
Disseminate
Dissipate

Dissolve
Dissuade
Distill
Distinguish
Distribute
Disunite
Diversify
Divert
Divest
Divide
Dock
Document
Dodge
Domesticate
Dominate
Double
Downsize
Draft
Drain
Dramatize
Drape
Draw
Dredge
Dress
Drill
Drive
Drop
Duplicate
Dust

E

Earmark
Earn
Ease
Economize
Edify
Edit
Educate
Effect
Effectuate
Eject
Elaborate
Elasticize
Elect
Electrify
Electroform
Electrolyze
Electroplate
Elevate
Elicit
Eliminate
Elude
E-mail
Emancipate
Embed

Embellish
Embody
Embrace
Empathize
Emphasize
Employ
Empower
Empty
Emulate
Emulsify
Enable
Enact
Enamor
Encage
Encapsulate
Encase
Encircle
Enclose
Encode
Encompass
Encourage
Encroach
Encumber
End
Endear
Endorse
Endow
Endure
Energize
Enforce
Engage (in)
Engineer
Engrave
Enhance
Enjoy
Enlarge
Enlighten
Enlist
Enliven
Enmesh
Enrich
Enroll
Ensure
Entangle
Enter
Entertain
Enthrall
Enthuse
Entice
Entitle
Entrench
Entrust
Entwine
Enumerate
Enunciate

Envelop
Envision
Enwrap
Equalize
Equate
Equip
Equivocate
Eradicate
Erase
Erect
Escalate
Escort
Escrow
Establish
Estimate
Etch
Euthanize
Evacuate
Evaluate
Even out
Evict
Evolve
Examine
Excavate
Exceed
Excel in
Excerpt
Exchange
Excite
Exclude
Excuse
Execute
Exemplify
Exempt
Exercise
Exert
Exfoliate
Exhibit
Exhume
Exit
Exonerate
Expand
Expedite
Expend
Experience
Experiment
Expire
Explain
Explore
Export
Expose
Expound
Express
Expunge
Extemporize

Extend
Exterminate
Externalize
Extinguish
Extract
Extrapolate
Extricate
Extrude
Exude

F

Fabricate
Face
Facilitate
Factor
Familiarize
Farm
Fashion
Fasten
Fathom
Feather
Feed
Fend (off)
Fertilize
Field
Figure
File
Fill
Film
Filter
Filtrate
Finalize
Finance
Find
Fine-tune
Finish
Fire
Fish
Fit
Fix
Flag
Flambé
Flank
Flare
Flash
Flatten
Flavor
Flex
Flight-test
Flip
Float
Flock
Flow
Fluidize
Fluoridate

Flush
Focalize
Focus (on)
Fold
Follow
Follow
  through
Follow up on
Forbid
Force
Forecast
Forego
Forerun
Foresee
Foreshadow
Forestall
Foretell
Forewarn
Forge
Forgo
Form
Formalize
Format
Formularize
Formulate
Fortify
Forward
Fossilize
Foster
Founded
Fractionalize
Fragment
Fragmentize
Frame
Franchise
Free (up)
Freelance
Freeze
Frequent
Fricassee
Frisk
Fry
Fuel
Fulfill
Fumigate
Function (as)
Fund
Fund-raise
Funnel
Furnish
Further
Fuse

G

Gain
Galvanize
Gang up
Garden
Garner
Garnish
Gather
Gauge
Gear up
Generalize
Generate
Get
Give
Glaze
Glorify
Glue
Go
Govern
Grade
Graduate
Grant
Graph
Grasp
Gravitate
Graze
Greet
Griddle
Grind
Groom
Gross
Ground
Group
Grout
Grow
Guarantee
Guard
Guide
Gut

H

Habilitate
Halt
Hand
Hand out
Hand over
Handcraft
Handcuff
Hand-feed
Handle
Handwrite
Hang
Harbor
Harden
Harmonize
Harvest

Hasten
Hatch
Haul
Head
Heal
Heat
Heave
Heed
Heighten
Help
Hem
Herd
Highlight
Hike
Hinge
Hire
Historicize
Hit
Hoe
Hoist
Hold
Hold off
Hold up
Home grow
Homogenize
Hone
Honor
Hook up
Hose
Host
House
House sit
Housekeep
Hover
Hunt
Hurry
Hustle
Hydrate
Hydrogenate
Hydrolyze
Hypercharge
Hyper-
  polarize
Hyphenate
Hypnotize
Hypostatize
Hypothesize

I

Idealize
Ideate
Identify
Ignite
  (creativity)
Illuminate
Illustrate
Imagine

Imagineer
Immerge
Immerse
Immobilize
Immunize
Impact
Impede
Implant
Implement
Import
Impound
Impress
Imprint
Imprison
Improve
Improvise
Inaugurate
Inbreed
Incant
Incarcerate
Incite
Include
Incorporate
Increase
Incubate
Incur
Indemnify
Index
Indicate
Individualize
Indoctrinate
Induce
Infer
Influence
Inform
Infuse
Initiate
Inject
Inlay
Innovate
Inoculate
Input
Inquire
Inscribe
Insert
Inspect
Inspire
Install
Instill
Institute
Instruct
Insulate
Insure
Integrate
Intensify
Interact with
Interbreed

Intercede
Intercept
Interchange
Intercrop
Interdiffuse
Interface with
Interject
Interlace
Interlink
Interlock
Intermediate
Intermix
Internalize
Interpolate
Interpret
Interrogate
Intersperse
Intervene
Interview
Interweave
Intrigue
Introduce
Intubate
Inundate
Invalidate
Invent
Inventory
Invert
Invest
Investigate
Invigorate
Invite
Invoke
Involve
Involved in
Ionize
Irradiate
Irrigate
Isolate
Issue
Itemize

J–K

Join
Judge
Juggle
Justify
Juxtapose
Keep
Keep up
Kern
Key
Keyboard
Keypunch
Kick off
Kindle
Knead

L

Label
Lacquer
Laminate
Landscape
Lasso
Latch
Launch
Launder
Lavish
Lay out
Layer
Lead
Learn
Leave
  (behind)
Lecture
Legislate
Legitimize
Lend
Lengthen
Lessen
Let
Letter
Level
Level off
Leverage
Levy
Liaise
Liberalize
Liberate
License
Lift
Light
Lighten
Liken
Limit
Line up
Linearize
Link
Liquidate
List
Listen
Litigate
Liven (up)
Load
Loan
Lobby
Localize
Locate
Lock
Lodge
Log
Look for
Look up
Loop

Loosen
Lower
Lubricate
Lure

M

Machine
Magnetize
Magnify
Mail
Mainstream
Maintain
Make
Make up
Manage
Mandate
Maneuver
Manicure
Manifest
Manifold
Manipulate
Manufacture
Map
Marbleize
March
Mark
Mark up
Market
Mask
Mason
Massage
Mass-produce
Master
Match
Mate
Materialize
Matriculate
Maturate
Maximize
Measure
Mechanize
Mediate
Meet
Meld
Melt
Memorialize
Memorize
Mend
Mention
Mentor
Merchandise
Merge
Merit
Mesh
Metabolize
Metalize
Meter

Methodize
Metricize
Micro-
  analyze
Micro-
  encapsulate
Microfilm
Migrate
Mill
Mimeograph
Mimic
Mind
Mineralize
Mingle
Minimize
Mint
Missionize
Mitigate
Mix
Mobilize
Model
Moderate
Modernize
Modify
Modulate
Moisten
Mold
Mollify
Monitor
Monogram
Monopolize
Moor
Mop (up)
Moralize
Mortar
Mortgage
Motion
Motivate
Motorize
Mount
Move
Mow
Mulch
Multiply
Multitask
Municipalize
Muse
Musicalize
Mute
Mutualize
Muzzle
Mythicize

Step 3

(continued)

ACTION VERBS FOR ALL PROFESSIONS *(continued)*

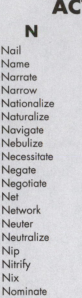

N

Nail
Name
Narrate
Narrow
Nationalize
Naturalize
Navigate
Nebulize
Necessitate
Negate
Negotiate
Net
Network
Neuter
Neutralize
Nip
Nitrify
Nix
Nominate
Nonretain
Normalize
Notice
Notify
Nourish
Nullify
Numerate
Nurse
Nurture

O

Objectify
Obligate
Oblige
Obliterate
Observe
Obsolete
Obtain
Occlude
Occupy
Offer
Officiate
Offset
Oil
Omit
Open
Operate
Oppose
Optimize
Orchestrate
Ordain
Order
Organize
Orient
Originate
Ossify
Oust

Outbreed
Outdistance
Outdo
Outfit
Outgrow
Outlay
Outline
Outperform
Outreach
Outsell
Overcome
Overhaul
Overlook
Override
Overrun
Oversee
Overtake
Overturn
Own
Oxidize
Oxygenate

P

Pace
Pacify
Pack
Package
Paddle
Page
Paginate
Paint
Pair
Palletize
Palliate
Palpate
Pamper
Pan
Panel
Parade
Parallel
Paraphrase
Parboil
Parcel
Parch
Pare
Parent
Park
Parlay
Parody
Parquet
Parse
Part
Participate
  (in)
Partition
Partner
  (with)

Pass
Pasteurize
Patch
Patent
Patrol
Pattern
Pause
Pave
Pay
Pay off
Peak
Peddle
Peel
Pen
Penalize
Penetrate
Perceive
Perch
Perfect
Perforate
Perform
Perfuse
Permeate
Permit
Perpetuate
Persevere
Persist
Personalize
Persuade
Peruse
Petition
Petrify
Phase (out)
Philosophize
Photocopy
Photograph
Photostat
Phrase
Pick
Pick up
Pickle
Pictorialize
Picture
Piece
  (together)
Pierce
Pigeonhole
Pigment
Pile (up)
Pilot
Pin (down)
Pinch
Pinch-hit
Pinnacle
Pinpoint
Pioneer
Pipe

Pit
Pitch
Pitch in
Pivot
Placate
Place
Plan
Plane
Plant
Plaster
Plasticize
Plate
Plateau
Play
Plea-bargain
Please
Pleat
Pledge
Plot
Plow
Pluck
Plumb
Poach
Poetize
Point (out)
Polarize
Police
Polish
Poll
Pollinate
Polymerize
Ponder
Pool
Popularize
Pore (over)
Portion
Portray
Pose
Position
Possess
Post
Postdate
Postmark
Postpone
Potentiate
Pour
Power
Practice
Praise
Preach
Preannounce
Preapprove
Prearrange
Preassign
Precast
Precede
Precode

Precondition
Precook
Precut
Predefine
Predesignate
Predetermine
Predicate
Predict
Predominate
Preedit
Preempt
Preen
Preestablish
Prefabricate
Preface
Prefer
Preformulate
Preharvest
Preheat
Prelaunch
Prelude
Premeasure
Premiere
Premix
Preoccupy
Preorder
Prep
Prepackage
Prepare
Prepaste
Preprint
Preprocess
Preprogram
Prequalify
Prerecord
Preregister
Preschedule
Prescore
Prescreen
Prescribe
Preselect
Present
Preserve
Preset
Preside
  (over)
Presort
Prespecify
Press
Pressure
Pressurize
Presume
Pretreat
Prevail
Prevent
Preview
Price

Price set
Prime
Print
Prioritize
Privatize
Probate
Probe (into)
Problem-
  solve
Proceed
Process
Proclaim
Procure
Produce
Profess
Professionalize
Profile
Profit
Program
Progress
Prohibit
Project
Proliferate
Prolong
Promise
Promote
Prompt
Promulgate
Pronounce
Proof
Proofread
Prop
Propagate
Propel
Proportion
Propose
Prorate
Prosecute
Prospect
Prosper
Protect
Protest
Prove
Provide
Prune
Pry (into)
Psychoanalyze
Psychologize
Publicize
Publish
Pull
Pull over
Pull through
Pulp
Pump
Punctuate
Puncture

Punish
Purchase
Purge
Purify
Purport
Pursue
Push
Put

Q

Quadrupled
Qualify
Quantify
Quarantine
Query
Quest
Question
Quicken
Quiet
Quill
Quilt
Quit
Quiz
Quote

R

Race
Radiate
Raise
Rake
Rally
Ramify
Randomize
Range
Rank
Rate
Ratify
Rationalize
Rattle
Ravel
Reacclimate
Reach (for)
Reach (out
  to)
Reacquaint
Reacquire
React
Reactivate
Read
Readdress
Readjust
Reaffirm
Reaffix
Realign
Realize

Reallocate
Reanalyze
Reapply
Reappraise
Reappropriate
Rearrange
Reason (with)
Reassemble
Reassert
Reassess
Reassign
Reassure
Reattach
Reattempt
Rebalance
Rebate
Rebid
Rebind
Rebook
Rebuild
Rebut
Recalculate
Recall
Recant
Recap
Recapitulate
Recapture
Recast
Receipt
Receive
Recharge
Recheck
Reciprocate
Recirculate
Recite
Reclaim
Reclassify
Recognize
Recoil
Recollect
Re-collect
Recommence
Recommend
Recompense
Recompile
Recompose
Recompute
Reconcile
Recondition
Reconfigure
Reconfirm
Reconsider

Reconstruct
Recontact
Reconvert
Reconvey
Record
Recoup
Recover
Re-create
Recruit
Rectify
Recultivate
Recycle
Redeem
Redeliver
Redeposit
Redesign
Redevelop
Redirect
Rediscount
Redistribute
Redistrict
Redraft
Redraw
Redress
Redrill
Reduce
Reduplicate
Reeducate
Reel
Reelect
Reemploy
Reengage
Reengineer
Reenroll
Reenter
Reerect
Reestablish
Reestimate
Reevaluate
Reexamine
Reexplore
Reface
Refer
Refile
Refill
Refinance
Refine
Reflect
Reflow
Refocus
Reforge
Reform
Re-form
Reformat

Reformulate
Refrain
Reframe
Refresh(en)
Refrigerate
Refuel
Refund
Refurbish
Refurnish
Refuse
Refute
Regain
Regard
Regenerate
Regiment
Regionalize
Register
Regrade
Regrow
Regulate
Rehabilitate
Rehear
Rehearse
Rehire
Rehouse
Rehydrate
Reimburse
Reinforce
Reink
Reinspect
Reinspire
Reinstall
Reinstate
Reintegrate
Reintroduce
Reinvent
Reinvest
Reinvestigate
Reissue
Reiterate
Reject
Rejoin
Rejuvenate
Rekey
Rekeyboard
Rekindle
Relabel
Relandscape
Relate
Relaunch
Relay
Relearn
Release
Re-lease

Relegate
Relieve
Relink
Relinquish
Relish
Reload
Relocate
Rely (on)
Remain
Remake
Remand
Remanufacture
Remarket
Remedy
Remerchandise
Remerge
Remind
Remit
Remix
Remobilize
Remodel
Remonetize
Remotivate
Remount
Remove
Rename
Render
Renegotiate
Renew
Renounce
Renovate
Rent
Reobserve
Reoccupy
Reopen
Reorchestrate
Reorder
Reorganize
Reorient
Repack
Repackage
Repaint
Repair
Repave
Repeal
Repeat
Repel
Rephotograph
Rephrase
Replace
Replan
Replant
Replay

Replenish
Replicate
Reply
Repolish
Repoll
Report
Reposit
Reposition
Repossess
Repot
Repower
Represent
Repress
Repressurize
Reprice
Reprint
Reprioritize
Reproach
Reprocess
Reproduce
Reprogram
Republish
Repunctuate
Repurchase
Repurify
Request
Require
Requisition
Reread
Rerecord
Reregister
Rereview
Reroute
Rerun
Resample
Reschedule
Rescind
Rescreen
Rescue
Reseal
Research
Reseason
Reseat
Resecure
Reseed
Reselect
Resell
Resend
Resentence
Reserve
Reservice
Resettle
Reshape
Reshingle

Reship
Reshoot
Reshow
Resign
Re-sign
Resist
Resize
Resod
Resolder
Resole
Resolidify
Resolve
Resonate
Re-sort
Resort (to)
Resow
Respecify
Respect
Respell
Respond to
Respray
Resprout
Restabilize
Restack
Restamp
Restandardize
Restart
Restock
Restore
Restrain
Restrengthen
Restress
Restrict
Restructure
Restuff
Restyle
Resubmit
Resume
Resupply
Resurrect
Resurvey
Resuscitate
Resynthesize
Retag
Retail
Retain
Retarget
Reteach
Reteam
Retest
Rethink
Reticulate
Retie
Retighten
Retire
Retool

Retouch
Retract
Retrain
Retranslate
Retransmit
Retread
Retrench
Retrieve
Retrofit
Retrospect
Retry
Retune
Return
Retype
Reunify
Reunite
Reupholster
Reuse
Reutilize
Revalidate
Revalue
Revamp
Reveal
Reverse
Revert (to)
Review
Revise
Revisit
Revitalize
Revive
Revoke
Revolutionize
Reward
Rewash
Reweigh
Rewind
Rewire
Rewrite
Ride
Rig
Ring
Rinse
Rip
Ripen
Rise
Risk
Rivet
Roast
Roll
Roll out
Root
Rope (off)
Rotate
Roughen
Round (up)
Route
Routinize
Row
Rub

(continued)

ACTION VERBS FOR ALL PROFESSIONS *(continued)*

Rub down
Rub out
Rule
Run
Run for
Run off
Rush
Rythmize

S

Sack
Saddle
Safeguard
Salinize
Salvage
Sample
Sanction
Sand
Sand-cast
Sanitate
Sanitize
Satiate
Satisfy
Saturate
Sauté
Save
Savor/
  Savour
Saw
Scale
Scale up
Scallop
Scan
Scatter
Schedule
Scheme
School
Scientize
Score
Scour
Scout
Scramble
Scrap
Screen
Screen test
Script
Scroll
Scrub
Scrutinize
Sculpt
Sculpture
Seal
Seal off

Search
Season
Seat
Seclude
Section
Secure
Sedate
Seed
Seek
Segment
Seize
Select
Sell
Send
Sense
Sensitize
Sentence
Separate
Sequence
Serve
Service
Set
Set off
Set up
Settle
Sever
Sew
Shade
Shake
Shape
Shape up
Share
Sharpen
Shave
Shear
Shed
Shell
Shelve
Shepherd
Shield
Shift
Shim
Shine
Shingle
Ship
Shoot
Shorten
Shoulder
Show
Showcase
Shred
Shrink
Shuffle

Shut off
Shut out
Side
Sift
Sign
Sign off
Sign out
Signal
Signify
Silence
Silhouette
Simmer
Simplify
Simulate
Sing
Sit (for)
Situate
Size
Sketch
Skim
Skip
Skiptrace
Slash
Smooth out
Snip
Soak
Soar
Socialize
  (with)
Sod
Soften
Solder
Solicit
Solidify
Solve
Soothe
Sort
Sound
Source
Sow
Space (out)
Spackle
Span
Spare
Spark
Spawn
Spay
Speak
Spear
Spearhead
Spec
Specialize in
Specify

Speculate
Speed up
Spell (out)
Spend
Spice (up)
Spin
Spin off
Spin out
Spindle
Spiral
Splice
Splint
Split
Sponge
Sponsor
Spool
Spoon-feed
Spot
Spot test
Spotlight
Spray
Spread
Sprinkle
Sprout
Spruce (up)
Spur
Spy
Square off
Stabilize
Stack
Staff
Stage
Stain
Stake out
Stall
Stamp
Stand (by)
Standardize
Staple
Star (in)
Stargaze
Start
State
Station
Stay
Steady
Steam
Steep
Steer
Step (in)
Step (up)
Sterilize
Stiffen

Stimulate
Stir
Stitch
Stock
Stockpile
Stop
Store
Straddle
Straighten
Strain
Strand
Strap
Strategize
Streamline
Strengthen
Stress
Stretch
Strike (a
  balance)
String
Stroke
Stroll
Structure
Struggle
Stud
Study
Stump
Stun
Style
Stylize
Sub out
Subcontract
Subdue
Subject
Sublease
Sublet
Submerge
Submit
Subpoena
Subscribe
  (to)
Subsidize
Subsist
Substantiate
Substitute
Substitute
  teach
Subtract
Succeed
Suggest
Suit
Sum (up)
Summarize

Summon
Supercede
Supervise
Supplement
Supply
Support
Suppress
Surcharge
Surpass
Surround
Survey
Suspect
Suspend
Sustain
Suture
Swap
Sway
Swear in
Sweep
Sweeten
Swim
Switch
Swoop (up)
Symbolize
Sympathize
Synchronize
Syndicate
Synergize
Synthesize
Systematize

T

Table
Tabulate
Tack
Tackle
Tail
Tailor
Take
Take in
Take off
Talk (to)
Tally
Tame
Tank
Tap (into)
Target
Tariff
Taste
Tattoo
Tax
Teach
Team (up)

Technologize
Telecast
Telegraph
Telephone
Televise
Tell
Temper
Temporize
Tempt
Tend (to)
Tenderize
Terminate
Territorialize
Test
Testify
Texturize
Thaw
Theatricalize
Theorize
Thicken
Thin (out)
Think
  (through)
Thought (out)
Thrash/
  thresh
Thread
Thrill
Throttle
Throw
Throw in
Throw off
Throw out
Thrust
Thwart
Tie (in)
Tighten
Tile
Time
Time stamp
Tint
Title
Toggle
Tolerate
Toll
Tone
Tool
Top
Toss (out)
Total
Touch off
Touch up
Tour

 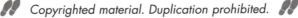

Tow	Tropicalize	Uncoil	Unplug	Vanish	Weather
Trace	Troubleshoot	Uncomplicate	Unravel	Vanquish	Weave
Track	Trowel	Uncover	Unreel	Vaporize	Weed
Trade	Trundle	Undercut	Unrush	Varnish	Weed out
Trade up	Try	Underdevelop	Unsaddle	Vary	Weigh
Trail	Tuck	Undergo	Unscrew	Vector	Welcome
Train	Tug	Underline	Unseal	Veil	Weld
Tranquilize	Tune	Underscore	Unsegment	Vent	Westernize
Transact	Tunnel	Understand	Unsell	Ventilate	Whisk
Transcend	Turn	Understudy	Unsoil	Verbalize	Whitewash
Transcribe	Turn around	Undertake	Unsort	Verify	Whittle
Transduce	Turn down	Underwrite	Untame	Versify	Widen
Transfer	Turn in	Unearth	Unthread	Veto	Win
Transfigure	Turn off	Unenforce	Untouch	Videotape	Wind
Transform	Turn on	Unfill	Untrain	View	Winterize
Transfuse	Turn over	Unfold	Unveil	Vindicate	Wipe out
Transilluminate	Turn up	Unharvest	Unwind	Visit	Wire
Transit	Tutor	Unhinge	Unwrap	Visualize	Withdraw
Transition	Tweak	Unhitch	Update	Vitalize	Withhold
Translate	Twine	Unify	Upgrade	Voice	Withstand
Transmit	Twist	Unimpair	Uphold	Void	Witness
Transplant	Type	Uninjure	Upholster	Volley	Work
Transport	Typecast	Uninsure	Uplift	Volunteer	Work closely
Transpose	Typeset	Unite	Upsell	Vote	with
Transshape	Typewrite	Universalize	Upsweep	Vow	Work out
Trap	**U**	Unlearn	Urbanize		Work up
Trash		Unlink	Urge	**W**	Wrap
Travel	Umpire	Unload	Use	Wade (through)	Write
Tread	Unaccept	Unlock	Utilize	Wager	Write off
Treat	Unaffect	Unloosen		Ward	
Trench	Unalter	Unmark	**V**	Warn	**X–Z**
Trigger	Unapprove	Unmask	Vacate	Warrant	X-ray
Trim	Uncancel	Unmount	Vaccinate	Wash	Yield
Trip	Unchange	Unmove	Validate	Watch	Zip
Triple	Uncharge	Unmuffle	Valuate	Water	Zone
Triumph	Unclassify	Unobstruct	Value	Waterproof	
Troop	Unclog	Unpack	Vamp	Wax	

Step 3

Getting Creative with Powerful Action Verbs

Having more than 2,800 action verbs available at your fingertips provides you the opportunity to write more descriptively and add more variety and impact to your resume. Once you have completed your responsibility bullets (which are covered next), come back to this section to see whether you can infuse some variety into your resume.

Here are some examples:

Old Wording	Revised Wording
Increased sales	Bolstered sales to a new level
Explained mortgage documents to clients	Demystified legal jargon for clients
Trained, developed, and motivated sales team	Energized and invigorated sales team to exceed goals by…
Developed a new (type of) program	Synthesized a new concept of…
Reversed falling sales	Rejuvenated (or Revitalized) declining product sales by…
Developed and negotiated win-win agreements with…	Mutualized all contracts into win-win agreements by…
Searched for and resolved incorrect accounting entries	Identified and eradicated all problem entries by…

Double-Playing Action Verbs

When you review the list of action verbs, you will find that a number of them are industry-specific. Take a look at these words from a new perspective. Instead of using a generic action verb, you can illustrate the action by using an industry-specific descriptive action word. You might even be able to come up with some clever, eye-catching wordings.

Here is an example: A home-decor retailer was advertising its spring specials. Instead of stating that they cut prices, they said "Pruned all floral prices by 20–50%"; "At 20% off, you'll take a shine to our candles"; and "Sitting down? Our seating collections are 20% off."

Here are some other examples:

- For a chef: **Confected** new menu planning ideas…
- For a sales associate: **Fortified** vitamin sales by…
- For a restaurant manager: **Cooked up** a new restaurant employee incentive program…
- For a farmer: **Cultivated** new harvesting methods for…
- For a retail manager: **Sweetened** bakery specials, which resulted in…
- For a construction project manager: **Retrofitted** unique construction techniques to overcome missing architectural details…
- For a landscaper: **Pruned** landscaping costs, which increased sales by…

START YOUR FIRST DRAFT

On the pages that follow, you will find worksheets for your first resume draft. You will include each of the jobs you identified in Step 1 and explain in full detail everything you do or did on a daily basis that is related to the focus of your resume. You can either write the information right into the worksheets in the book or

copy the worksheets from the accompanying CD onto your hard drive and type your information into them. To get started, follow these steps:

1. Starting with your current or most recent position, write or type each of the positions (employers) you came up with in Step 1—that is, your job titles, companies, and the years at each position—under jobs 1 to 5 right into the worksheets on pages 64–73.

2. Transfer over the first and second bullets from pages 45 and 50 for each of your positions.

3. Carry over your circled action verbs from pages 52–59 directly under each position title where they are applicable. When you do this, put similar functions together in their natural sequence. These will become your bullet starters. (You can use a piece of scrap paper first if that helps you organize the action verbs.) Here's an example:

Action Verb Examples		Put in Natural Sequence
• Configure	• Correct	• Install, configure, and monitor…
• Design	• Develop	• Design and develop…
• Diagnose	• Install	• Research, troubleshoot, diagnose, and correct…
• Monitor	• Provide	• Provide…
• Research	• Troubleshoot	

4. Next, review your bullet starters (action verbs) and determine which ones are most important to your targeted profession, are your most significant work functions, and are the first in order of function sequence. Then number them accordingly. Here's an example for an information technology professional:

(2) Install, configure, and monitor…

(1) Design and develop…

(4) Research, troubleshoot, diagnose, and correct…

(3) Provide…

5. Your bullet starters are already helping you define the work functions you perform. Now start to fill in the nouns in the sentences with what you do in this process. Using the same example, this is how your bullets might start to look:

1. Design and develop _____ (what?)
2. Install, configure, and monitor _____ (what?)
3. Provide _____ (what?)
4. Research, troubleshoot, diagnose, and correct _____ (what?)

Here's an example:

1. Design and develop <u>computer solutions and user-friendly systems…</u>
2. Install, configure, and monitor <u>hardware and software…</u>
3. Provide <u>technical support and solutions…</u>
4. Research, troubleshoot, diagnose, and correct <u>all system bugs.</u>

6. Taking this one step further, answer the question "for whom?" or "for what?" do you perform these functions. Try to quantify your answers with numbers whenever possible.

Here's an example:

1. Design and develop computer solutions and user-friendly systems <u>for all corporate divisions of this manufacturing company with 250 employees.</u>
2. Install, configure, and monitor hardware and software <u>to meet the needs of end users...</u>
3. Provide technical support and solutions <u>for 15 branches...</u>
4. Research, troubleshoot, diagnose, and correct all system bugs.

7. For the bullets that need to be developed further, ask yourself "What does this include?" or "What is the purpose?" In this case, bullets 2 and 3 can be further defined. You'll leave the other bullets alone for now.

Here's the example text with further development:

1. Design and develop computer solutions and user-friendly systems for all corporate divisions of this manufacturing company with 250 employees.
2. Install, configure, and monitor hardware and software to meet the needs of end users, <u>including operating systems, office suites, peripherals, and output devices.</u>
3. Provide technical support and solutions for 15 branches <u>in the network migration from system 0.0 to system 0.0.</u>
4. Research, troubleshoot, diagnose, and correct all system bugs.

8. Ask yourself whether there is a resultant benefit to what you performed. If so, be sure to include it. In this example, bullet 3 can show a benefit:

1. Design and develop computer solutions and user-friendly systems for all corporate divisions of this manufacturing company with 250 employees.
2. Install, configure, and monitor hardware and software to meet the needs of end users, including operating systems, office suites, peripherals, and output devices.
3. Provided technical support and solutions for 15 branches in the network migration from system 0.0 to system 0.0, <u>which resulted in a smooth and timely conversion.</u>
4. Research, troubleshoot, diagnose, and correct all system bugs.

9. A descriptive word properly placed can answer the "How well?" or "What type?" question. Review each of your bullets and determine whether there is a descriptive adverb or adjective that can precede any of your functions (action verbs) to show how effectively you performed that responsibility. Here are some sample adverbs and adjectives.

Adverbs (Answer the Question "How Well?"):

- <u>Creatively</u> develop…
- <u>Professionally</u> greet…
- <u>Actively</u> work with…
- <u>Successfully</u> transitioned…
- <u>Significantly</u> surpassed…
- <u>Consistently</u> attain…
- <u>Accurately</u> prepare…
- <u>Dramatically</u> reduced…
- <u>Regularly</u> maintain…
- <u>Persistently</u> follow up on…
- <u>Appropriately</u> allocate…
- <u>Quickly</u> intervene…
- <u>Diplomatically</u> negotiate…
- <u>Persuasively</u> upsell…
- <u>Efficiently</u> answer…
- <u>Strategically</u> forecast…
- <u>Patiently</u> cater to…
- <u>Carefully</u> inspect…
- <u>Effectively</u> enhance…
- <u>Diligently</u> perform…
- <u>Concisely</u> edit…
- <u>Successfully</u> spearheaded…
- <u>Thoughtfully</u> address…
- <u>Thoroughly</u> review…

Adjectives (Show "How Well" by Describing "What Type?"):

- Develop <u>creative</u> lesson plans…
- Implement <u>successful</u> new policies…
- Prepare <u>accurate</u> records…
- Negotiate <u>diplomatic</u> relations…
- Conduct <u>regular</u> compliance reviews…
- Develop <u>effective</u> solutions…
- Allocate <u>appropriate</u> resources…
- Make <u>thorough</u> recommendations…

You can add an adverb or adjective to each of the four bullets, as follows:

- Design and develop <u>total</u> computer solutions and <u>user-friendly</u> systems for all corporate divisions of this manufacturing company with 250 employees.
- <u>Successfully</u> install, configure, and monitor hardware and software to meet the needs of end users, including operating systems, office suites, peripherals, and output devices.
- Provide <u>thorough</u> technical support and <u>effective</u> solutions for 15 branches in the network migration from system 0.0 to system 0.0, which resulted in a smooth and timely conversion.
- <u>Accurately</u> research, troubleshoot, diagnose, and correct all system bugs.

10. Before finalizing this step, think through all of your responsibilities for each of your positions and check them against what you have documented so far (here and in earlier steps) to determine whether you left out any important functions. Write these as you have done with the others. Provide as much detail as possible at this stage; you will get back to the wording in the editing stage in Step 9.

That's it for your responsibilities for now. Be sure you follow the same process for each of your position titles.

In Step 4, you will tackle your achievements for each position. The bullets you work up (your achievements) will be the next bullets you will include in the Professional Experience section of your first resume draft. Those bullets will follow right after the responsibility bullets you just completed.

In the Resume ClipBullets™ section (Step 6), you will find many additional "heavy-hitter" bullets that are specific to your position, which will also fall under the Professional Experience section of your resume. You will review them for applicability and inclusion in your resume draft as well.

Between the various methods of working up your resume bullets in this book, you should wind up with a terrific Professional Experience section!

RESUME DRAFT WORKSHEET

List your most recent position first. Take this from Step 2. Your most recent position is usually the one you will describe in the most detail. Use the two pages provided for your first position to work up your bullets thoroughly. Write as many responsibility bullets as you can right now. Be thorough in each. You will edit them later.

Job 1 (from Step 2)

Years: _____–_____: Job title:_____
                            Company:_____
                            Town:_____ State:_____

Responsibilities: Provide a detailed description of all related job functions. Start with action verbs and be sure to quantify everything.

Bullet 1
(from Steps
3 and 6):   ❏ _____
             _____
             _____
             _____

Bullet 2
(from Step 3): ❏ _____
             _____
             _____
             _____

Responsibility
bullets starting
with action verbs
(from Steps
3 and 6):   ❏ _____
             _____
             _____
             _____

             ❏ _____
             _____
             _____
             _____

             ❏ _____
             _____
             _____
             _____

             ❏ _____
             _____
             _____
             _____

             ❏ _____
             _____
             _____
             _____

             ❏ _____
             _____
             _____

Achievements: Include all achievement bullets you work up in Step 4 and Resume ClipBullets™ from Step 6. Write up as many achievement bullets as you can think of. Use additional sheets as needed to be sure your first draft is thorough.

Achievement bullets (from Steps 4 and 6) —leave blank for now.

❏ _____
_____
_____
_____

❏ _____
_____
_____
_____

❏ _____
_____
_____
_____

❏ _____
_____
_____
_____

❏ _____
_____
_____
_____

❏ _____
_____
_____
_____

❏ _____
_____
_____
_____

❏ _____
_____
_____
_____

❏ _____
_____
_____
_____

❏ _____
_____
_____
_____

Step 3

(continued)

RESUME DRAFT WORKSHEET *(continued)*

Job 2 (from Step 2)

Years: _____–_____ :   Job title:_____

Company:_____

Town:_____   State:_____

Responsibilities: Provide a detailed description of all related job functions. Start with action verbs and be sure to quantify everything.

Bullet 1 (from Steps 3 and 6):	❑	_____ _____ _____ _____
Bullet 2 (from Step 3):	❑	_____ _____ _____ _____
Responsibility bullets starting with action verbs (from Steps 3 and 6):	❑	_____ _____ _____ _____
	❑	_____ _____ _____ _____
	❑	_____ _____ _____ _____
	❑	_____ _____ _____ _____
	❑	_____ _____ _____ _____
	❑	_____ _____ _____ _____

Achievements: Include all achievement bullets you work up in Step 4 and Resume ClipBullets™ from Step 6. Write up as many achievement bullets as you can think of. Use additional sheets as needed to be sure your first draft is thorough.

Achievement bullets (from Steps 4 and 6) —leave blank for now.	❑ _____ _____ _____ _____
	❑ _____ _____ _____ _____
	❑ _____ _____ _____ _____
	❑ _____ _____ _____ _____
	❑ _____ _____ _____ _____
	❑ _____ _____ _____ _____
	❑ _____ _____ _____ _____
	❑ _____ _____ _____ _____
	❑ _____ _____ _____ _____

Step 3

(continued)

RESUME DRAFT WORKSHEET *(continued)*

Job 3 (from Step 2)

Years: _____ – _____: Job title:_____

Company:_____

Town:_____ State:_____

Responsibilities: Provide a detailed description of all related job functions. Start with action verbs and be sure to quantify everything.

Bullet 1 (from Steps 3 and 6):	❏
Bullet 2 (from Step 3):	❏
Responsibility bullets starting with action verbs (from Steps 3 and 6):	❏
	❏
	❏
	❏
	❏
	❏

Achievements: Include all achievement bullets you work up in Step 4 and Resume ClipBullets™ from Step 6. Write up as many achievement bullets as you can think of. Use additional sheets as needed to be sure your first draft is thorough.

Achievement bullets (from Steps 4 and 6) —leave blank for now.	❏ _____
	❏ _____
	❏ _____
	❏ _____
	❏ _____
	❏ _____
	❏ _____
	❏ _____
	❏ _____

(continued)

RESUME DRAFT WORKSHEET *(continued)*

Job 4 (from Step 2)

Years: _____ – _____ :   Job title: _____

Company: _____

Town: _____ State: _____

Responsibilities: Provide a detailed description of all related job functions. Start with action verbs and be sure to quantify everything.

Bullet 1 (from Steps 3 and 6):	❑ _____
Bullet 2 (from Step 3):	❑ _____
Responsibility bullets starting with action verbs (from Steps 3 and 6):	❑ _____
	❑ _____
	❑ _____
	❑ _____
	❑ _____
	❑ _____

Achievements: Include all achievement bullets you work up in Step 4 and Resume ClipBullets™ from Step 6. Write up as many achievement bullets as you can think of. Use additional sheets as needed to be sure your first draft is thorough.

Achievement bullets (from Steps 4 and 6) —leave blank for now.

❏ _____
_____
_____
_____

❏ _____
_____
_____
_____

❏ _____
_____
_____
_____

❏ _____
_____
_____
_____

❏ _____
_____
_____
_____

❏ _____
_____
_____
_____

❏ _____
_____
_____
_____

❏ _____
_____
_____
_____

❏ _____
_____
_____
_____

❏ _____
_____
_____
_____

Step 3

(continued)

RESUME DRAFT WORKSHEET *(continued)*

Job 5 (from Step 2)

Years: _____–_____: Job title:_____

Company:_____

Town:_____ State:_____

Responsibilities: Provide a detailed description of all related job functions. Start with action verbs and be sure to quantify everything.

Bullet 1 (from Steps 3 and 6):	❏ _____
Bullet 2 (from Step 3):	❏ _____
Responsibility bullets starting with action verbs (from Steps 3 and 6):	❏ _____
	❏ _____
	❏ _____
	❏ _____
	❏ _____
	❏ _____

Achievements: Include all achievement bullets you work up in Step 4 and Resume ClipBullets™ from Step 6. Write up as many achievement bullets as you can think of. Use additional sheets as needed to be sure your first draft is thorough.

Achievement bullets (from Steps 4 and 6) —leave blank for now.	❏
	❏
	❏
	❏
	❏
	❏
	❏
	❏
	❏
	❏

step 4

Identify Your
Achievements

ACHIEVEMENTS: THE MOST IMPORTANT PART OF YOUR RESUME

In this step, you will identify your achievements. Achievements (also known as accomplishments) are the most important part of your resume. Not including or improperly stating achievements is where 98 percent of people fall short when they prepare their own resumes. Your achievements are what set you apart from your peers and what will help you to gain significantly more interviews than the norm. So the worksheets in this step are critical components in the preparation of your resume.

Achievement bullets that intrigue recruiters show not only what you did, but how well you did it and what the results and benefits of your efforts were to your employers and its customers or clients. These statements are called "CAR" statements because they state the **C**hallenge you faced, the **A**ction you took, and the **R**esults you achieved. Remember, employers have a "what's in it for me?" mindset. You have to show them what they will get for their money—just as a salesperson has to sell the benefits of his or her product to consumers in order to make the sale. Employers, like consumers, want to get the best value for their money.

From my 20 years of experience as a professional resume writer, I can tell you that my colleagues and I nationwide find the quest to obtain achievement-related information from our clients to be the toughest part of preparing their resumes. The reason for this? It is obviously the toughest part for our clients to provide. That is why I created profession-specific worksheet solutions that are all-inclusive and work for everyone.

What Do Employers Want?

It's simple and it makes sense when you think about it: Employers seek to fill positions with applicants who come closest to the job description they need to fill, and they want to do so with someone they feel can help save them money, increase profits, or fulfill some other goal in some way. In other words, applicants who correctly target their resumes and showcase how their achievements helped benefit their employers have a greater chance of being offered positions than those who do not. In this way, the prospective employer can make a determination as to your suitability for their organization.

That is why achievements are the most important part of your resume. Successful resumes—ones that receive interview calls—are targeted and achievement-based. I can't tell you how often professional resume writers receive calls from prospective clients who say, "I just want a basic (or general) resume." There's no such thing—if you want it to be successful, that is! This chapter will help you identify your achievements and mesh those with what employers seek.

The Importance of Achievements

Everyone has achievements, although many people believe they don't. I will show you that you do have achievements and how simple it really is to determine your relevant achievements—whether you are seeking an entry-level job or an executive position.

For example, when I asked an auto painter about his achievements, he swore he had none. In fact, even getting him to tell me his responsibilities was like pulling teeth. He said, "I paint cars, that's it. I don't know what else to tell you." After asking him achievement-related questions, it became apparent that he saved the company more than $350,000 a year by eliminating the need for a prime coat (which took two people a day to apply) through the use of a certain kind of paint. This achievement saved the company not only the extra paint, but all the manhours to apply it. That $350,000 was worth more than 10 times his annual salary, which certainly answered the prospective employer's question "what's in it for me?" In fact, in essence, hiring an applicant who could save an employer this amount of money could actually be considered "free" for the employer.

Achievements set you apart from your peers and help you out-compete your competition, thereby helping you gain significantly more interviews. Your resume is the link between you and the right job for you. And achievements are the major component of this link.

Achievement Questions on the Worksheets

The type of questions contained in the worksheets varies. To strike an effective balance between providing as many options as possible from which you can select and not constricting or limiting your responses, there is a good mix of the various types of questions, as follows:

- ✔ **Check-off options:** The worksheets contain many check-off options from which you can select applicable answers based on your own unique situation. Having job functions and achievement options visually available helps job seekers remember and include all of their primary responsibilities and accomplishments. To help you develop your resume quickly, I've included information garnered from actual resumes I have written over the years. Experience has shown that sometimes people just need to see achievements in order to realize that what they performed was, indeed, an accomplishment.

- ✔ **Fill-in-the-blank answers:** You will also find fill-in-the-blank quantifying questions for information such as dollar amounts, percentages, number of employees supervised, and so on to help you gather your quantifying job information as well as other profession-specific details.

- ✔ **Open-ended responses:** Many of the questions require open-ended responses because it is important for you to capture your own unique accomplishments.

- ✔ **Yes-or-no answers:** Occasionally questions require just a simple "yes" or "no" answer. Those questions are easy to convert to bullets for your resume.

Converting Your Worksheet Answers to Resume Bullets

The questions on the worksheets have been formulated using resume language, so you can easily convert the questions along with your responses into resume bullets. When you have completed them, you will have almost all of the information you will need at your fingertips. As a result, the resume writing process will be much easier for you.

The examples on the following pages are ones that I use when instructing professional resume writers. I am sharing them with you so that you can see how easy it is to complete the questions in the worksheets and convert your responses into actual resume bullets. I've chosen a variety of question types for various positions and converted the answers to resume bullets as examples.

Keep in mind the basics:

1. Convert the question into the beginning of your bullet and add your answer to make a sentence.
2. Don't try to be flowery; keep it simple by making very clear statements about what you performed.

ACHIEVEMENT CONVERSION EXAMPLES

In these examples, notice how a string of specifically worded questions together with sample responses is more than sufficient to put together a concise but effective resume bullet. Think of it as going back to fourth-grade English, where you include the question within the answer.

Example 1 (Service Positions)

1. What services do you provide?
2. To whom do you provide these services?
3. How do your services help your clients?

The bullet foundation that I used to convert the questions and answers into resume bullets is boldfaced.

- **Provide** _____ [type of] **services to** _____ [whom?] **to help them**
  _____ [do what?].

COUNSELOR/SOCIAL WORKER

1. **What services do you provide?** counseling, advocacy, and linkage.
2. **To whom do you provide these services?** clients with a history of drug abuse.
3. **How do your services help your clients?** help them overcome their addictions and locate community resources.

- **Provide** counseling, advocacy, and linkage **services to** clients with a history of drug abuse **to help them** overcome their addictions and locate community resources.

OCCUPATIONAL THERAPIST

1. **What services do you provide?** occupational therapy and assessment services.
2. **To whom do you provide these services?** elementary students with learning disabilities, physical limitations, and/or communication impairments.
3. **How do your services help your clients?** help them enhance their abilities and function in an academic setting.

- **Provide** occupational therapy and assessment **services to** elementary students with learning disabilities, physical limitations, and/or communication impairments **to help them** enhance their abilities and function in an academic setting.

REGISTERED NURSE

1. **What services do you provide?** nursing health care and self-care instruction.
2. **To whom do you provide these services?** cardiac patients and their families.
3. **How do your services help your clients?** help them recuperate and return home.

- **Provide** nursing health care and self-care instruction to cardiac patients and their families **to help** patients recuperate and return home.

LIBRARIAN

1. **What services do you provide?** specialized library and technical services, including referencing, cataloging, and researching on the Internet.
2. **To whom do you provide these services?** the general public.
3. **How do your services help your clients?** help them find the books, periodicals, videos, and information they seek.

- **Provide** specialized library and technical **services to** the general public, including referencing, cataloging, and researching on the Internet **to help** patrons find the books, periodicals, videos, and information they seek.

Example 2 (Sales Associate)

In this example, all of the specifics needed to quantify this sales associate's achievements are provided via check-off options, fill-in-the-blank questions, and additional input. (You might not have all of the statistics; however, the question requests three ways to answer it, and even one of those statistics would suffice.)

1. How have you helped develop/increase the client base?

- ☑ Personalized service
- ☐ Attending client functions
- ☐ Networking
- ☐ Cold-call sales
- ☑ Creative presentations
- ☐ Trade shows

- ☑ Persistent follow-up
- ☐ Building client relationships
- ☐ Selling trust
- ☐ Educating consumers
- ☑ Community outreach programs
- ☑ Other: <u>knowing when to close the deal</u>

2. By how much have you increased the client base? <u>   20   </u>%
Increased by $<u>   .5 million   </u> (from: $<u> 2.5 million </u> to $<u> 3 million </u>)
(#) <u>   125   </u> (from: # <u>   750   </u> to # <u>   875   </u>)

- **Increased client base** by 20% ($.5 million) by opening 125 new accounts **through** effective community outreach, personalized service, creative presentations, persistent follow-up, and knowing when to close the deal.

Example 3 (Teacher)

You will note in this example that it took no time to provide a lot of relevant and specific information. You actually have more information than you need to use, so you can select the information that will have the most impact to include in your resume. Sometimes people have to see it in writing to understand what works!

1. What type of classroom-management and disciplinary techniques do you use that prove most successful with your students?

- ☐ Provide clear, consistent directions and follow-through.
- ☐ Use behavior-modification strategies.
- ☐ Establish a reward system.
- ☐ Use Assertive Discipline model.
- ☑ Develop a positive rapport with all students.
- ☐ Use Cooperative Discipline model.
- ☐ Place emphasis on structure and following school rules and regulations.
- ☐ Use positive reinforcement.
- ☐ Handle challenging behavioral populations.
- ☐ Mediation of peer conflicts.
- ☐ Utilize the point system.
- ☐ Ensure students remain on task.

- ☑ Exhibit confidence.
- ☑ Set clear behavior guidelines.
- ☐ Incorporate a sense of humor.
- ☑ Make learning fun.
- ☐ Actively engage students in lessons.
- ☐ Utilize individual charts and sticker reward system.
- ☑ Exhibit mutual respect.
- ☐ Set a work-oriented and relaxed atmosphere.
- ☑ Create a calm learning environment.
- ☐ Use a firm vocal tone.
- ☐ Set up and follow a class routine.
- ☐ Implement a token economy.
- ☑ Exhibit a friendly demeanor.
- ☐ Other: _____

- Successfully maintain effective classroom management by setting clear behavior guidelines, exhibiting mutual respect, creating a calm learning environment, and making learning fun.

ACHIEVEMENTS WORKSHEET INSTRUCTIONS

The Achievements worksheets are broken down by function (type of work) or position categories. Review each of the worksheets and answer all of the achievement questions that relate to your background and targeted position as thoroughly as you can. Start with the category that is most relevant to your job target; then review each of the other sections for relative functions, as applicable.

> **note** To create the best possible resume, it is important that you complete the worksheets as thoroughly as possible. Be detailed when explaining your achievements, and pay particular attention to areas that are most relevant to your job target. Sample fill-in-the-blank bullets are provided on pages 77–79 to start you off with some ideas for documenting your resume bullets; more will come in Step 6, "Round Out Your Resume with ClipBullets™."

When you answer the questions in the worksheets that follow, write your answers using the conversion method by converting the question into a sentence (your foundation) and follow with your answer (as the earlier examples show). Then transfer your resume bullets into your resume draft. (All worksheets are also on the CD at the back of this book, in case you would prefer to work on them in your word-processing program.) Don't worry too much about finalizing your bullets now. You will edit them in Steps 6 and 9.

Okay, got your cup of coffee and pencil? Let's proceed!

GENERAL ACHIEVEMENTS WORKSHEET

1. What was your number-one achievement in each of your positions? Explain how you accomplished each and what the results were. For example:

   ❑ Successfully achieved _____ [your accomplishment] by _____ [doing what?], which resulted in _____ [benefit to company].

   ❑ Spearheaded the _____ [type of] initiative to _____ [do what?], which benefited the organization in the areas of _____, _____, and _____.

   Position 1: _____

   _____

   _____

   Position 2: _____

   _____

   _____

   _____

   Position 3: _____

   _____

   _____

   _____

   Position 4: _____

   _____

   _____

   _____

   Position 5: _____

   _____

   _____

2. What was the biggest hurdle you overcame at each position? Explain how you accomplished each and what the results were. Indicate the applicable position. Here are some examples:

   ❑ Tackled _____ [what challenge?] by _____ [using what methods or techniques?], which resulted in _____ [what benefits?].

(continued)

GENERAL ACHIEVEMENTS WORKSHEET *(continued)*

❏ Successfully overcame the _____ [what problem or obstacle?] by implementing _____ _____ [type of] strategies, which benefited the organization by _____ [how?].

Position 1: _____
_____
_____
_____

Position 2: _____
_____
_____
_____

Position 3: _____
_____
_____
_____

Position 4: _____
_____
_____
_____

Position 5: _____
_____
_____
_____

3. Did your company or department adopt any suggestion you made? ❏ Yes ❏ No
What was the suggestion and corresponding benefit to the company? (Indicate which position.)

❏ Suggested and implemented a new method to _____ [do what?], which the company adopted [nationwide/company-wide/division-wide/throughout the department/other: _____], resulting in _____ _____ [what benefit to company?].

❏ The _____ department adopted my suggestion to _____ _____ [do what?], which [attracted new business/resulted in _____ (#) new accounts totaling $_____ / other benefit: _____].

❏ After successfully developing and implementing the _____ _____ [process, strategy, method, etc.], the company made it a corporate policy to _____ [do what?].

4. Have you been the recipient of any special awards for outstanding performance in any area? ❏ Yes ❏ No
If so, what award and in what area did you earn recognition?

❏ Recipient of ["Annual High Performer"/"Salesman of the Month"/"Customer Service"/"Exceeding Goals in District"/"Monthly Service Quality"/other: _____] Award for perform-ance in _____ [what area?].

❏ Awarded company-wide ["Most Valuable Player"/"Top Achiever"/"High Performer"/other: _____] _____ [type of] Award in recognition of _____ _____ [what?].

❏ Achieved _____ Award _____ [#] consecutive [years/months] for exceeding _____ [what?] goals by _____ %.

❏ Recipient of various top achievement awards throughout my employment, including _____, _____, and _____.

❏ Won the ["Customer Service Contract Sales"/other: _____] Award on _____ [#] occasions for selling the highest percentage of contracts to total sales—which was _____% over the average.

❏ Made ["Top Salesperson"/"Top Sales Achiever"/"Quota Club Performer"/other status: _____] in _____ [month and year] by [meeting or exceeding all quotas/opening up the most new accounts/other achievement: _____].

❏ _____
_____
_____

5. Have you been recognized by superiors, customers, or others for outstanding performance in any area? What did you do to earn this recognition? **Tip:** Review past performance evaluations and select the areas in which you were a high achiever.

❏ Recognized by supervisors for my performance in _____, _____, and _____ [what areas?].

❏ Consistently [ranked/evaluated] as [achiever/top performer] in _____ [what genre?] for _____ [what areas?].

❏ Commended by customers for [achieving/exceeding] expectations in the areas of _____, _____, and _____ [what?].

❏ _____
_____
_____

(continued)

GENERAL ACHIEVEMENTS WORKSHEET *(continued)*

6. Were you selected over other employees to perform a certain function due to some unique skill, attribute, or talent? For what were you selected? Why?

❑ Selected by _____ [whom?] as the _____ [what title or function?] to handle _____ [what?] for _____
_____ [purpose] due to my [dependability/quality control/organization skills/other: _____].

❑ Chosen to represent the company at the _____ [occasion or event], which resulted in _____ [what benefits?].

❑ Chosen as the company liaison with _____ [what agency or function?] to represent the firm in the area(s) of _____.

❑ Elected ["Team Leader"/"Company Sponsor"/"Project Manager"/other: _____] for excelling in [problem resolution/sales/customer relations/project management/other: _____], which resulted in [increased customer base/increased sales/a smooth and timely project completion/other: _____].

❑ Act in the capacity of the _____ [superior's title] in the areas of _____, _____, and _____ in supervisor's absence.

❑ _____
_____
_____
_____

7. In what ways have you contributed to the success of your employers? How did you accomplish this? What were the results? [Indicate which position.]

❑ Contributed to the success of the company by _____
_____ [doing what?], which had a direct impact on _____ [what area or function?] and resulted in _____
_____ [benefit].

❑ Contributed to the growth of the firm by _____
_____ [doing what?], which resulted in _____
_____[what benefit?].

❑ _____
_____
_____
_____

8. What projects or achievements have you accomplished that you are most proud of? Explain the challenges, actions, and results. [Indicate which position.]

❑ No. 1 Challenge: _____
_____
_____

Action(s): _____
_____
_____

Results: _____

_____

_____ Position No. _____

❑ No. 2 Challenge: _____

_____

_____

Action(s): _____

_____

_____

Results: _____

_____

_____ Position No. _____

❑ No. 3 Challenge: _____

_____

_____

Action(s): _____

_____

_____

Results: _____

_____

_____ Position No. _____

9. What type of professional expertise did you gain/learn from working in any of your positions? In what ways did you employ this newly acquired knowledge? How has it helped you do your job better and benefit the company?

❑ Gained expertise in the areas of _____ and _____ [what areas?], which helped me to perform _____ [what?] and benefited the company by _____ [how?].

❑ Successfully learned new _____ [type of] [industry/procedure/methods/other: _____] within _____ [what time period?] through [observation/ studying all available materials/attending trade shows/other methods: _____].

❑ _____

_____

_____

(continued)

GENERAL ACHIEVEMENTS WORKSHEET *(continued)*

10. Did you have to overcome adversity, ambiguity, or boundaries to accomplish what you knew was important to the company? ❑ Yes ❑ No

What type of people, mediation, and leadership skills did you use? What was the end result?

❑ Overcame _____ [type of]
[adversity/ambiguity/boundaries/other: _____] by strategically
_____ [performing what?], **which resulted in** [a more cohesive
environment/increased sales/other benefits: _____].

❑ _____
_____
_____

11. Have you met any hard-to-accomplish goals? ❑ Yes ❑ No

What were they and how did you accomplish this?

❑ Successfully achieved _____ [type of] goals while
combining and implementing various _____
_____ [type of] strategies, which resulted in _____
_____ [what benefit?].

❑ Efficiently [accomplished/processed/managed/other: _____]
_____ [what?] in a fast-
paced environment with tight deadlines by devising and implementing a means to _____
_____ [do what?].

❑ _____
_____
_____

12. Have you increased sales or profitability in any way? ❑ Yes ❑ No

If so, by how much? $_____ How did you accomplish this?

❑ Increased [sales/profitability/client base] by $_____ annually by _____
_____ [doing what?].

❑ _____
_____
_____

13. Have you helped streamline operations in any way? ❏ Yes ❏ No

If so, explain how you accomplished this. What were the results of your efforts?

❏ Streamlined operations in the area(s) of _____
by _____ [doing what?], which resulted
in _____ [what benefit?].

❏ Increased the efficiency of _____ [what
function?] by _____ [doing what?],
which resulted in _____ [what benefit?].

❏ _____
_____
_____

14. Have you increased productivity in any way? ❏ Yes ❏ No

Explain how you accomplished this. What were the results of your efforts?

❏ Increased _____ [type of] productivity by
devising a [new/revised] [method/procedure/other: _____] to
_____ [do what?], which resulted in
_____ [what benefit?].

❏ Increased productivity in the area(s) of _____ by
_____ [doing what?], thereby saving the company $_____ annually.

❏ _____
_____
_____

15. Have you helped your employer cut costs in any way? ❏ Yes ❏ No

If so, by how much? $_____ How did you accomplish this?

❏ Decreased _____ [type of] costs by _____
_____ [doing what?], which resulted in _____
_____ [what benefit?].

❏ Saved $_____ annually by cutting costs in the area(s) of _____
_____ by _____
_____ [doing what?].

❏ _____
_____
_____

(continued)

GENERAL ACHIEVEMENTS WORKSHEET *(continued)*

16. Have you helped your company grow its business or benefit in any other way? ❏ Yes ❏ No

If so, explain how you accomplished this and what the results were.

❏ _____

_____

_____

_____ Position No. _____

❏ _____

_____

_____

_____ Position No. _____

❏ _____

_____

_____

_____ Position No. _____

❏ _____

_____

_____

_____ Position No. _____

❏ _____

_____

_____

_____ Position No. _____

Step 4

ENTRY-LEVEL/NEW GRADUATE ACHIEVEMENTS WORKSHEET

If you are a college graduate who has internship experience, complete a worksheet for your specific field and explain each of your job functions and achievements (learning experiences are achievements!) as you would any other job. You will incorporate this experience right into your resume under the "Professional Employment" heading. Excerpts from evaluations make excellent testimonials in your resume. I'll explain where and how to include them in Step 8.

College attended: _____

City/State: _____ Dates attended: From _____ to _____

1. What degree did you receive? _____

   Year degree received: _____ Major? _____

   Minor? _____

2. Have you made the Dean's List? ❑ Yes ❑ No   President's List? ❑ Yes ❑ No

3. What was your overall GPA? _____ GPA in your major? _____

4. Are you a member of an Honor Society? ❑ Yes ❑ No

   Which one(s)? _____

   _____

5. Were you the recipient of any special awards? ❑ Yes ❑ No

   What was the award and what did you achieve it for?

   _____

   _____

   _____

6. Were you a student representative, officer, or member of any particular college function or fraternity? ❑ Yes ❑ No

   If so, what were your roles/functions? _____

   _____

   _____

   _____

7. Are you a member of any professional associations related to your major or your target career? ❑ Yes ❑ No

   If so, which ones? _____

   _____

8. If you have completed a senior project or any thesis work, explain the project and focus. (Attach additional sheets if needed.)

   _____

   _____

   _____

9. List your primary related courses of study.

   _____

   _____

   _____

Step 4

SUPERVISORY ACHIEVEMENTS WORKSHEET

1. What divisions, departments, or units do you supervise or oversee?

_____

_____

_____

_____

_____

2. How many employees are in your division/department/unit? _____

How many employees do you directly supervise? _____

How many do you indirectly supervise? _____

What are their titles?

_____

_____

_____

_____

3. List all functions you supervise, coordinate, or oversee.

a. _____

_____

b. _____

_____

c. _____

_____

d. _____

_____

e. _____

_____

f. _____

_____

g. _____

_____

h. _____

4. What is your involvement with the hiring process, if any?

_____

_____

_____

Step 4

5. What do you do to train, develop, coach, or mentor your subordinates?

_____

_____

_____

In what areas (topics) do you train and develop your staff?

_____

_____

_____

6. What do you do to ensure your staff completes all assigned functions correctly and in accordance with policies, procedures, and regulations?

_____

_____

_____

How do you know your methods are successful?

_____

_____

_____

What are the end results?

_____

_____

_____

7. How do you handle difficult employees? Explain your methods and results.

_____

_____

_____

8. What types of challenging employee situations have you had to overcome to keep the workflow running smoothly?

_____

_____

_____

How did you tackle these challenges?

_____

_____

_____

What was the end result?

_____

_____

_____

Step 4

(continued)

SUPERVISORY ACHIEVEMENTS WORKSHEET *(continued)*

9. What methods or means do you use to motivate your staff to produce high-quality products, meet high levels of customer service, and meet difficult deadlines or challenges?

_____

_____

_____

_____

10. What means do you use to evaluate your staff?

_____

_____

_____

How do you ensure that these methods are fair to all?

_____

_____

_____

11. Have you decreased turnover? ❏ Yes ❏ No. If so, by how much? _____

How did you accomplish this? _____

_____

_____

_____

12. What is the ❏ production, ❏ sales, ❏ customer service, or ❏ other quota for your department?

_____

By what percentage does your staff meet this quota? _____ %

How do they accomplish this?

_____

_____

_____

13. Have you developed any programs or procedures that cut down the workload or made your area run more smoothly? ❏ Yes ❏ No

If so, what programs did you develop and what process(es) did they help?

_____

_____

_____

How did you accomplish this?

_____

_____

_____

What were the results/benefits of your efforts?

_____

_____

_____

14. What methods, techniques, and personal attributes do you use that help you maintain a productive, quality-producing staff?

_____

_____

_____

How do you know these methods are effective/why do they work?

_____

_____

_____

15. If you asked your staff to rate your supervisory abilities, fairness, and the way you manage your employees and the work load, what would they say?

_____

_____

_____

Do they generally like working for you? ❑ Yes ❑ No. Why or why not?

_____

_____

_____

16. How does management rate your supervisory abilities? In what areas?
(Use or attach excerpts from performance evaluations, if available.)

_____

_____

_____

_____

Step 4

MANAGEMENT AND EXECUTIVE ACHIEVEMENTS WORKSHEET

1. In what ways have you helped the company increase revenue, profitability, or market share?

_____

_____

_____

_____

How did you achieve this growth?

_____

_____

_____

_____

What were the results/benefits to the company?

_____

_____

_____

2. If you decreased company costs or streamlined operations in any way, how did you accomplish this? What savings did you realize through this effort?

_____

_____

_____

_____

_____

3. In what ways have you helped increase your company's competitive edge? How did you accomplish this? What were the results?

_____

_____

_____

_____

4. What types of training initiatives have you put in place or have you directed and overseen? What were the results/benefits to the company?

_____

_____

_____

_____

Step 4

5. What initiatives have you put in place to develop new business?

_____

_____

_____

How did you accomplish this?

_____

_____

_____

What were the results/benefits to the company?

_____

_____

_____

6. How have you ensured that your company and products remain reputable, economically viable, current, and groundbreaking?

_____

_____

_____

What were the benefits to the company?

_____

_____

_____

7. How do you think outside the box?

_____

_____

_____

What have you accomplished to prove this? Show how using your visionary, nonconforming, innovative talents has helped your company break new ground or helped its people to flourish and the business to grow.

_____

_____

_____

_____

(continued)

MANAGEMENT AND EXECUTIVE ACHIEVEMENTS
WORKSHEET *(continued)*

8. In what ways have you increased employee morale and minimized turnover?

_____

_____

_____

_____

How did you accomplish this?

_____

_____

_____

_____

What were the results/benefits to the company?

_____

_____

_____

9. How do you coach, motivate, and develop a winning team and develop loyalty in your staff?

_____

_____

_____

_____

What incentive programs or motivation efforts have you used that proved successful?

_____

_____

_____

_____

What were the results?

_____

_____

10. In what ways do you effectively use the following personal attributes, which are critical to successful managers? Being approachable? Having composure? Being a mentor? Inspiring teams? Ethics and values? Integrity? Listening skills? Conflict management? Morale building? Decision-making? Critical thinking? Other?

_____

_____

_____

_____

11. What was the worst hand you were dealt? (Did you take over a failing company? Have to work with a noncreative, old-world senior management team?)

_____

_____

_____

_____

How did you successfully tackle and overcome this?

_____

_____

_____

_____

12. How do you balance being able to closely monitor all aspects of the business while at the same time delegating responsibilities to and making others accountable for their own creative initiatives so that you can be a "One-Minute Manager" and your employees can produce valuable results and feel good about themselves and the organization?

_____

_____

_____

_____

_____

_____

13. What types of products or programs have you launched?

_____

_____

_____

_____

What were the results?

_____

_____

_____

14. Have you created any departments or divisions? ❑ Yes ❑ No. How did you accomplish this?

_____

_____

_____

_____

(continued)

Step 4

MANAGEMENT AND EXECUTIVE ACHIEVEMENTS
WORKSHEET *(continued)*

How did it benefit the company?

_____

_____

_____

_____

15. What types of business-development initiatives have you spearheaded?

_____

_____

_____

_____

Through what means?

_____

_____

_____

_____

What were the results?

_____

_____

_____

_____

16. Have you established any state-of-the art programs or technological advances? ❏ Yes ❏ No

How did you accomplish this?

_____

_____

_____

What were the results?

_____

_____

_____

17. Have you reduced payroll costs? ❏ Yes ❏ No. What is the annual savings? $_____. How did you do it?

_____

_____

_____

_____

18. Have you increased productivity or efficiency in any way in any area? ❑ Yes ❑ No. What specific initiatives did you put in place to do this?

_____

_____

_____

_____

What were the results?

_____

_____

19. Have you reduced purchasing or other overhead costs in any way? ❑ Yes ❑ No. How did you accomplish this? What were the results?

_____

_____

_____

_____

_____

20. What types of corporate information technology systems or improvements did you spearhead? What business functions did these systems improve? What were the results?

_____

_____

_____

_____

_____

21. Have you negotiated any major contracts for your firm? ❑ Yes ❑ No. With whom and for how much? Did you increase profits for your company or reduce any costs associated with these contracts? How did you accomplish this?

_____

_____

_____

_____

_____

_____

Step 4

(continued)

MANAGEMENT AND EXECUTIVE ACHIEVEMENTS WORKSHEET *(continued)*

22. Have you secured any preferred provider, wholesale distributor, or other agreements? ❑ Yes ❑ No. If so, how did you accomplish this?

_____

_____

_____

_____

23. Have you increased purchasing service levels? ❑ Yes ❑ No. If so, how did you accomplish this? What were the results?

_____

_____

_____

_____

24. How and by how much have you increased customer satisfaction levels?

_____

_____

_____

_____

25. Have you improved safety performance levels? ❑ Yes ❑ No. If so, how?

_____

_____

_____

_____

26. Who do you manage? How do you inspire teamwork? What are the results?

_____

_____

_____

_____

27. Do you have any other achievements that you have not identified here? ❑ Yes ❑ No. What was your mission? Your actions? The results?

_____

_____

_____

_____

_____

ADMINISTRATIVE ACHIEVEMENTS WORKSHEET

1. What types of office, administrative, and support functions do you perform, coordinate, or supervise? What is involved?

_____

_____

_____

_____

2. Do you perform secretarial or executive assistant functions? ❏ Yes ❏ No. If so, what?

_____

_____

_____

_____

3. If your responsibilities include answering phones, greeting visitors, or handling customers, how well do you perform these functions? Give examples.

_____

_____

_____

_____

4. In what ways, if any, has your technical expertise helped your employer? (For example, did you provide office computer support, help improve any processing systems, provide scheduled maintenance, and so on?)

_____

_____

_____

_____

5. Do you perform any billing, data entry, or payroll responsibilities? ❏ Yes ❏ No. If so, how do you perform these functions well?

_____

_____

_____

_____

6. If your work is of a clerical nature, what type of clerical functions do you perform? How do you handle these functions in an exemplary way?

_____

_____

_____

_____

(continued)

ADMINISTRATIVE ACHIEVEMENTS WORKSHEET (continued)

7. What types of reports, contracts, or publications do you prepare, process, generate, or oversee the preparation of?

_____

_____

_____

_____

8. What types of correspondence, e-mails, and memoranda do you prepare? What is the purpose of this correspondence?

_____

_____

_____

Explain any independent judgment required as to their content and what you research, compile, or analyze when preparing them.

_____

_____

_____

_____

9. Do you act as a liaison between management, other departments, or customers? ❑ Yes ❑ No. If so, explain your involvement and how you perform this well.

_____

_____

_____

_____

_____

10. If you schedule or coordinate meetings, conferences, trade shows, or special events, what is your involvement?

_____

_____

_____

11. What methods or attributes do you use to handle visitors with the utmost of professionalism and follow-through, making every contact feel that he or she is important?

_____

_____

_____

_____

Step 4

12. If you have authority to coordinate or make independent decisions for certain nonroutine administrative functions, what are they and how do you perform them well?

_____

_____

_____

_____

13. What spreadsheet and database programs do you use to create, process, and maintain documents, charts, and administrative records?

_____

_____

_____

Do these documents contain technical information or difficult formats? ❑ Yes ❑ No. If so, describe them.

_____

_____

_____

14. Do you have responsibility for financial recordkeeping, such as monitoring budgets or preparing financial transactions? ❑ Yes ❑ No. If so, explain your involvement.

_____

_____

_____

_____

15. If you supervise a support staff, what functions do you oversee?

_____

_____

_____

_____

16. What other office-support, word-processing, filing, and other functions do you perform or oversee?

_____

_____

_____

_____

(continued)

ADMINISTRATIVE ACHIEVEMENTS WORKSHEET *(continued)*

17. What types of independent research, analysis, or compilation of information do you handle?

_____

_____

_____

What types of problems do you resolve independently? Explain the purpose and process.

_____

_____

_____

_____

18. If you handle customer or staff complaints or resolve time-sensitive problems, explain your involvement and the results you achieve.

_____

_____

_____

_____

19. If you interpret or apply complex information such as regulations, policies, or services, what type of information is it and how do you handle this?

_____

_____

_____

_____

20. Provide examples of functioning with independence or exercising discretion in applying policies and procedures.

_____

_____

_____

_____

21. How do you effectively balance and coordinate a workload of multiple projects, or, if applicable, a workload for several executives?

_____

_____

_____

_____

_____

Step 4

22. What functions does your boss rely on you to handle in his or her absence? _____

_____

_____

_____

Cite examples of how well you perform these functions.

_____

_____

_____

_____

23. Have you had any other administrative responsibilities or achievements that you have not identified here? What were the challenges, your actions, and the results of your efforts?

_____

_____

_____

_____

_____

_____

_____

_____

_____

_____

_____

Step 4

CREATIVE ACHIEVEMENTS WORKSHEET

The following resume worksheet is excerpted from Evelyn Salvador's profession-specific *Resume Worksheets for Creative Professions* book (Creative Image Builders), which can be ordered using the form at the end of this book.

1. What have you created or designed that has benefited the company?

_____

_____

_____

_____

What were the results?

_____

_____

_____

What was the importance of this achievement?

_____

_____

_____

_____

2. What types of innovative initiatives have you developed or promoted?

_____

_____

_____

_____

How did you accomplish this?

_____

_____

_____

What were the results?

_____

_____

_____

3. What types of design concepts/techniques do you use that have proven successful? What was the purpose/result of these concepts?

_____

_____

_____

_____

_____

Step 4

4. Do you meet with clients or others to strategize their creative needs? ❑ Yes ❑ No. What is involved in these meetings?

_____

_____

_____

_____

5. Are you involved in the creative design, marketing, or advertising process? ❑ Yes ❑ No. In what way? What are the results?

_____

_____

_____

_____

6. Are you involved in the production process of your designs? ❑ Yes ❑ No. What is your involvement?

_____

_____

_____

Did you save the company any money in this process? ❑ Yes ❑ No

_____

_____

7. Have your creative efforts increased sales or decreased costs for your company or its clients? ❑ Yes ❑ No. How did you accomplish this?

_____

_____

_____

What was the result?

_____

_____

_____

CUSTOMER SERVICE ACHIEVEMENTS WORKSHEET

The following resume worksheet is excerpted from Evelyn Salvador's profession-specific *Resume Worksheets for Sales and Marketing Professions* book (Creative Image Builders), which can be ordered using the form at the end of this book.

1. What type of customer service do you provide?

   _____
   _____
   _____
   _____

2. In what ways do you assist your customers (such as product selections, decision-making, catalog orders, purchasing, customizing, and so on)?

   _____
   _____
   _____
   _____

3. If you manage customer service, are you in charge of ❑ national, ❑ regional, ❑ international, ❑ local, ❑ area, or ❑ other [which? _____] customer service?

4. Besides customer service, do you oversee or handle any other areas, such as merchandising, cashiering, inventory control, shipping and receiving, or catalog order fulfillment? ❑ Yes ❑ No. If so, which areas?

   _____
   _____
   _____

5. Do you have profit-and-loss (P&L) responsibility? ❑ Yes ❑ No. Amount: $_____

6. Are you accountable for a budget? ❑ Yes ❑ No. Amount: $_____

7. What methods do you use to help improve customer service and to elevate customer satisfaction levels?

   _____
   _____
   _____
   _____

   What is your overall percentage of customer satisfaction? _____

8. What type of advice or consultation do you provide to your customers?

   _____
   _____
   _____
   _____

9. How many accounts do you service?: _____ . What is your involvement with clients on a daily, weekly, or other basis?

_____

_____

_____

_____

10. How do you keep your composure during difficult situations?

_____

_____

_____

What is the result? Provide examples/situations:

_____

_____

_____

11. Have you developed or implemented any new programs? ❑ Yes ❑ No. If so, what types of programs?

_____

_____

_____

_____

What was the intended purpose and resulting benefit of these programs?

_____

_____

_____

_____

12. Do you utilize market, competition, product, and pricing awareness in your position? ❑ Yes ❑ No. In what ways?

_____

_____

_____

_____

What are the benefits and results?

_____

_____

_____

_____

(continued)

CUSTOMER SERVICE ACHIEVEMENTS WORKSHEET *(continued)*

13. What cash-management/inventory-control functions do you supervise or handle (such as cash drawers, petty cash, bank deposits, receivables monitoring and reporting, asset protection, inventory control and management, payroll, and so on)?

_____

_____

_____

14. Have you helped increase customer satisfaction levels? ❑ Yes ❑ No. If so, from what to what? From _____ % to _____ %. How did you accomplish this?

_____

_____

_____

_____

15. How do you ensure optimum personnel utilization and that work activities are completed in a timely and efficient manner to meet customer needs?

_____

_____

_____

_____

16. Have you been instrumental in turning around a department? ❑ Yes ❑ No. If so, in what ways?

_____

_____

_____

What was the challenge? What types of obstacles did you face?

_____

_____

_____

_____

What were the results?

_____

_____

_____

17. Have you reduced customer service delivery time? ❑ Yes ❑ No. If so, from what time frame to what time frame? From _____ to _____. How did you accomplish this?

_____

_____

_____

18. Have you identified and implemented cross-sell or upsell opportunities? ❑ Yes ❑ No. What were they?

_____

_____

What were the results?

_____

_____

19. How do you handle customer complaints and problems in a way that keeps the customer satisfied without "giving away the store"?

_____

_____

_____

20. What is the average customer ticket amount? $_____. Has this amount increased since you have managed the department? ❑ Yes ❑ No. If so, what did you do to help increase the amount?

_____

_____

_____

21. What types of difficult customer service problems have you had to resolve? Provide the challenge, your actions, and the end result of your efforts.

_____

_____

_____

_____

_____

(continued)

CUSTOMER SERVICE ACHIEVEMENTS WORKSHEET *(continued)*

22. In what ways have you helped the company increase sales or profitability? How did you accomplish this? What were the dollar amounts/percentages?

_____

_____

_____

_____

23. Have you conducted any feasibility studies that resulted in increased profits? ❏ Yes ❏ No. What were they? What were the results of these studies?

_____

_____

_____

_____

24. Have you made any recommendations for new product development or improvement in existing products? ❏ Yes ❏ No. If so, what were they? Were your recommendations implemented? ❏ Yes ❏ No

_____

_____

_____

_____

25. What types of goals have you set or do you have to meet for your department or division? Do you or your staff generally meet these goals?

_____

_____

_____

26. What methods do you use to ensure floor coverage during peak periods?

_____

_____

_____

27. What is your involvement with developing and implementing floor-sales-promotion campaigns?

_____

_____

_____

28. What retail floor-sales techniques do you use to help increase sales? What has been the result?

_____

_____

_____

29. Are you involved in any retail advertising or sales promotions? ❏ Yes ❏ No. If so, explain your involvement.

_____

_____

_____

30. What effective stock-management methods do you use?

_____

_____

_____

31. Have you implemented any new customer service standards or increased any existing ones for your division/department/unit? ❏ Yes ❏ No. If so, what did you accomplish?

_____

_____

_____

32. What methods do you use to appease dissatisfied customers?

_____

_____

_____

33. Are you involved with coordinating shipping or delivery of merchandise to customers? ❏ Yes ❏ No. What is your involvement?

_____

_____

_____

34. What type of sales or other reports do you manage, compile, or prepare (such as sales reports, credit card receipts, bank deposits, accounts receivable/payable reports, and so on)? How do you ensure their accuracy?

_____

_____

_____

_____

MARKETING ACHIEVEMENTS WORKSHEET

The following resume worksheet is excerpted from Evelyn Salvador's profession-specific *Resume Worksheets for Sales and Marketing Professions* book (Creative Image Builders), which can be ordered using the form at the end of this book.

1. What types of products or services do you or your firm promote and market? To whom do you market these products or services? What is the price range?

_____

_____

_____

_____

2. Were you a pioneer in the startup of the firm, a division, or a new product-development effort? ❑ Yes ❑ No. If so, what was involved? What were the results?

_____

_____

_____

_____

_____

3. What types of market-research methods or techniques do you use? (Examples: focus groups, one-on-one interviews, Internet surveys, quantitative techniques, telephone opinion surveys, and so on.) How have these methods proven successful?

_____

_____

_____

_____

4. What types of market research, analysis, or assessment have you performed? Have you identified new markets? If so, which one(s)? Explain your involvement and the results.

_____

_____

_____

_____

5. Are you involved in researching, analyzing, monitoring, tracking, or forecasting trends? ❑ Yes ❑ No. If so, which trends?

_____

_____

Have you recommended, developed, or implemented any new products or services to meet those trends? ❑ Yes ❑ No. What products/services?

_____

_____

_____

Step 4

What was your involvement and what were the results?

_____

_____

_____

_____

6. Have you conducted competitive, demographic, or psychographic analyses or costing and budgeting? ❏ Yes ❏ No. For what? What was the end result?

_____

_____

_____

_____

_____

7. Have you created, coordinated, or implemented any new marketing campaigns, promotions, trade shows, or special events? ❏ Yes ❏ No. If so, what was your involvement and what were the results?

_____

_____

_____

_____

_____

8. What is your involvement with new business development or marketing programs? What are the benefits/results of your efforts?

_____

_____

_____

_____

_____

9. In what ways, if any, have you contributed to the firm's increased sales or profits? By how much? How did you accomplish this?

_____

_____

_____

_____

_____

Step 4

(continued)

MARKETING ACHIEVEMENTS WORKSHEET *(continued)*

10. Have you been involved in developing marketing strategy for your firm? ❑ Yes ❑ No. Determining product demand? ❑ Yes ❑ No. Identifying new potential markets? ❑ Yes ❑ No. What was your involvement and what were the results?

_____

_____

_____

_____

11. Have you performed any product analysis or testing? ❑ Yes ❑ No. On what product(s)? What was the final result?

_____

_____

_____

12. Have you designed or developed any promotional materials for direct-mail or marketing campaigns? ❑ Yes ❑ No. Worked with a design team on layout and production? ❑ Yes ❑ No. What was your involvement and the results of the campaign?

_____

_____

_____

_____

13. Have you written any advertising or promotional copy for consumer or corporate campaigns? ❑ Yes ❑ No. What was it for?

_____

_____

_____

_____

14. What type of research and analysis do you conduct?

_____

_____

_____

What is this research and analysis used for?

_____

_____

_____

_____

Step 4

15. Have you devised methods for obtaining data; evaluated data; or conducted telephone, mail, or Internet surveys to do so? ❑ Yes ❑ No. If so, what type of data? What was it used for? (Examples: required to make decisions on promotions, distribution, design, or pricing of products; for adding new merchandise lines; opening new branches; and so on.)

_____

_____

_____

_____

_____

16. Have you created or delivered any client presentations? ❑ Yes ❑ No. If so, on what? What was the result of your efforts?

_____

_____

_____

_____

17. What type of marketing reports do you prepare? What are they used for?

_____

_____

_____

_____

18. Have you helped establish brand recognition, product visibility, or consumer awareness of any products? ❑ Yes ❑ No. Was this for your company or a client? _____

What type of branding, visibility, or awareness did you create?

_____

_____

How did you accomplish this and what were the results?

_____

_____

_____

_____

_____

Step 4

(continued)

MARKETING ACHIEVEMENTS WORKSHEET *(continued)*

19. Have you helped identify any sales opportunities or new product concepts? ❏ Yes ❏ No. In what way? What was the result?

_____

_____

_____

20. Have you developed a pricing strategy for any new products or services to maximize your firm's share of the market? ❏ Yes ❏ No. If so, what was it for?

_____

_____

_____

_____

21. Are you responsible for any budgets, advertising sales, or cost management? ❏ Yes ❏ No. If so, which ones and for what amounts?

_____

_____

_____

What means do you use to manage them effectively?

_____

_____

_____

22. Have you been involved in corporate giveaways, community events, or fund-raising endeavors? ❏ Yes ❏ No. If so, explain your involvement and the results.

_____

_____

_____

_____

23. Have you helped elevate market penetration by meeting or exceeding sales goals? ❏ Yes ❏ No. If so, how did you accomplish this, and by what percentage did you exceed goals? What closing ratio did you achieve?

_____

_____

_____

_____

Step 4

24. Have you handled any public relations functions? ❏ Yes ❏ No. Written or distributed news releases? ❏ Yes ❏ No. Obtained press coverage? ❏ Yes ❏ No. How did you achieve this and what were the results?

_____

_____

_____

_____

_____

25. Have you ever been a speaker or presenter at any conventions, conferences, workshops, or public engagements? ❏ Yes ❏ No. On what topic did you speak? Who were your attendees? How did it turn out?

_____

_____

_____

_____

_____

26. Have you played a role in the creation of any other marketing programs or plans, such as the structure and development of a business plan or market analysis? ❏ Yes ❏ No. If so, what was your involvement and what were the results?

_____

_____

_____

_____

_____

27. Have you developed online marketing initiatives such as blogs, Twitter, Facebook, etc.? ❏ Yes ❏ No. How many followers have you garnered for the company?

_____

_____

_____

_____

_____

PRODUCTION ACHIEVEMENTS WORKSHEET

The following resume worksheet is excerpted from Evelyn Salvador's profession-specific *Resume Worksheets for Business Professions* book (Creative Image Builders), which can be ordered using the form at the end of this book.

1. What involvement do you have in the production process?

_____

_____

_____

_____

   How do you ensure a smooth process and quality control?

_____

_____

_____

_____

2. Have you increased productivity rates in any way? How? What were the results?

_____

_____

_____

_____

3. Have you decreased production costs? ❏ Yes ❏ No. If so, how did you achieve this?

_____

_____

_____

_____

   What were the results?

_____

_____

_____

4. How do you ensure production accuracy? What are the results?

_____

_____

_____

_____

5. What types of products or parts assembly do you manage, supervise, perform, monitor, inspect, or coordinate the production of?

_____

_____

Step 4

_____

_____

6. What is your primary involvement in the manufacturing and production processes?

_____

_____

_____

7. What production/manufacturing functions do you manage or supervise?

- ❑ Manage production process
- ❑ Direct manufacturing/production functions
- ❑ Establish production timelines
- ❑ Establish production methods and applications
- ❑ Determine required resources
- ❑ Supervise production assembly work
- ❑ Supervise production work
- ❑ Control manufacturing projects
- ❑ Supervise machine shop
- ❑ Manage production schedules
- ❑ Plan and schedule workload
- ❑ Expedite parts flow through production stages
- ❑ Review production schedules
- ❑ Direct production operations and processes
- ❑ Monitor budget and expenses
- ❑ Troubleshoot and correct production problems

- ❑ Provide work direction
- ❑ Monitor production schedules
- ❑ Communicate with suppliers
- ❑ Direct quality assurance program/operations
- ❑ Meet performance objectives
- ❑ Identify and resolve quality problem areas
- ❑ Handle inventory control
- ❑ Record testing procedure results
- ❑ Ensure product quality
- ❑ Prepare reports and documentation
- ❑ Monitor and inspect production
- ❑ Conduct quality-assurance training
- ❑ Evaluate vendors
- ❑ Approve/reject finished products
- ❑ Other: _____

8. What tools, machinery, and equipment do you set up, operate, or oversee?

_____

_____

_____

_____

9. What production/manufacturing functions do you perform?

_____

_____

_____

_____

(continued)

PRODUCTION ACHIEVEMENTS WORKSHEET *(continued)*

10. How do you perform these functions in an exceptional manner?

❏ Assemble products

❏ Perform subassembly of products

❏ Meet performance deadlines

❏ Read/follow assembly sketches/blueprints

❏ Apply labels

❏ Assemble materials into product packaging/cartons

❏ Collate materials

❏ Adhere to all performance standards

❏ Perform pre-assembly work

❏ Recommend quality improvement changes

❏ Set up belts

❏ Test manufactured parts for quality

❏ Other: _____
_____

11. If you have scheduled equipment use, sequence of operations, or manpower, explain and quantify your involvement for each.

_____
_____
_____
_____
_____

12. If you are involved in the estimation process of costs, labor, materials, or time, explain and quantify your involvement.

_____
_____
_____
_____
_____

13. What methods do you use to ensure production accuracy and quality control?

_____
_____
_____
_____

14. How do you ensure a smooth and timely workflow process in all production phases or those in which you perform?

_____
_____
_____
_____

Step 4

15. Have you increased productivity rates in any way? ❏ Yes ❏ No. If so, how did you achieve this?

_____

_____

_____

What were the results (provide percentages)?

_____

_____

_____

16. Have you decreased production costs in any way? ❏ Yes ❏ No. If so, in what area(s)?

_____

_____

_____

How did you accomplish this and what were the results?

_____

_____

_____

17. If you develop and monitor a budget, which one(s) and for how much?

_____

_____

_____

18. Have you established any new production methods or applications? ❏ Yes ❏ No. If so, what were they and what process did they involve?

_____

_____

_____

How is this method better than a prior one?

_____

_____

_____

What process did it improve? What are the benefits?

_____

_____

_____

19. If you helped decrease final product turnaround time, by what means did you accomplish this and what was the end result?

_____

_____

_____

(continued)

PRODUCTION ACHIEVEMENTS WORKSHEET *(continued)*

20. If you supervise production assembly work, a machine shop, or other manufacturing process, how many shifts and workers do you oversee? What titles? What functions?

_____

_____

_____

_____

21. Describe a typical production schedule. What are the timelines? The challenges? How many people are involved in the process?

_____

_____

_____

_____

_____

_____

_____

22. What is your involvement in the evaluation and selection of vendors?

_____

_____

23. How do you ensure that the end product meets your firm's (or clients') needs, specifications, and technical standards?

_____

_____

24. What types of production problems do you troubleshoot and correct? How do you identify and resolve quality problem areas?

_____

_____

_____

Step 4

25. What types of production reports and documentation do you prepare? What do you do to ensure that all required details are included?

_____

_____

26. What types of performance objectives must you meet?

_____

_____

27. Describe the largest manufacturing projects you have been involved in performing, supervising, or managing. Include the project scope and cost. Indicate for which position. (Use additional sheet if needed.)

(a) _____

_____

_____ $ _____

(b) _____

_____

_____ $ _____

(c) _____

_____

_____ $ _____

(d) _____

_____

_____ $ _____

(e) _____

_____

_____ $ _____

(f) _____

_____

_____ $ _____

28. What other manufacturing/production challenges have you tackled? Explain the process and results.

_____

_____

_____

_____

_____

Step 4

SALES ACHIEVEMENTS WORKSHEET

The following resume worksheet is excerpted from Evelyn Salvador's profession-specific *Resume Worksheets for Sales and Marketing Professions* book (Creative Image Builders), which can be ordered using the form at the end of this book.

1. What does your firm sell and to whom? Are you involved in the sale of all of these products or certain ones? A particular division or region? Which?

_____

_____

2. Do you conduct or manage inside or outside sales? Local, regional, national, or global sales?

❏ Inside Sales ❏ Outside Sales ❏ Local ❏ Regional ❏ National ❏ Global

3. Who is your target market?

_____

4. What is the price range of, and company and regional sales amounts for, these products/services?

Product price range: $_____ Annual company sales: $_____

Your regional sales: $_____ Average regional sales: $_____

Your average ticket: $_____ Company average ticket: $_____

5. What is the price range of, and company or division sales amounts for, these products/services?

Price range: $_____ Annual sales? $_____

Daily average sales? $_____ Peak sales day? $_____

Weekly average sales? $_____ Peak sales week? $_____

6. What is the average ticket size of your sales? $_____ What is the normal average ticket size for your division? $_____ If your average ticket is higher than the norm, how do you accomplish this?

_____

_____

7. Have you increased the sales/account base? By how much? $_____ Percent: _____%

Increased by $_____ (from $_____ to $_____)

#_____ (from: #_____ to #_____)

To what do you primarily attribute the increase?

❏ Concentrating on higher-end sales

❏ Increasing loyalty of existing client base

❏ Promoting a consumer-sensitive approach

❏ Increasing product and customer needs awareness

❏ Launching direct-mail campaigns

❏ Developing programs/promotions that encouraged cross-selling or add-on sales

❏ Other:

_____

_____

Step 4

8. What sales methods do you use to sell your company's products or services?

❏ Personalized service   ❏ Creative presentations   ❏ Selling trust

❏ Attending client functions   ❏ Trade shows   ❏ Educating consumers

❏ Networking   ❏ Persistent follow-up   ❏ Community outreach programs

❏ Cold-call sales   ❏ Building client relationships   ❏ Other: _____

What has been your success rate/benefit to the company?

_____

_____

_____

_____

9. Do you generally meet or exceed sales quotas? ❏ Meet ❏ Exceed. What percentage of quota do you meet? _____%. What is the norm for your company versus your annual sales amount?

Company Norm: $_____ Your Annual Sales: $_____

10. What is the highest percentage of quota you have made? _____%. How do you accomplish this?

_____

_____

_____

_____

11. How does your region/division fare next to others? _____. If your region's/division's sales are higher, to what do you attribute this?

_____

_____

_____

_____

12. Has your region ever come in as No. 1 or in the top 10 in annual sales? What was your contribution? Explain.

_____

_____

_____

_____

Step 4

(continued)

SALES ACHIEVEMENTS WORKSHEET *(continued)*

13. Have you spearheaded the development and implementation of any new products or remerchandised existing ones? ❑ Yes ❑ No. What were the results?

_____

_____

_____

_____

14. What types of sales programs or promotions have you developed or implemented? What did this entail? What were the results?

_____

_____

_____

_____

15. Have you helped increase your company's competitive edge in any way? ❑ Yes ❑ No. If so, how did you accomplish this? Explain how this benefited the company.

_____

_____

_____

_____

16. In what ways have you helped increase customer loyalty or satisfaction and gained repeat business or referrals?

_____

_____

_____

_____

17. What types of proactive business-development/marketing initiatives have you spearheaded? Through what means? What were the results?

_____

_____

_____

_____

_____

_____

Step 4

18. What other initiatives have you put in place to develop new business, expand growth potential, or bring clientele up to a new level?

_____

_____

_____

_____

How did you accomplish this?

_____

_____

_____

What were the results?

_____

_____

19. How do you coach, motivate, and mentor a winning sales team and develop loyalty in your staff? What incentive programs or motivation efforts have you used that proved successful? What were the results?

_____

_____

_____

20. What skills or attributes do you use that help you build relationships, overcome objections, close sales, and achieve higher sales results?

_____

_____

_____

_____

21. In what ways, if any, have you have helped your company increase ROI?

_____

_____

_____

_____

22. Have you received any special awards for meeting or exceeding sales goals, customer service, etc.?
❏ Yes ❏ No. What were you recognized for?

_____

_____

_____

(continued)

SALES ACHIEVEMENTS WORKSHEET *(continued)*

23. Have you represented your company at any trade shows, conferences, or conventions? ❑ Yes ❑ No. If so, what benefits have you reaped?

_____

_____

_____

_____

24. How do you handle customer complaints?

_____

_____

_____

_____

25. How do you convert customer desires into needs? What is the result?

_____

_____

_____

_____

26. Do you have a low kill rate on your orders? If so, how do you accomplish this?

_____

_____

_____

_____

27. What is the largest sale you made or contract you negotiated? With whom did you make this sale? What was involved? Did this sale help your company attain higher national or global positioning?

_____

_____

_____

_____

28. Have you made any sales to Fortune 100/500/1000 companies? ❑ Yes ❑ No. Which companies (if you would not be breaking any confidentiality agreements to say this) and what did you sell? What was involved in the process?

_____

_____

_____

_____

SERVICE ACHIEVEMENTS WORKSHEET

The following resume worksheet is excerpted from Evelyn Salvador's profession-specific *Resume Worksheets for Business Professions* book (Creative Image Builders), which can be ordered using the form at the end of this book.

1. What types of services do you provide and to whom? What is the service's intended purpose and the resultant benefit?

   _____

   _____

   _____

   _____

2. What types of plans, programs, goals, or procedures do you develop to facilitate these services? What is their intended purpose? What are the benefits?

   _____

   _____

   _____

   _____

3. What types of methods, techniques, and strategies do you use that have proven successful? What is their intended purpose? What benefits have they provided?

   _____

   _____

   _____

   _____

4. What types of functions/projects/areas do you coordinate, manage, or supervise? What has been the resultant benefit?

   _____

   _____

   _____

   _____

5. Who do you work or meet with to benefit your clients? What do you develop?

   _____

   _____

   _____

   _____

6. Who have you helped? How did you accomplish this? What were the results?

   _____

   _____

   _____

   _____

(continued)

SERVICE ACHIEVEMENTS WORKSHEET (continued)

7. What types of evaluations/assessments do you make? What are their purposes? How have they benefited your clients/patients/students/other?

_____

_____

_____

_____

8. How do you plan for future needs?

_____

_____

_____

_____

9. How do the services you perform help your clients? What are their intended purposes and the resultant benefits of your services?

_____

_____

_____

_____

10. What types of techniques, methods, or strategies do you use in performing these services? How are these methods successful? What benefits do they provide?

_____

_____

_____

_____

11. If you manage or oversee any aspects of providing client services, what functions do you oversee and how do you ensure effectiveness?

_____

_____

_____

_____

12. Is there any client or group of clients you feel especially proud of helping? How did/do you accomplish this? What were the results?

_____

_____

_____

_____

Step 4

13. What types of evaluations/assessments do you make? What is their purpose? How have they benefited your clients?

_____

_____

_____

_____

14. How do you ensure that your evaluations/assessments are thorough and correct?

_____

_____

_____

15. What types of findings and recommendations do you prepare?

_____

_____

_____

16. Have you negotiated any large contracts? For what amount and what type of services? How did you accomplish this?

_____

_____

_____

_____

17. In what way, if any, have you helped build the company's reputation or competitive edge? What did you do to accomplish this?

_____

_____

_____

_____

Step 4

step 5

Put Together Your First Draft

- Prepare Your First Draft
  - 1. Write Your Professional Summary
  - 2. Transfer Your Information
  - 3. Start Your Bullets with Action Verbs
  - 4. Expand Your Sentences to Include All Functions
  - 5. Omit All Unnecessary or Redundant Words
  - 6. Type Your Text into Your Draft
- Write Your Professional Summary
  - Additional Professional Summary Bullets
  - Standalone Sentences
- Choose Your Format Template and Compile Your Resume

PREPARE YOUR FIRST DRAFT

Now you're at the stage of putting all your hard work together by preparing your first resume draft! You will use the resume format—reverse-chronological, functional, combination, or curriculum vitae—you selected in Step 2 and transfer the information from the worksheets and check-off lists in the preceding steps into the appropriate blank resume format. (Obviously, you can skip over all the other formats that do not apply to you.) You will do this according to the steps in the following sections.

1. Write Your Professional Summary

Start by completing the Professional Summary Template in the next section of this step. When you have done that, transfer your completed summary paragraph directly into your resume draft.

2. Transfer Your Information

Then carry over the information from Step 2 and from the General Worksheet pages in Step 3 to your resume draft. Do the same with the Responsibility bullets from Step 3 and the Achievement bullets from Step 4.

Always use bullets rather than paragraphs to describe your experience in the Professional Experience section. Bullets are easier to read and give the reader permission to stop in short intervals, as opposed to paragraphs, which can be overwhelming to the reader and can cause the reader to skip your resume and go to the next one.

3. Start Your Bullets with Action Verbs

Remember, almost without exception, every bullet in your Professional Experience section should start with an action verb (except where you have preceded it with an adverb). Check to be sure they do.

4. Expand Your Sentences to Include All Functions

Take a look at all of your sentences. When you have stated a function and can add "including…" to create more clarity and impact to your sentence, do so.

Examples:

- Successfully install, configure, and monitor hardware and software to meet the needs of end users, <u>including operating systems, office suites, peripherals, and output devices.</u>

- Provide specialized library and technical services, <u>including referencing, cataloging, organization of information, and researching on the Internet,</u> to help community patrons find the books, periodicals, videos, and information they seek.

5. Omit All Unnecessary or Redundant Words

Check all of your sentences for fluff words, unnecessary (understood) words, and superfluous words. Omit these words or rewrite:

- ✔ The words "I," "me," and "my" do not belong in your resume (they are understood).
- ✔ Omit the words "the," "that," and any other words that your sentence can flow without.
- ✔ If you have more than one bullet that explains similar functions, combine them.
- ✔ If you have included similar information within the same bullet, edit it down to its most concise form without deleting important content.

6. Type Your Text into Your Draft

At this stage, you should be typing your information into your word-processing program if you are not already doing so (in no particular format at the moment—just type it).

Step 5

WRITE YOUR PROFESSIONAL SUMMARY

The Professional Summary section will become the very first section on your resume, following your contact information. This section of your resume is an all-important one. It could determine whether a potential employer will read your resume or toss it. The summary is an encapsulated profile of who you are and what you can offer an employer, in one paragraph. This one paragraph must show the experience you have gained throughout your career (or education) that can serve to help a potential employer in your targeted job. It should whet the appetite of the reader to read further. The information it contains will be supported by the content of the rest of the resume.

Through the years, I have found that there are a few tried-and-true methods that work well in preparing profile information for just about everyone. I have developed the following four templates to help you create your summary. Fill in the blanks with your customized information (applicable skills, attributes, qualifications, and so on) and select the paragraph that says the most about what you do. Truthfully, all the templates have impact, and you can use almost any of them for almost any position, so you should be fine with whichever one you select.

After you fill in the blanks, your Professional Summary will be so highly customized that if an employer read several resumes prepared in the same format, he or she would be hard-pressed to tell that the same template was used for both. That's because the template itself is only a foundation and the information you supply will be the meat of the summary. Also, these templates are scientifically developed so that they can be used pretty much across the board for whatever position you are targeting.

 note All four of these professional summary templates are available in Microsoft Word format on the CD at the back of this book.

Each template contains a number of sentences. You can delete the sentences that are not applicable. You can also mix and match sentences from the various templates to come up with the most suitable Professional Summary for you. Following the templates are additional Professional Summary bullets and standalone sentences that you can infuse into your profile information.

Select a template and fill in the blanks. When completing the templates, refer to your skill areas and attributes assessment, which you did in Step 2. Also remember to target the job requirements you specified in Step 1.

A Word About Career Goals/Objectives

Your career goal or objective is simply your targeted job title. When you use one of the Professional Summary templates that follow, your career goal/objective will be contained within it; it will not be necessary to state your objective again in a separate section.

When applicants use a Career Goal or Objective section in their resume, they generally do it for the wrong reason. They either use it to state what they want in a job, or they include a fuzzy sentence seeking some "rewarding position" that is "challenging," "provides advancement," or "utilizes their expertise." This is not only redundant and superfluous, but it turns off the employer because your resume's job is to sell you, not to demand at the outset that the employer promote you.

Remember, you are the product and you are selling your benefits to the employer. If you picked up a sales brochure selling appliances, would you want to read the benefits of purchasing this product to determine whether it is the right appliance for you? Or would you want to read "Dishwasher seeking a contemporary home to use its features to clean your dishes"?

Step 5

PROFESSIONAL SUMMARY FOUNDATION 1

_____ [#] years of _____ [type of] experience [in the _____ field, including _____, _____, _____, and _____ (primary skills) **OR** _____ (doing what?) in various settings, including _____, _____, and _____]. Proven proficiency in _____, _____, _____, and _____, with knowledge of _____ and _____ [additional skill areas]. Clientele/projects have included _____, _____, and _____. A(n) _____ [industry] professional with excellent _____ and _____ skills and ability to [establish and build positive, solid relationships with _____/other: _____].

Following are some sample Professional Summary statements that were written using Foundation 1. The boldfaced words came from the template, and the rest are applicable to the job seeker.

EXAMPLE: SOCIAL WORKER

Eight **years of** social-work **experience** counseling adolescents at various cognitive and emotional levels **in various settings, including** group homes, schools, **and** mental-health facilities. **Proven proficiency in** advocacy and linkage, casework, client needs assessments, goal planning, **and** life-skills training **with knowledge of** housing coordination **and** referral servicing. **Clientele have included** emotionally disturbed, learning disabled, developmentally delayed, and depressed adolescents as well as those diagnosed with ADHD, schizophrenia, autism, cerebral palsy, and mental retardation. **A** mental-health **professional with excellent** communications, advocacy, **and** troubleshooting **skills. Ability to establish and build positive, solid relationships with** clients, associates, and all mental-health professionals.

EXAMPLE: EXECUTIVE CHEF

Fourteen **years of experience in** restaurant and hotel management in an Executive or Head Chef position **in the** culinary-arts **field, including** hiring and training sous chefs and cooks, menu planning **and** cooking, buying, catering, maintaining inventory, controlling and negotiating food costs, **and** delegating tasks. **Proficient in** Continental and Italian culinary arts, butchering, and food decoration. **A** culinary-management **professional with excellent** creativity **and** staff-development **skills and ability to** motivate staff to achieve highest quality of culinary arts standards encompassing appetizers, entrees, and desserts.

EXAMPLE: GRAPHIC DESIGNER

Three **years of** graphic design **experience in the** advertising **field, including** client needs assessment, layout and design, illustration, **and** photo retouching. **Proven proficiency in** creating logos, ads, brochures, newsletters, stationery, **and** publications **with knowledge of** Web site design **and** development. **Clientele have included** Fortune 500 firms, industrial manufacturers, and small businesses. **An** advertising **professional with excellent** client relations, design, **and** problem-solving **skills.**

PROFESSIONAL SUMMARY FOUNDATION 2

A(n) _____ and _____ [primary personal attributes] _____
_____ [type of] [professional/executive/manager] experienced in _____,
_____, _____, and _____. [Fully versed in/
Background encompasses ability to] _____ [do what?]. High degree of responsibility in
_____. [Demonstrated/Proven] ability to work effectively both independently and as an integral part of a team effort to achieve goals. A strong _____ [title/function] with a high degree of responsibility [in _____ **OR** who works well with _____, _____, and _____] alike. Adept at handling _____ and developing proactive _____ [type of strategies, methods, or procedures]. Computer experience includes _____.

EXAMPLE: DATABASE MANAGER

A results-oriented information technology **professional experienced in** database installation, implementation, troubleshooting, and management, as well as office management **and** customer relations. **Fully versed** in tracking customer information, report generation, account management, estimate development, and project scheduling. **Demonstrated ability to work effectively both independently and as an integral part of a team effort to achieve goals. A strong** problem-solver **with a high degree of responsibility in** tackling challenges with automated solutions.

An IT professional would include his or her specific computer expertise in a separate section later in the resume.

EXAMPLE: ACCOUNTING VICE PRESIDENT

A seasoned upper-level financial **executive with** extensive **expertise in** accounting management. **Background encompasses the ability to** reduce overall costs while increasing levels of productivity and profitability. **Proven ability to** train and develop staff to exceed goals while raising morale. **Fully versed in** addressing and resolving client concerns **and** maintaining positive rapport with all levels of clients. Analytically inclined problem-solver **with** leadership **skills. Computer experience includes** Windows, MS Word and Excel, Simply Accounting, Filemaker Pro, PowerPoint, and ACCPAC.

EXAMPLE: SCHOOL PSYCHOLOGIST

A caring **and** patient mental-health **professional experienced in** psychology, early childhood intervention and evaluation, **and** testing gifted to multi-handicapped children. **Fully versed in** psychological assessments, designing IEP goals, identifying and interpreting situations, counseling, running parent workshops, representing the school district at impartial hearings, and working with various clientele. **High degree of responsibility in** problem-solving with resolution follow-up, client relations, and crisis intervention. **A strong** advocate **who works well with** staff, clients, **and** resource personnel **alike. Adept at handling** crises **and developing proactive** counseling plans to assist students in realizing their fullest potential.

PROFESSIONAL SUMMARY FOUNDATION 3 (MANAGEMENT)

A(n) _____ [attribute] _____ [title] with a distinctive career in _____ and _____ [primary targeted areas] management, including _____, _____, and _____, with full responsibility for _____ and _____. A progressive career within diverse business atmospheres, including _____, _____, and _____. Broad-based experience encompasses _____, _____, and _____. Recognized for ability to _____. An effective _____ and _____. A self-directed and motivated [professional/executive/manager/other: _____] with the ability to consistently achieve objectives. Computer experience includes _____.

EXAMPLE: CHIEF FINANCIAL OFFICER

A results-oriented senior financial officer **with a distinctive career in** general and financial **management, including** the direction and streamlining of corporate financial operations **with full responsibility for** financial reporting and cost reduction. **A progressive career within diverse business spheres, including** manufacturing, distribution, **and** entrepreneurial business startup. **Broad-based experience encompasses** business restructuring and reengineering, strategic planning, **and** cost containment. **Recognized for ability to** coach and develop staff. **A self-directed and motivated executive with the ability to consistently achieve objectives. Computer experience includes** Microsoft Access, Excel, Word, Outlook, and Explorer; ACT!; Visual Manufacturing; Crystal Report Writer; and UNIX.

EXAMPLE: IT SALES AND MARKETING EXECUTIVE

A proactive information technology executive **with a distinctive career in** the high-tech industry and the electronic communications field **with full responsibility for** sales, marketing, advertising, **and** public relations functions. **A progressive career within diverse business spheres, including** the systems integration marketplace interfacing with distribution **and** manufacturing channels. **Broad-based experience encompasses** systems analysis, LAN-to-host connectivity, system component design, heterogeneous network solutions, **and** software customization. **Recognized for ability to** stay on top of the high-tech industry and consistently increase profits. **An effective** problem-solver **and** staff motivator.

EXAMPLE: QUALITY ASSURANCE MANAGER

A seasoned quality assurance manager **with a distinctive career in** quality assurance, operations, **and** front-line **management, including** customer service, research and analysis, quality control, auditing, **and** personnel management. **Recognized for ability to** manage multi-counter operations, service agent productivity, and revenue performance. **An effective** leader and team builder skilled in training, developing, coaching, and motivating others **with the ability to consistently achieve objectives.**

Step 5

PROFESSIONAL SUMMARY FOUNDATION 4

_____ [#] years of professional _____ and _____ [type of] experience in the _____ [field/industry] working for various _____ [type of] facilities. Full knowledge of _____, _____, and _____ [primary skill areas]. Proven ability to _____, _____, _____, and _____. Highly skilled in _____ and _____ [additional skill areas]. [Multiskilled _____ (type of) professional who is _____, _____, and _____. **OR** Attributes include _____, _____, and _____.] Proficient in _____ with knowledge of _____, _____, _____, and _____ [computer literacy].

EXAMPLE: MEDICAL BILLING AND COLLECTION SPECIALIST

Ten **years of** billing, collection, and supervisory **experience in the** medical **field working for various** multimodality **facilities. Full knowledge of** medical terminology; insurance laws; insurance codes; and policies of Medicare, No-Fault, Workers' Compensation, HMOs, **and** third-party payers. **Highly skilled in** productivity improvement, quality assurance, research and analysis, bookkeeping, and general accounting. **Multiskilled** medical **professional who is** honest, hardworking, and detail-oriented **with ability to** work in a fast-paced environment, establish effective relationships, and work as a team player with patients, staff, and management. **Proficient in** Versyss, AccuMed, and Medic Vision systems, with knowledge of ADS, Windows, and word processing.

EXAMPLE: SECURITY DIRECTOR

Ten **years of experience in the** security and investigations **field. Full knowledge of** security investigations, employee and premises security, building integrity, product security, transporting of valuable items, bomb threat investigations, and handling volatile situations. **Proven ability** in managing personnel functions, including scheduling, evaluations, and training. **Skilled in** making cost-effective recommendations regarding surveillance **and** detection equipment technology. **Attributes include** integrity, honesty, and ability to interact with all levels of management.

EXAMPLE: MOVIE SCREENING COORDINATOR

Three **years of professional** communications **experience in the** entertainment **industry. Full knowledge of** public relations, public speaking, and speech preparation. **Proven ability to** handle national and international special events coordination **and** movie screenings. **Highly skilled in** interpersonal communication **and** listening. **Attributes include** creativity, strong organization and conflict resolution skills, **and** outstanding public speaking abilities. **Ability to** take on difficult challenges and get things done in an impeccable manner while being deadline-conscious. **Proficient in** Windows with familiarity in Excel, Kedit, SPSS, and SAS.

Step 5

Additional Professional Summary Bullets

Following are a number of professional summary foundation sentences you can also use in your resume. Check off the ones you find appropriate for your situation and add them or substitute them for other sentences in the foundation you selected.

❑ A seasoned upper-level _____ [type of] executive with extensive expertise in _____ [what field?] management. Background encompasses the ability to _____ [do what?].

- **A seasoned upper-level** financial **executive with extensive expertise in** accounting **management. Background encompasses the ability to** reduce overall costs while increasing levels of productivity and profitability.

❑ Strong _____ ability, _____ knowledge, _____ skills, and _____ with a good understanding of the _____ business and company success goals.

- **Strong** sales **ability,** operational **knowledge,** merchandising **skills, and** work ethic **with a good understanding of the** retail **business and company success goals.**

❑ Proven track record in _____ [primary area of expertise] with emphasis on _____ and _____ [primary functions].

- **Proven track record in** client satisfaction **with emphasis on** reliability **and** follow-up.

❑ Seasoned, _____, and _____ [attributes] _____ [title] specializing in _____.

- **Seasoned,** energetic, **and** enthusiastic teacher **specializing in** developing innovative, interactive lesson plans utilizing the integration of technology and basic math principles.

❑ A _____, _____, _____ [primary attributes] professional _____ [title] offering substantial experience in _____ and _____ in _____ [which?] settings.

- **A** dedicated, compassionate, results-oriented **professional** nurse **offering substantial experience in** shift management **and** patient care **in** acute-care **settings.**

❑ Possess excellent _____, _____, and _____ skills coupled with the ability to _____.

- **Possess excellent** interpersonal, critical thinking, **and** assessment **skills coupled with the ability to** put individuals at ease.

❑ Proven _____ and _____ adeptness and the ability to maintain superior levels of _____ [primary function] under all types of circumstances.

- **Proven** planning **and** organizational **adeptness and the ability to maintain superior levels of** quality care **under all types of circumstances.**

❑ Innate ability to _____ [do what?].

- **Innate ability to** create a positive working atmosphere for staff and patients alike.

❑ Interface directly with _____ [whom] regarding _____ [primary areas of expertise].

- **Interface directly with** key advertising agents and PR firms **regarding** marketing, press coverage, publicity, and design of visual communications.

Standalone Sentences

You can add any of the following standalone sentences to your Professional Summary paragraph as appropriate. Check off the ones you find appropriate for your situation and add them or substitute them for other sentences in the foundation you selected.

❑ Strong leadership qualities with ability to take charge and follow through with a commitment to excellence.

❑ A self-motivated professional who works well under pressure, enjoys new challenges, is a team player, and is dedicated to the profession.

❑ An able problem solver with the tenacity to successfully complete assignments and the flexibility to adapt to changing situations and requirements.

❑ Excellent knowledge of industry terminology and strategies.

❑ Sound commonsense decision-maker with well-rounded experience.

❑ A self-motivated team builder with the ability to manage multiple projects simultaneously while maintaining a clear perspective of goals and objectives.

❑ Demonstrated skills in assessing problem areas and offering recommendations resulting in [increased productivity/streamlined operations/ increased sales/increased profits/decreased expenses/cost reductions/other: _____].

❑ A hands-on professional who works well under pressure and leads by example.

❑ An experienced manager with the ability to motivate and guide staff and build a solid team environment with superior work ethic and a commitment to excellence.

❑ Successful team builder skilled in training, developing, coaching, and motivating others.

❑ Ability to work well under pressure and function effectively under all types of circumstances.

❑ Ability to plan, coordinate, and implement multiple projects simultaneously.

❑ Recruit, train, and develop employees, ensuring compliance with federal and state employment regulations.

❑ Demonstrated skills in assessing problem areas and offering recommendations, resulting in increased productivity and profitability while reducing expenses.

❑ Possess excellent interpersonal, critical thinking, and assessment skills coupled with the ability to put individuals at ease.

❑ Ability to plan and implement new ideas and to evaluate problem situations and arrive at practical decisions.

❑ Ability to lead, train, motivate, and inspire others to [sell/produce/work/other: _____] at their optimum potential.

Step 5

CHOOSE YOUR FORMAT TEMPLATE AND COMPILE YOUR RESUME

On the following pages you will find templates for the four resume format types discussed in Step 2:

- ✔ Reverse-chronological
- ✔ Combination
- ✔ Functional
- ✔ Curriculum vitae (CV)

Find the template that corresponds to the resume format you selected in Step 2. Pull together all of the components you have completed in previous steps and place them in their appropriate places within your selected resume format template by following the instructions in the template. You can either write them on the following pages or select the appropriate format from the accompanying CD and type your resume draft in Microsoft Word.

 note For the reverse-chronological format (which is the resume format most preferred by recruiters), if the pages you completed earlier while compiling your Professional Experience section are neat and readable, there is no need to rewrite that section. Use those pages for "Jobs 1– 5" and then jump to the last page of this format (page 149) to complete the remainder.

REVERSE-CHRONOLOGICAL FORMAT

YOUR NAME_____

Address_____

Phone #_____ • Cellular #_____

E-Mail Address_____

PROFESSIONAL SUMMARY *(Pick up from Step 5.)*

_____
_____
_____
_____
_____

LICENSES / CERTIFICATIONS

• _____   • _____

AREAS OF EXPERTISE *(Pick up from Step 1.)*

• _____   • _____   • _____
• _____   • _____   • _____
• _____   • _____   • _____
• _____   • _____   • _____
• _____   • _____   • _____

PROFESSIONAL EXPERIENCE *(Pick up from Steps 2, 3, and 4.)*

_____–_____: JOB TITLE:_____

Company_____, Town_____, State____

• _____
_____
• _____
_____
• _____
_____
• _____
_____
• _____
_____
• _____
_____
• _____
_____
• _____
_____

Step 5

_____ – _____: **JOB TITLE:**_____

Company_____, **Town**_____, **State**____

- _____
- _____
- _____
- _____
- _____
- _____
- _____
- _____
- _____
- _____

_____ – _____: **JOB TITLE:**_____

Company_____, **Town**_____, **State**____

- _____
- _____
- _____
- _____
- _____
- _____
- _____
- _____
- _____

Step 5

(continued)

REVERSE-CHRONOLOGICAL FORMAT *(continued)*

_____–_____: JOB TITLE:_____

Company_____, Town_____, State_____

- _____
  _____
- _____
  _____
- _____
  _____
- _____
  _____
- _____
  _____
- _____
  _____
- _____
  _____
- _____
  _____

_____–_____: JOB TITLE:_____

Company_____, Town_____, State_____

- _____
  _____
- _____
  _____
- _____
  _____
- _____
  _____
- _____
  _____
- _____
  _____
- _____
  _____

Step 5

EDUCATION *(If you are entry level, list education at the beginning of your resume.)*

College:_____ **Town:**_____ **State:**____

_____Degree in _____ (year) • GPA: ____

Achievements:_____

_____

_____

_____

College:_____ **Town:**_____ **State:**____

_____Degree in _____ (year) • GPA: ____

PROFESSIONAL AFFILIATIONS

- _____
- _____
- _____

- _____
- _____
- _____

TESTIMONIALS *(Pick up from Step 8.)*

_____

_____

_____

_____

_____

_____

                         Name:_____ Title:_____

                         Company:_____, Town / State:_____

_____

_____

_____

_____

                         Name:_____ Title:_____

                         Company:_____, Town / State:_____

_____

_____

_____

_____

                         Name:_____ Title:_____

                         Company:_____, Town / State:_____

Step 5

COMBINATION FORMAT

YOUR NAME_____

Address_____

Phone #_____ • Cellular #_____

E-Mail Address_____

PROFESSIONAL SUMMARY *(Pick up from Step 5.)*

_____
_____
_____
_____
_____

CERTIFICATIONS

• _____   • _____

AREAS OF EXPERTISE *(Pick up from Step 1.)*

• _____   • _____   • _____
• _____   • _____   • _____
• _____   • _____   • _____
• _____   • _____

ACHIEVEMENT HIGHLIGHTS *(Pick up from Steps 4 and 6.)*

• _____
_____
_____

• _____
_____
_____

• _____
_____
_____

• _____
_____
_____

• _____
_____
_____

Step 5

- _____
  _____
  _____
  _____

- _____
  _____
  _____
  _____

- _____
  _____
  _____

PROFESSIONAL EXPERIENCE *(Pick up from Steps 2, 3, and 4.)*

JOB TITLE:_____ (_____ – _____)

Company_____, **Town**_____, **State**_____

- _____
  _____
  _____

JOB TITLE:_____ (_____ – _____)

Company_____, **Town**_____, **State**_____

- _____
  _____
  _____

JOB TITLE:_____ (_____ – _____)

Company_____, **Town**_____, **State**_____

- _____
  _____
  _____

JOB TITLE:_____ (_____ – _____)

Company_____, **Town**_____, **State**_____

- _____
  _____

JOB TITLE:_____ (_____ – _____)

Company_____, **Town**_____, **State**_____

- _____
  _____

Step 5

(continued)

COMBINATION FORMAT *(continued)*

EDUCATION *(If you are entry level, list education at the beginning of your resume.)*

College:_____ **Town:**_____ **State:**____

_____Degree in _____ (year) • GPA: ____

Achievements:_____

_____

_____

_____

College:_____ **Town:**_____ **State:**____

_____Degree in _____ (year) • GPA: ____

PROFESSIONAL AFFILIATIONS

- _____   • _____
- _____   • _____

TESTIMONIALS *(Pick up from Step 8.)*

_____

_____

_____

_____

_____

_____

Name:_____ Title:_____

Company:_____, Town / State:_____

_____

_____

_____

_____

_____

Name:_____ Title:_____

Company:_____, Town / State:_____

_____

_____

_____

_____

_____

Name:_____ Title:_____

Company:_____, Town / State:_____

Step 5

FUNCTIONAL FORMAT

YOUR NAME_____

Address_____

Phone #_____ • **Cellular #**_____

E-Mail Address_____

PROFESSIONAL SUMMARY *(Pick up from Step 5.)*

_____

_____

_____

_____

_____

AREAS OF STRENGTH *(Pick up from Step 1.)*

- _____
- _____
- _____
- _____

- _____
- _____
- _____
- _____

- _____
- _____
- _____
- _____

ACHIEVEMENT HIGHLIGHTS *(Pick up from Steps 4 and 6.)*

- _____

  _____

  _____

- _____

  _____

  _____

- _____

  _____

  _____

- _____

  _____

  _____

- _____

  _____

  _____

- _____

  _____

  _____

Step 5

(continued)

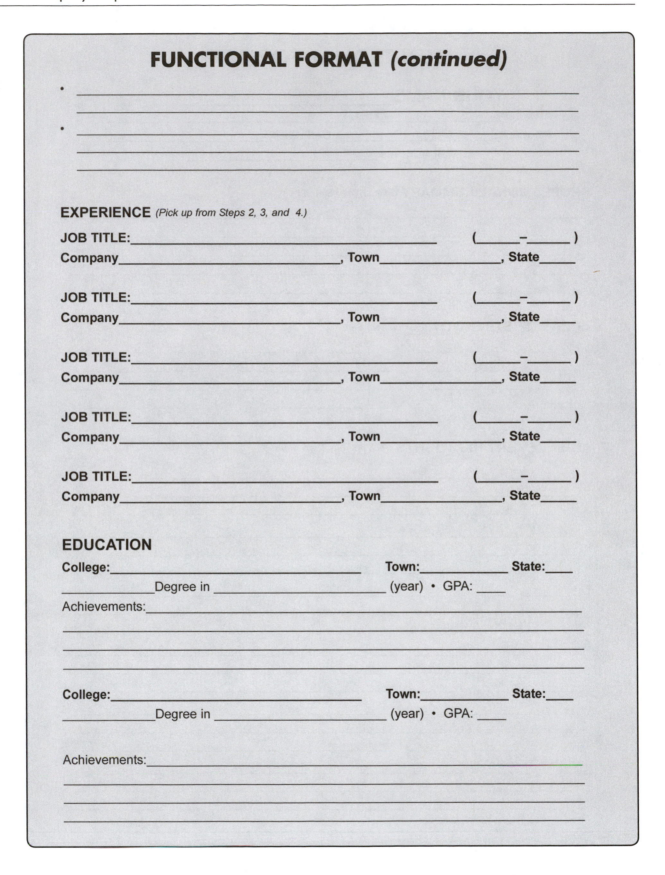

FUNCTIONAL FORMAT *(continued)*

- _____
  _____
  _____
- _____
  _____
  _____

EXPERIENCE *(Pick up from Steps 2, 3, and 4.)*

JOB TITLE:_____ (_____ – _____)
Company_____, Town_____, State_____

JOB TITLE:_____ (_____ – _____)
Company_____, Town_____, State_____

JOB TITLE:_____ (_____ – _____)
Company_____, Town_____, State_____

JOB TITLE:_____ (_____ – _____)
Company_____, Town_____, State_____

JOB TITLE:_____ (_____ – _____)
Company_____, Town_____, State_____

EDUCATION

College:_____ Town:_____ State:____
_____Degree in _____ (year) • GPA: _____
Achievements:_____
_____
_____
_____

College:_____ Town:_____ State:____
_____Degree in _____ (year) • GPA: _____

Achievements:_____
_____
_____
_____

TESTIMONIALS *(Pick up from Step #8.)*

_____
_____
_____
_____
_____
_____

Name:_____ Title:_____
Company:_____, Town / State:_____

_____
_____
_____
_____
_____
_____

Name:_____ Title:_____
Company:_____, Town / State:_____

_____
_____
_____
_____
_____
_____

Name:_____ Title:_____
Company:_____, Town / State:_____

CURRICULUM VITAE (CV) FORMAT

NAME

ADDRESS _____

PHONE NO._____ FAX NO._____

CELLULAR NO. _____ E-MAIL _____

Current Position

Fellow in:
_____

Division of:
_____

Name of Hospital / Facility: _____

Hospital / Facility Address: _____

Education

POST-GRADUATE EDUCATION:

_____ (year): _____

_____

_____ (year): _____

_____

MEDICAL SCHOOL:

_____ (year): _____

_____

UNDERGRADUATE:

_____ (year): _____

_____

Post-Graduate Training

_____ (year): _____

_____

_____ (year): _____

_____

Licenses / Board Certifications

- _____ # _____ (year)
- _____ # _____ (year)

Professional Affiliations

- _____   - _____
- _____   - _____

Appointments

____-____: _____
_____

____-____: _____
_____

____-____: _____
_____

____-____: _____
_____

Presentations & Conferences

- _____
- _____
- _____
- _____

Articles

"_____," featured in _____ _(year)_
"_____," featured in _____ _(year)_
"_____," featured in _____ _(year)_

Current Research

_____
_____
_____
_____

(continued)

CURRICULUM VITAE (CV) FORMAT *(continued)*

Abstracts

- _____
- _____
- _____
- _____

Manuscripts

- _____
- _____
- _____
- _____

Book Chapters

- _____
- _____
- _____
- _____

Works in Progress

- _____
- _____
- _____
- _____

Awards

- _____
- _____
- _____
- _____

Step 5

step 6

Round Out Your Resume with ClipBullets™

RESUME CLIPBULLETS™: AN EASY WAY TO COMPLETE YOUR RESUME

I have saved the Resume ClipBullets™ for last because in order to work up your resume to the best it can be, you should include all of your own uniquely developed responsibilities and accomplishments first. Although the ClipBullets™ allow you to fully customize your expertise, using various methods to work up your resume will give your resume the greatest impact on prospective employers. At this point, you have completed the greater portion of your resume. The easiest part of the process follows.

What Are Resume ClipBullets™?

Resume ClipBullets™ are prewritten, customizable, fill-in-the-blank resume bullets for the Professional Experience section of your resume. I have provided the Resume ClipBullets™ in this later chapter so that you can review each functional achievement specific to your position to determine whether you have left out any important functions or achievements, and to help you in the final resume writing stage.

These Resume ClipBullets™ include many professional functions and achievements in a format that you can customize to your own situation. I have developed these ClipBullets™ from resumes I have written over the years, a lot of research, and a painstaking writing and editing process via a scientific approach so that everyone can have heavy-hitting customizable responsibility and achievement bullets to "wow" recruiters further—without all the hard work. I have written each of the bullets as I would if you came to me in my private practice. You can incorporate the ones that are applicable to you into what you have already created to help enhance and polish your overall resume.

Instructions for Using ClipBullets™

1. As before, first review the worksheet sections that are most applicable to your specific position.
2. Review the remaining worksheets to determine whether there are any functions or achievements that might also be applicable to you and target your goal. Be sure to include all functions
   - ✔ From all of your current and past positions
   - ✔ That would be required in the position you are targeting
   - ✔ That you might have performed for your supervisor or manager
   - ✔ In any lateral positions that might include similar functions to the ones you performed

   Put a star at the top of each of these pages because these are the ones you will be working with.
3. Carefully review each of the bullets on the starred pages. Check off all bullets that are the same as or similar to functions and achievements you have performed. Fill in the blanks with information about what you actually performed in your positions. (See the CD at the back of this book for Word files containing all ClipBullets™. You can copy and paste them into your resume instead of retyping them.)
4. Adjust the wording of the bullets as required to make each a true statement of your performance.
5. Review the bullets in your rough draft and eliminate any duplicates.
6. Infuse the new resume bullets into your resume draft.
7. Prioritize them in your resume draft according to importance in your targeted field.
8. For additional functions and achievements you have performed, review the wording contained in the ClipBullets™ for ideas of how to proceed to complete your remaining bullets.

RESUME CLIPBULLETS™ BY PROFESSION

MANAGEMENT AND EXECUTIVE BULLETS

Review the following fill-in-the-blank Resume ClipBullets™ samples to see whether any of the functions and achievements apply to your work. Fill in the blanks and adjust the wording as appropriate. Incorporate these bullets into your resume draft where applicable.

What You Manage

❑ Direct day-to-day [corporate affairs/operations/other: _____] of this [multibillion/multimillion/$_____] _____ [type of] firm, including _____, _____, and _____ [primary activities].

❑ Direct and operate a [multilevel] _____ [type of] firm providing _____[type of] products and services to the _____ [type of] market(s).

❑ Direct the _____ [which?] division, including ____ [#] direct reports and ____ [#] indirect reports of this [multibillion/multimillion/$_____] _____ [type of] firm specializing in _____ [type of products or services].

❑ Conceptualized, developed, and manage a(n) [multibillion/multimillion/$_____] _____ [type of] [firm/network/division/other: _____] by [networking and brainstorming with experts/other method: _____], resulting in it becoming [the backbone of the company's growth from _____ [what size or measure?] to _____ [what size or measure?]/other result: _____].

❑ Recruited as right hand to _____ [title] to save a once-profitable company from a then-floundering situation [($_____ loss on $_____ in sales)] through effective [strategic and tactical efforts/other: _____] as instrumental to its turnaround to $_____ profit on $_____ sales.

New-Business Startups

❑ Developed, built, and operate a startup _____ [type of] firm from the ground up, culminating in ____ [#] locations with ____ [#] employees, and resulting in annual revenues of $_____ over a(n) ____ [#]-year period.

❑ One of _____ [#] pioneers of this startup _____ [type of] firm specializing in _____ [type of products/services] to the _____ market within the [national/international] _____ [type of] industries.

❑ Created a successful [company/division] from the ground up to $_____ in annual sales by [networking and building an account base of ____ [#]/hiring talented sales representatives to sell our lines/improving the quality of the _____ lines/targeting the _____ market/building strong relationships with _____ (whom?)].

(continued)

MANAGEMENT AND EXECUTIVE BULLETS *(continued)*
Creating New Departments or Divisions

❏ Created the _____ [department(s)/division(s)] from the ground up, which entailed _____ and resulted in _____ [what benefits?].

❏ [Started a new/Consolidated the] _____ [division(s)/department(s)] [after company acquired _____ (what company?) with $_____ in net worth]. [Achieved/Exceeded] firm's _____[#]-month goal to do $_____ in sales by _____% by_____ [doing what?].

❏ Started up a new outbound _____ [name of] group selling _____ [type of] [products/services], which resulted in growing the client base by [$_____/_____%] through sales and marketing efforts, including [direct mail/seminars/trade shows/other: _____].

❏ Opened new local office with an annual quota of $_____, achieving 100% of quota by _____ [doing what?] within _____ [#] months.

❏ Spurred the growth of _____'s [company name] world headquarters, built its turnkey sales offices throughout the country, handled all vendors, purchased all supplies, and negotiated all agreements from _____ [what?] to _____ [what?].

Rescuing the Firm, a Division, or a Department

❏ Turned around a struggling _____ [name of] division, which in _____ [year] was achieving only _____% of quota by [making staffing changes/creating marketing programs to enhance all sales opportunities/other method: _____], bringing quota up to _____% [within _____[#] months/by _____ (year)].

❏ Rescued the floundering _____ [type of] [firm/division/department], which sold _____ [type of] products to the _____ market by [establishing contacts with various channels, including _____/other: _____]. The successful turnaround of [the firm/this division/the department] resulted in _____[benefits].

Increasing Sales, Revenue, and Profitability

❏ Spearheaded the _____ [type of] initiative to _____ [do what?], which resulted in [increased sales/profits of $_____/market share/other benefit: _____].

❏ Drove annual sales from $_____ to $_____ by developing and implementing the _____ [type of product, campaign, program, or project] designed to _____ [do what?].

❏ Increased [sales/profits/revenue] in the _____ marketplace from $_____ to $_____ by creating a(n) _____ [type of program], which enabled _____ [what benefit?].

❏ Spearheaded the acquisition of _____ [#] facilities, which increased gross annual sales from $_____ to more than $_____ in the area of _____.

Increasing Market Share

❑ Successfully managed and fulfilled mission to develop company into a major full-service _____ [type of] firm by penetrating the _____ [type of] marketplace and _____ [doing what?].

❑ Increased market share by [_____%/$_____] in the _____ market, bringing annual sales to $_____ by _____ [doing what?].

Reducing Overhead Costs and Maximizing ROI

❑ Reduced total [operating expenses/overhead costs] [by _____%/in excess of $_____] annually by establishing a _____ [type of] initiative to _____ [do what?].

❑ Implemented a cost-effective method to _____ [do what?], which improved _____ [what process?] and reduced operating expenses by [$_____/_____%].

❑ Decreased [purchasing/overhead/payroll/corporate tax exposure/other: _____] [$_____/_____%] annually by successfully introducing the _____ [concept/program/procedure] and eliminating the need for _____ [what process?].

❑ Successfully spearheaded a _____ [type of] cost-reduction program by [evaluating business bottlenecks and turning them into assets/other method: _____].

❑ Maximized return on investment by purchasing _____ [type of] raw materials to produce finished _____ [type of] goods.

❑ Saved $_____ annually by implementing a cost-effective _____ [type of] [policy/procedure/program/campaign/other: _____], which improved _____ [what process?].

Spearheading New Business-Development Initiatives

❑ Actively and successfully explore new business-development opportunities to expand growth potential by _____ [doing what?], resulting in _____ [benefit].

❑ Spearheaded proactive business development of _____ [what?], which resulted in _____ and _____ .

❑ Devised and implemented various new business-development initiatives, including _____ , _____ , and _____ , resulting in annual sales increases of $_____ and _____ [other benefits].

(continued)

MANAGEMENT AND EXECUTIVE BULLETS *(continued)*
Ensuring That the Company and Products Remain Reputable, Economically Viable, Current, and Groundbreaking

❑ Ensure company and programs remain reputable, economically viable, and current by [providing a clear vision/proactive leadership/other: _____] through strategically sound [mission statements/business plans/ongoing planning and implementation/other method: _____], which resulted in [sales increases of $_____/other benefit: _____].

Training Initiatives

❑ Recruit, train, and develop [corporate officers/key management personnel/a winning sales team/other: _____], resulting in [a well-trained management staff/exceptionally low turnover rate/increased profits/other: _____].

❑ Devised and implemented a _____ [type of] training program to [enhance employees' product knowledge/help them learn to close sales quickly/other: _____], which resulted in _____ [what benefits?].

❑ Incorporated an ongoing staff-development training effort to enhance employees' _____ [type of] knowledge, which entailed _____, _____, and _____.

Increasing Employee Morale and Minimizing Turnover

❑ Increased morale and minimized turnover through [mutual respect/honesty/effective two-way communication/other: _____], which provided a healthy and positive environment that allowed employees to succeed and the company to grow.

❑ Through effective use of _____ [strategies you used or initiatives you put in place], increased morale and minimized turnover, which resulted in [an extremely low turnover rate for the industry/an annual cost savings of $_____/other: _____].

Coaching, Motivating, and Developing a Winning Team

❑ Coach, motivate, and develop a winning [sales/other: _____] team through effective _____ [what methods?], resulting in _____ [what benefit?].

❑ Manage and direct a team of _____ [#] _____ [what staff?] personnel and inspire teamwork among staff by _____ [doing what?] to develop measurable outcomes, resulting in _____ [results of your initiatives].

Thinking Outside the Box

❑ Using visionary _____ [type of] [methods/skills/techniques] in _____ [what areas?], helped the business flourish in the areas of _____.

Effectively Using Personal Attributes Critical to Successful Managers

❑ By employing use of effective _____ and _____ [type of] skills, was successfully able to _____ [do what?], resulting in _____ [what benefit?].

❑ Successfully utilizing _____ and _____ [what?] has served to _____ [do what?], resulting in _____ [what benefit?].

❑ Through effective use of _____ [what skills?], overcame _____ [type of] challenges, resulting in _____ [what benefit?].

❑ Utilizing effective _____ [type of] skills has helped others to _____ [do what?], resulting in _____ [what benefit?].

Successfully Tackling Difficult Challenges

❑ Successfully turned around _____ [what challenge?] by _____ [doing what?], which resulted in _____ [what benefit?].

❑ Rescued the floundering _____ division, which sold _____ [type of] products to the _____ market, by [establishing contacts with various channels, including _____/other: _____]. The successful turnaround of this division resulted in _____.

❑ Successfully met difficult challenges faced by _____ by _____ [doing what?].

❑ Turned around a struggling _____ division that was achieving only _____% of quota by [making changes in _____ personnel/creating marketing programs to enhance all sales opportunities/other: _____], bringing quota up to _____% within _____ [#] months.

Balancing Monitoring the Business While Making Others Accountable for Their Own Creative Initiatives

❑ Successfully balance _____ [what with what?], resulting in _____ [what benefit?].

Launching New Products or Programs

❑ Launched numerous _____ [type of] [products/programs] for _____, resulting in _____ [what benefit?].

❑ Increased competitive edge and cost-effectiveness of _____ [type of] programs by developing and implementing _____ [state initiatives], resulting in [a steady increase of clients/high referral rate/other company benefits: _____].

(continued)

MANADGEMENT AND EXECUTIVE BULLETS *(continued)*

Spearheading State-of-the-Art Programs or Technological Advances

❑ Established a state-of-the-art _____ [type of] program for _____ [what purpose?], which resulted in _____ .

❑ Spearheaded the corporate-wide _____ [type of] initiative to _____ [purpose], which realized gains in _____ [what areas?].

❑ Adopted _____ [type of] technological resources to convert _____ [what?] from [manual/semiautomated] to automated systems, which improved [records/files/document retention/ease of use/other: _____] and streamlined processing.

❑ Established and successfully implemented a company-wide [policy/procedure/initiative] to _____ [do what?], which significantly improved _____ [what archaic method?].

Increasing Productivity and Streamlining Operations

❑ Increased productivity by _____% by _____ [doing what?], which resulted in _____ _____ [benefits to company].

❑ Streamlined operations by _____ [doing or implementing what?], which resulted in _____ , _____ [what benefit?].

❑ Spearheaded the _____ [type of] initiative to _____ [do what?], which aided in _____ [what functions?].

❑ Increased daily production from _____ to _____ without raising overhead by _____ [doing what?].

Negotiating Major Contracts

❑ Negotiated and ratified _____ [#] _____ [type of] agreements with various _____ [type of] firms [overseas/abroad], resulting in _____ [what benefit?].

❑ Played an integral role in obtaining a $_____ contract from _____ [whom?] to replace its current _____ [methodology/technology/products/other: _____] with _____ [what?].

Step 6

❑ Led negotiations with _____ [whom?] for long-term _____ [type of] agreements with fore-
casted savings of $_____ over a _____[#]-year period.

❑ Secured _____ [preferred provider/wholesale distribution/other: _____] agreements for
_____ [purpose] by developing _____ [what?].

❑ Negotiated a $_____ contract with _____ [whom?], which served to _____
[purpose] and resulted in _____ [what was the win-win for the firm and the client?].

❑ Led negotiations with _____ [whom?] [and investment bankers] in acquiring company's most profitable [facility/
plant/distribution center/store/branch/other: _____]. With an appraised value versus purchase price of ____ [#]
to 1, profits exceeded acquisition costs in less than _____ [what time period?].

Increasing Purchasing Service Levels

❑ Increased purchasing service levels from _____% to _____% efficiency by _____ [achievement].

Increasing Customer Satisfaction Levels

❑ Increased customer satisfaction levels from _____% to _____% at a value of $_____ annually by
_____ [doing what?].

❑ Fostered good business relationships with all [clients/customers/referral sources/payers/other: _____] by
[successfully meeting their needs/being above board with all communiqués/other: _____].

Improving Safety Performance Levels

❑ Achieved safety performance levels to _____ from previous incident rate of _____ by
_____ [doing what?].

SUPERVISORY BULLETS

Review the following fill-in-the-blank Resume ClipBullets™ samples to see whether any of the functions and achievements apply to your work. Fill in the blanks and adjust wording as appropriate. Incorporate these bullets into your resume where applicable.

Divisions, Departments, or Units You Supervise

❑ Supervise and oversee _____ [#] employees in the [department/unit/store/other: _____], including _____ [#] directly and _____ [#] indirectly for this _____ [type of] firm.

❑ Coordinate, delegate, and supervise all _____ [type of] functions in the _____ [division/department/unit/store/other: _____], including _____, _____, _____, and _____ [type of functions].

❑ Coordinate and oversee _____ [which?] operations for this $_____ _____ [type of] firm with _____ [#] [locations/branches/employees/customers/other: _____].

Training and Developing Staff

❑ Coordinate and implement [formal/informal] on-the-job training programs to enhance _____ [which?] staff's level of performance and personal development.

❑ Coach, mentor, and motivate [new/existing] _____ [type of] staff to achieve corporate objectives via _____ [type of] methods, resulting in _____ [what benefits?].

❑ Developed and implemented an ongoing training program that serves to keep [offices/departments/stores/employees/other: _____] current on changes in [product lines/procedures/industry standards/market trends/sales forecasting/other: _____].

❑ Train and develop the _____ [which?] staff in [the expertise required for the profession/a thorough understanding of the _____ (type of) industry/new product offerings/core business development/other: _____] via [regular meetings/hands-on training/individual coaching sessions/other: _____].

❑ Schedule and coordinate all staff training for _____ [#] [departments/corporate offices/franchise stores/other: _____] and _____ [#] employees.

Staff Scheduling

❑ Plan and organize _____ [type of] staff's work schedule to ensure [excellent customer service/optimum personnel utilization/the efficient completion of daily work activities/other: _____].

❑ Schedule and coordinate all employee _____ [type of] functions for _____ [#] [departments/corporate offices/franchise stores/other: _____] by effectively _____ [doing what?].

❑ Develop _____ [type of] staff schedules to [maintain continuity/ensure adequate levels of coverage during peak hours of operations/reduce overtime/be sensitive to personnel needs/other: _____].

Step 6

Delegation and Follow-Up

❏ Successfully _____ [do what?] to ensure staff completes all assigned functions correctly and in accordance with [policies and procedures/rules and regulations/other: _____], resulting in _____ [what benefits?].

Motivating Staff

❏ Energize and motivate a _____ [type of] staff of _____ [#] to [produce high-quality products/meet high levels of customer service/exceed sales goals/meet difficult deadlines/other: _____] by _____ [doing what?].

❏ Developed and implemented a _____ [type of] employee incentive program to _____ [accomplish what?], which resulted in _____ [what benefits?].

Evaluating Staff Performance

❏ Developed a _____ [type of] [program/procedure/other: _____] to evaluate staff's progress, which has resulted in _____ [what benefits?].

❏ Monitor, fairly evaluate, and document subordinates' progress to ensure that [all required goals are met for the position/quality of work or customer service delivered meets firm's high standards of excellence/other requirements:_____].

❏ Utilize _____, _____, and _____ [what?] means to evaluate staff's progress, resulting in _____ [what benefits?].

Handling Challenging Employee Situations

❏ Tackle challenging employee situations through the means of _____ [what?] methods, which has resulted in [a smooth workflow/less downtime/more productivity/more motivated employees/other: _____].

Streamlining Operations/Increasing Productivity

❏ Created and implemented a successful _____ [type of] program to [cut down the workload/increase sales/reduce overtime/increase productivity/streamline operations/cut expenses/other: _____], which has resulted in _____ [what benefits?].

❏ Utilize _____ [type of] [methods/techniques/attributes/skills/other: _____] to maintain a productive, quality-producing staff, which has resulted in _____ [what benefits?].

Step 6

ADMINISTRATIVE BULLETS

Review the following fill-in-the-blank Resume ClipBullets™ samples to see whether any of the functions and achievements apply to your work. Fill in the blanks and adjust wording as appropriate. Incorporate these bullets into your resume where applicable.

Managing Office and Administrative Functions

❏ Manage various [operational aspects of/administrative support services for] this $_____ _____ [type of firm], including [administration/payroll/secretarial pool/data processing/mailroom/materials distribution/printing/records management/security/telecommunications/computer troubleshooting/other: _____].

❏ [Direct and oversee/Supervise] all administrative support services, including [inventory/purchasing/payroll/invoicing/other: _____] for all _____ [#] [departments/offices/stores/other: _____] requiring [calculating current stock/determining ordering needs/accurate data entry of all information/other: _____].

Supervising an Office-Support Staff and Administrative Functions

❏ Supervise an office-support staff of _____ [#] _____ [position titles] in the functions of [word processing/filing/billing/other: _____].

❏ Oversee _____ [#] first-line supervisors from _____ [which?] departments, including the [administrative/secretarial/clerical/other: _____] staff(s), which involves hiring and dismissing employees.

❏ Supervise diversified office activities, including [correspondence/bookkeeping/billing/travel arrangements/insurance/dispatch/timekeeping/job inquiries/payroll reports/other: _____].

❏ Prioritize work assignments and project tasks by [determining deadlines/analyzing scope and importance of work/strategizing best approach to meet commitments/other: _____].

Performing Office and Administrative Functions

❏ Perform various office and administrative functions, including [switchboard operations/word processing/data entry/client correspondence/document processing/opening and sorting mail/filing/basic bookkeeping/making bank deposits/other: _____] for this $_____ _____ [type of] firm.

❏ Provide support to the _____ [which?] departments, handling all [order taking/correspondence/memoranda/faxes/phone messages/mailings/deliveries/copying/scanning/e-mailing/other: _____] in a timely and professional fashion.

❏ Handle [general office administration/account servicing/daily customer service matters/payroll issues/health insurance/401(k) matters/other: _____] for an office staff of _____ [#].

Step 6

Performing Secretarial or Executive Assistance Functions

❑ Perform all [secretarial/administrative/executive assistance/operations/office management] functions for _____ [management titles], **including** [taking dictation, scheduling appointments/making phone contacts/typing correspondence/filing/other: _____] in a professional manner.

❑ Serve as "right hand" to the [president/other title(s): _____], assisting with [developing departmental plans/setting goals and deadlines/developing and implementing procedures/banking matters/writing correspondence/generating client e-mail/all facets of business operations/other: _____].

❑ Perform word processing in [Microsoft Word/WordPerfect/other: _____] at _____ [#] words per minute with accurate proofreading, punctuation, grammar, and editing.

❑ Take and transcribe shorthand for _____ [#] [executives/senior management/partners/other: _____] using [Gregg Shorthand/Pittman/digital voice recording/other method: _____].

❑ Accurately take and transcribe [letter dictation/interoffice correspondence/reports/speeches/other: _____] at _____ [#] words per minute, ensuring correct spelling, grammar, and sentence structure at all times.

❑ Schedule the executive's day while ensuring sufficient time for her daily objectives to be met by [developing good rapport with peers and execs/being firm or flexible, as appropriate, in evaluating requests made for his time/other method: _____].

❑ Being very attuned to the pressures of my boss' job as it relates to my functions, prioritize workload and meet day-to-day functions with [impeccable timing/good business sense/other: _____].

Handling Correspondence and Mail

❑ Sort and process all [incoming correspondence/mail/e-mail/customer invoices/payments/orders/other: _____] and respond to those of a general nature.

❑ Accurately type [correspondence/e-mail/memoranda/speeches/invoices/other: _____] on a daily basis using [MS Word/WordPerfect/other: _____].

❑ [Research/Analyze/Compile/Prepare/Coordinate] _____ [type of] [correspondence/e-mails/memoranda/other: _____] using independent judgment in the areas of _____ and _____.

❑ Carefully examine all incoming mail and other materials and code them [numerically/alphabetically/by subject matter/other: _____], and correctly file all [forms/letters/receipts/reports/correspondence/invoices/other: _____].

Answering Phones

❑ Professionally answer _____ [#] phone lines [within two rings/other: _____], directing callers to proper recipients in a courteous manner and [in accordance with company procedures/as quickly as possible/other: _____].

❑ Screen and service all internal and external calls to _____ [whom?] in a polite and professional manner, ensuring that all callers get the help they need—with [confidentiality/courtesy/follow-up/other: _____].

❑ Handle heavy telephone contact with [clients/suppliers/_____ (#) stores/business associates/vendors/other: _____] in a professional, friendly manner, always ensuring appropriate follow-through within a _____ [#]-[hour/minute] timeframe.

(continued)

ADMINISTRATIVE BULLETS *(continued)*
Greeting and Handling Visitors

❑ Greet _____ [type of] [executives/clients/customers/vendors/other: _____] from [within the company/other stores/the community/around the world/other: _____] in a [friendly/professional/culturally respectful/other: _____] manner.

❑ Greet and direct all customers in a professional manner, assisting them with [account information/product specifications and decisions/other: _____] while promoting the company and going above and beyond to fulfill customers' needs.

❑ Ensure all greetings leave a positive first impression by being [courteous/professional/helpful/businesslike/other: _____] to all company visitors and callers.

Handling Customers

❑ Provide information to prospective clients regarding [products/services/membership packages/other: _____], starting initial sales process by attracting interest and directing prospects to appropriate sales associate.

❑ Handle all customer complaints by successfully appeasing dissatisfied customers and turning them into satisfied clients through [effective listening/patience/understanding/a caring manner/other methods: _____].

Technical Expertise

❑ Utilize _____ [which?] [spreadsheet/database/other: _____] programs to [create/process/maintain] [documents/charts/administrative records/other: _____] for all _____ [what?].

❑ Maintain automated [computer databases/reports/inventory supply/work schedules/payroll/other: _____] via [PC/MAC]-based _____ [type of] systems.

❑ Conduct [Internet research/other: _____], assist in [Web site development/other: _____], and perform [desktop publishing/other: _____] for all company [marketing/training/other: _____] materials.

❑ Instruct staff and provide computer support on [QuickBooks Pro/Microsoft Word/InDesign/other: _____] and various other programs.

Step 6

Automating Manual Systems

❑ Automated company's manual _____ [type of] system to a computerized [account database/payroll/other: _____] system [increasing overall productivity and efficiency/other benefit: _____].

❑ Converted manual processing [office/administrative/other: _____] systems to a functional [peer-to-peer/vendor-to-office/other: _____] computer environment, including [billing/payroll/accounting/word processing/desktop publishing/other: _____].

❑ Implemented [Microsoft Access/other: _____] program designed to [generate quarterly reports/track customer information/target demographic information/other:_____], which resulted in [more accurate and up-to-date records/ easily obtaining all relative customer data/other benefits: _____].

❑ Revamped and automated company's entire [accounting/bookkeeping/payroll/data entry/other: _____] [records/system/program] by _____ [how?], which resulted in _____ [what benefits?].

❑ Converted manual [payroll/invoicing/budget tracking/other: _____] system to [Lotus/QuickBooks/other: _____], providing [executives/staff/vendors/customers/other: _____] with [better reporting/more accurate and up-to-date information/other benefit: _____].

❑ Sought and obtained approval to have a _____ [type of] program written [eliminating duplication of input efforts in _____[#] departments/other process: _____], which [simplified tracking of _____ (type of) charges/cut _____ (type of) costs/other result: _____].

Performing Billing, Data Entry, or Payroll Responsibilities

❑ [Manage/Supervise/Prepare/Coordinate] [payroll/bookkeeping/billing/accounts payable/accounts receivable/general ledger/ inventory/purchasing/other: _____] for a staff of _____ [#], keeping all records current and ensuring their accuracy.

❑ Perform data entry of [customer/contractual/sales/other: _____] information, including _____, _____, and _____ on _____ [name of] system.

❑ [Conduct/Supervise] computer entry of daily [appointments/billing/payments/recordkeeping/client communiqué/payroll/other: _____], ensuring accurate data entry at all times.

❑ Accurately complete and verify data entry of _____ [#] weekly invoices using [QuickBooks/Excel/Quicken/other: _____].

❑ Process approximately _____ [#] [invoice pages/sales contracts/letters of credit/other: _____] weekly, compared to a norm of _____ [#]—completing a five-day workload in only _____ [#] days.

❑ Research, determine, and correct all billing errors, saving company $_____ by exercising [patience/diligence/ability to overcome frustration when numbers don't balance/other: _____].

Step 6

(continued)

ADMINISTRATIVE BULLETS *(continued)*
Performing Clerical Functions

❑ Assist _____ [office/department/store/other: _____] with [filing/answering phones/messenger service/office work/other: _____].

❑ In charge of filing all customer account paperwork and maintaining records of _____[#] accounts so they are [organized/up-to-date/easily retrievable/other: _____].

❑ Process bulk [mail/faxing/other: _____] of approximately _____ [#] items per week, compared to a standard of _____ [#].

❑ Neatly format [articles/reports/files/correspondence/other: _____] and expediently route to _____ [#] departments daily.

❑ Accurately [file/classify/store/retrieve/update/other: _____] daily [receipts/invoices/contracts/reports/client files/other documents: _____], keeping on top of workload without accumulating a backlog.

❑ Maintain all office equipment, including [multiline telephone systems/personal computers/photocopiers/postal stamp machines/fax machines/other: _____].

❑ Successfully overcame challenge of learning an in-depth filing system and familiarizing myself with employer's accounts. Resulted in [working faster/filing records correctly/the ability for others to locate files without guesswork/other: _____].

Desktop Publishing and Creating Publications

❑ Create and generate [in-office/client/other: _____] publications, including [newsletters/financials/proposals/manuals/reports/other: _____] using [MS Publisher/MS Word/InDesign/QuarkXPress/other: _____].

❑ Use advanced word-processing functions such as [calculating tables/style add-ins/columns/charts and graphs/headers and footers/mail merges/cross-referencing/borders and shading/other: _____] to prepare [newsletters/brochures/sales materials/procedure manuals/training manuals/other: _____].

Preparing and Generating Reports or Contacts

❑ Oversee the [preparation/analysis/negotiation/review] of [contracts/invoices/estimates/billing/other: _____] related to the [purchase/sale] of [equipment/materials/supplies/products/services/other: _____].

❑ Facilitate distribution of [financial statements/journal entries/articles/publications/other: _____] and oversee the [compilation/coordination/accuracy/other: _____] of all _____ [what data or info?].

❑ Maintain _____ [type of] reports, and follow up with _____ [departments/divisions/writers/other: _____] to ensure timely submissions of _____ [type of] items.

❑ Developed a(n) [invoice/report/billing chart/template/form/other: _____] to record _____ [what information?] superceding the manual method and saving the company $_____ in the area of _____.

Step 6

Providing Liaison Between Various Parties

❑ Act as liaison between [management/company/other: _____] and [other departments/customers/vendors/other: _____] _____] in the area of _____.

Scheduling and Coordinating Meetings, Conferences, Trade Shows, Travel Arrangements, or Special Events

❑ Schedule and coordinate all [travel and itinerary arrangements/expense reporting/other: _____] for _____ [#] [executives/sales staff/other: _____] with an eye toward travelers' time constraints and convenience, including all [plane/car/hotel] reservations and [dinner/conference/meeting/other: _____] arrangements.

❑ Coordinate and orchestrate [national conventions/trade shows/special events/conferences/other: _____], resulting in [obtaining _____ (#) new accounts/meeting prospective clients/generating leads/gaining new customer accounts/increasing company exposure to industry professionals/other benefits: _____].

Coordinating or Making Independent Decisions for Certain Administrative Functions

❑ Coordinate _____ [which?] functions, making independent decisions for _____ [which?] administrative functions in the areas of _____, _____, and _____.

Financial Recordkeeping

❑ Handle all recordkeeping of all [purchases and supplies/monthly billing/budget monitoring/financial transaction processing/other process: _____] for _____ [#] accounts.

❑ Coordinate payroll operations and accounting for _____ [#] employees, including [accurate recordkeeping/reporting of all employee hours, absences and vacations/other: _____].

❑ Accurately handle all monthly billing for _____ [#] accounts with recordkeeping of all purchases and supplies per account using _____ [program or method].

❑ Managed the automated payroll for _____ [#] employees, and handled bookkeeping and accounts receivables/payables for _____.

(continued)

Step 6

ADMINISTRATIVE BULLETS *(continued)*

Handling Independent Research and Analysis

❑ Conduct [independent research/analysis/compilation of data/other: _____] in the areas of _____, _____, and _____ for the purpose of _____.

Resolving Customer or Staff Complaints

❑ Handle and resolve all [customer/staff/other: _____] complaints, resolving time-sensitive issues in an expedient manner to the [customer's/staff's/company's/other: _____] satisfaction.

❑ Successfully resolve [customer account problems/conflicts with employees/account discrepancies/other: _____] through effective [customer service/teamwork/troubleshooting/patience/other: _____].

Balancing Multiple Projects and Workload

❑ Effectively balance and coordinate a workload [of multiple projects/for several executives/other: _____] by _____ [methods you use successfully].

❑ Successfully handle multiple [projects/activities/tasks] simultaneously with nonstop interaction—serving approximately _____ [#] [accounts/customers/members/patients/other: _____] daily.

❑ Successfully and efficiently worked in a fast-paced environment with ability to change direction midstream as needed.

Other Administrative Responsibilities or Achievements

❑ Created a _____ [type of] [filing/data entry/other: _____] [system/procedure/program/other: _____], which resulted in _____ [what benefits?].

❑ Conduct [telesales/cold calling/other: _____], making approximately _____ [#] calls per day and generating more than _____ [#] new clients annually, resulting in [repeat business/new leads/other: _____].

❑ Increased sales and revenues by generating new and maintaining existing clientele through [phone contact/e-mail blasts/telemarketing/strong follow-up/other: _____].

Step 6

CREATIVE BULLETS

Review the following fill-in-the-blank Resume ClipBullets™ samples to see whether any of the functions and achievements apply to your work. Fill in the blanks and adjust the wording as appropriate. Incorporate the bullets into your resume where applicable.

The following Resume ClipBullets™ are excerpted from Evelyn Salvador's profession-specific *Resume ClipBullets™ for Creative Professions* book (Creative Image Builders), which you can order using the form at the end of this book.

Your Creations or Designs

❏ Created and implemented _____ [what?] designed to _____ [do what?], resulting in _____ [what benefits?].

❏ Developed _____ [what?], which focused on _____ [what?] and resulted in _____ [what benefit?].

❏ [Designed/Planned/Managed/Implemented/Coordinated] _____ [what?], which resulted in _____ .

Innovative Initiatives You Have Developed or Promoted

❏ Developed and implemented innovative _____ [type of] programs for _____ [what?], which resulted in _____ [achievement].

❏ Instrumental in creating and formulating the _____ [what initiative?], which significantly improved _____ [what?].

❏ Initiated and implemented the _____ [what?] initiative, which generated volume sales in _____ by _____ [doing what?].

❏ Launched and aggressively promoted the "_____ Program" by _____ [doing what?], which resulted in _____ .

❏ Strengthened company's growth potential through various initiatives, including _____ .

Types of Design Concepts and Techniques You Use

❏ Successfully created _____ [type of] [design concepts/techniques] for _____ [what?], utilizing _____ [type of] methods to [create/perform] _____ [what?].

Meeting with Clients to Strategize Their Needs

❏ Strategize with _____ [whom?] to [develop comprehensive print media needs/develop marketing concepts/ascertain budget/determine direction best to meet user needs/other: _____].

❏ Meet with clients to strategize and assess their [graphic design/multimedia/other: _____] needs, create design concepts, and make recommendations in various areas, including _____ [what areas?].

(continued)

CREATIVE BULLETS *(continued)*
Involvement with Creative Design, Marketing, or Advertising

❏ Conceptualize, design, and implement _____ [type of] projects from concept to completion, including integration of _____ [what?] using _____ [what programs or methods?].

❏ Design and produce [effective visual communications/marketing campaigns/camera-ready art/interior decorating plans/apparel design/architectural layouts/other: _____] to meet client _____ [type of] needs, including _____ [what?].

❏ Lay out and design [marketing brochures/promotional displays/distinctive company logos/ad campaigns/catalogs/Web sites/video-cable spots/trade shows/other: _____] for _____ [what?], which have resulted in _____ [benefit].

❏ [Oversee/Manage/Coordinate/Perform] the [layout/design/production/prepress/other: _____] of all marketing communications, including final output of the piece.

❏ Create [illustrations/graphics/line drawings/sketches/technical illustrations/CADD drawings/other] for _____.

❏ Edit, proofread, and rewrite text for content, clarity, spelling, grammar, and punctuation, including [articles/news releases/publication materials/blog posts/other:_____] for _____ [what?].

❏ Assist _____ [whom?] in the creation of [promotional pieces/advertising design/newspaper layouts/Web research/selection of stock photography/photo retouching/other:_____] for _____ [what?].

❏ Synthesize input from a variety of sources to design _____ [what?] to meet the budget, timeframes, and marketing objectives of _____ [type of] clients.

Your Involvement with the Production Process

❏ Streamlined in-house operations and increased production accuracy of _____ [what?] by _____ [doing what?].

❏ Saved [production time/paper/printing/other:_____] costs by _____ [doing what?].

❏ Manage and coordinate a smooth and timely work-flow process from [prepress to press/other:_____], including quality control of _____ [what processes?].

❏ Streamlined production and decreased final product turnaround time by _____ [doing what?].

❏ Perform prepress flight checks and press checks to ensure quality control of printed pieces by _____ [doing what?].

Increasing Sales or Decreasing Costs Due to Your Creativity

❏ Increased sales by $_____ by designing _____ [what?] for _____ [whom or what promotion?], **which resulted in** [significant business for company/rave reviews from client/other: _____].

❏ Decreased costs by coming in $_____ under budget by _____ [doing what?].

❏ Generate sales through [attractive visual presentations/three-dimensional models/attaining referrals through word of mouth from satisfied clients/other: _____].

Step 6

CUSTOMER SERVICE BULLETS

Review the following fill-in-the-blank Resume ClipBullet™ samples to see whether any of the functions and achievements apply to your work. Fill in the blanks and adjust the wording as appropriate. Incorporate these bullets into your resume where applicable.

The following Resume ClipBullets™ are excerpted from Evelyn Salvador's profession-specific *Resume ClipBullets™ for Sales and Marketing Professions* book (Creative Image Builders), which you can order using the form at the end of the book.

What You Manage or Supervise

❑ [Manage/Supervise] [customer service operations/the distribution center/purchasing/other: _____] of _____ [type of] firm, which sells _____ [type of] [products/services] to the _____[type of] market.

❑ Oversee total [customer service/purchasing/merchandising/inter-company supply/other: _____], including [import/export/distribution/other: _____] with operational budget responsibilities of $_____ .

❑ Manage the [customer service operations/total sales support/other: _____] of [recognized world standard setter for] _____ [type of] projects previously averaging $_____ per project, and with my redirection put them in the $_____ per-project market.

Types of Services You Provide and How You Assist Customers

❑ Handle all facets of customer service—from assisting customers with their buying decisions to resolving problems with difficult customers for $_____ [revenues] _____ [type of] [firm/store/other: _____], which sells _____ [type of] [products/services].

❑ Provide [pre-/post-] sales support to [customers/clients/other: _____] in the areas of _____, _____, and _____.

❑ Successfully handle various customer service functions daily, including [managing all sales transactions/processing sales orders/handling all facets of register operations/providing customers with merchandise information/coordinating shipping and delivery of merchandise/other: _____].

❑ Provide customers with [advice/professional help/consultation/other: _____] in _____ [what functions?] for [multimillion-dollar/$_____] _____ [type of] firm with _____ [#] [locations/employees].

❑ Assist customers with [merchandise/product/service/delivery/other: _____] inquiries both in person and via telephone by _____ [how you do this in an exceptional manner].

❑ Work with customers by [processing and expediting all sales orders/providing product information/informing them of sale items and monthly specials/solving credit problems/providing follow-up and advisement/checking orders on computer/other: _____] [in person/by mail/by phone/by e-mail/via online chat].

❑ As the primary customer contact, act as liaison between _____[which?] department and the customer in the areas of _____, _____, _____, and _____.

❑ Service _____ [#] accounts by setting up _____ [#] [daily/weekly] [delivery routes/account or product servicing/follow-up/sales support/other: _____] and providing _____ [what?].

(continued)

CUSTOMER SERVICE BULLETS *(continued)*
Other Customer-Service Functions You Perform

❑ Compile and prepare [sales reports/credit-card receipts/monthly statements/bank deposits/accounts receivable and accounts payable reports/other: _____], ensuring their accuracy and _____ [what else?] by _____ [doing what?].

❑ Balance _____ [#] [cash drawers/safe/other: _____] daily, ensuring [proper documentation for all sales transactions/ balancing all voids, returns, and credits/other: _____].

❑ Fill and prove all cash drawers on a daily basis to ensure accuracy at the start of each business day.

Improving Customer Service

❑ Developed and implemented a new _____ [name of] customer service program, which _____ [program purpose] and resulted in $_____ in new business.

❑ Reduced customer service delivery time from _____ [#] minutes to _____ [#] minutes by _____ [doing what?].

❑ Spearheaded successful high-quality [customer service/sales support] programs for company's _____ [division/store(s)/department(s)], which resulted in _____ [what benefits?].

❑ Elevated levels of client satisfaction by _____% by [providing knowledgeable service in a friendly manner/increasing number of registers to reduce client wait times/researching and resolving customer complaints in a timely fashion/other: _____].

❑ Conceptualize and develop seamless, cost-effective customer service and sales-support strategies such as _____, _____, and _____, resulting in _____ [benefit].

Increasing Sales or Profitability

❑ Increased average sales ticket from $_____ to $_____ through [suggestive selling/upselling/cross-selling/catering to customer needs/overcoming obstacles/knowing when to close a sale/other method: _____].

❑ Successfully contributed to increased sales and obtained many customer referrals by [providing excellent customer service/working well under pressure/exhibiting patience/solving problems/meeting customer needs/other methods: _____].

❑ Increased _____ [type of] sales by [gaining a strong knowledge of products and inventory/providing customers with superior levels of service/other: _____].

Step 6

❏ Increased sales of _____ [what?] by $_____ by turning proposals into signed contracts via [presenting in-depth performance reports/competition analysis sales proposals/contract results analyses detailing project scope and descriptions/ profitable but user-friendly pricing/other method: _____].

❏ Conceived and negotiated an exclusive contract with _____ [what company?] for one of its major _____ [type of] products by [identifying and defining a market niche/other: _____], resulting in _____ [what benefits?].

❏ Increased sales from $_____ to $_____ and profitability ratio from_____% to _____% by [researching and analyzing historic activities/performing feasibility studies/brainstorming with long-time employees, customers, and distributors/strategizing a successful marketing plan/other: _____].

❏ Developed and implemented a _____ [name of] program, which _____ [program purpose] resulted in $_____ in new business annually.

Cash Management and Inventory Control

❏ Supervise [cash-management/inventory control/other: _____] functions, including [cash drawers/petty cash/bank deposits/receivables monitoring and reporting/asset protection/inventory control and management/payroll/other: _____].

❏ Develop _____ [type of] cashier schedules to maintain continuity and ensure adequate levels of coverage during peak hours of operations.

❏ Increased productivity by _____% by [working with cashiers to develop proactive cash-management systems/other method: _____].

Providing High-Quality Customer Service

❏ Spearheaded cost-effective, high-quality [customer service/sales support] program(s) that resulted in [increased annual sales of $_____/ other: _____].

❏ Plan and organize [sales associates'/cashiers'/customer service representatives'/other: _____] work schedules to ensure [excellent customer service/availability of staff/optimum personnel utilization/successful completion of work activities/other benefits: _____].

❏ Ensure the quality of customer service delivered meets high standards of excellence by [monitoring and evaluating staff's progress/other: _____].

❏ Received many customer commendations due to [having a positive attitude/being efficient/my quest for excellence/going beyond the expected/other trait: _____], resulting in more satisfied customers and repeat business for the company.

Step 6

(continued)

CUSTOMER SERVICE BULLETS *(continued)*
Handling Customer Complaints and Difficult Situations

❑ Work with a wide range of clientele and handle difficult customer problems in a [calm/diplomatic/patient/friendly/courteous/positive/knowledgeable/professional] manner.

❑ Handle all customer complaints and problems by _____ [doing what?], which balances keeping the customer satisfied without "giving away the store."

❑ Keep composure during peak times by [tackling each situation as it arises/remaining calm/soliciting and obtaining help from peers in making short-staff situations transparent to customers/other methods: _____].

❑ Appease dissatisfied customers by _____, _____, and _____ [doing what?].

Other Customer-Service Achievements

❑ Received _____ [how many?] client commendations for _____, _____, and _____ [why commended], resulting in [more satisfied customers/repeat business/referrals/other: _____] for company.

❑ Organized a [hodgepodge order-as-you-need-it supply system/other area: _____] by focusing on centralization, resulting in [a streamlined supply flow/more on-time deliveries/elimination of panic order situations/other: _____].

❑ Identified and implemented [cross-sell/upsell/other: _____] opportunities—including _____ and _____—by [providing employee incentives/other method: _____], resulting in _____ [what benefit?].

❑ Reduced receivable exposure from an average of _____ [#] days down to _____ [#] days by establishing [checks and balances/feedback/control procedures/other: _____]. (Reduction of _____% on $_____ in average monthly sales totaled a savings of _____% per month or $_____ savings in annual interest.)

Step 6

PRODUCTION AND MANUFACTURING BULLETS

Review the following fill-in-the-blank Resume ClipBullet™ samples to see whether any of the functions and achievements apply to your work. Fill in the blanks and adjust the wording as appropriate. Incorporate these bullets into your resume where applicable.

The following Resume ClipBullets™ are excerpted from Evelyn Salvador's profession-specific *Resume ClipBullets™ for Business Professions* book (Creative Image Builders), which you can order using the form at the back of this book.

What You Manage or Supervise

❑ Manage the [manufacture/production/distribution/other: _____] of _____ [type of] products for this _____ [type of] firm with revenues over $_____ and _____ [#] locations [nationally/globally].

❑ Perform production supervision and coordination of the manufacturing of all product lines, including _____ [type of product lines] in accordance with _____ [what?] regulations.

❑ Manage overall [domestic/international/regional/other: _____] operations—from ordering piece goods to overseeing _____ [what?].

❑ Direct and manage daily activities of _____ [#] managers and oversee production operations of _____ [#] employees for this [worldwide manufacturer of/industry leader in/other: _____] _____ [what genre?].

❑ Manage the manufacturing and installation of _____ [type of] products for this _____ [type of] manufacturer specializing in _____ [what genre?] with _____ [#] locations and annual revenues in excess of $_____.

❑ Manage staff of _____ [#] in the installation of all products, including _____, _____, and _____ at [residential/commercial] customer sites.

❑ Manage and oversee a production staff of _____ [#], and coordinate production and distribution with staff of various subsidiary divisions for this $_____ [total revenues] _____ [type of] firm specializing in _____ [what?].

❑ Supervise the day-to-day activities of _____ [#] managers overseeing the operations of up to _____ [#] employees.

Production Functions You Perform

❑ Handle raw materials purchasing of _____ [type of raw materials], quality control of all manufacturing components, and production of _____ for this $_____ [revenues] _____ [type of] manufacturing firm.

❑ Manage and coordinate a smooth and timely work-flow process from raw materials to finished goods, including [supervising the machine shop and production assembly process/determining required resources/establishing production methods, applications, and timelines/controlling manufacturing projects/managing production schedules/evaluating vendors/planning, supervising, and monitoring production schedules/scheduling workload/expediting parts flow through production stages/monitoring budget and expenses/troubleshooting and correcting production problems/communicating with suppliers/directing quality-assurance operations/meeting performance objectives/identifying and resolving quality problem areas/handling inventory control/recording testing procedure results/ensuring product quality/preparing reports and documentation/monitoring and inspecting production/conducting quality-assurance training/approving finished products/other: _____].

(continued)

PRODUCTION AND MANUFACTURING BULLETS *(continued)*

❏ Coordinate all facets of [manufacturing/production/distribution/packaging/shipping/other: _____], ensuring scheduling is reviewed [weekly/daily/other: _____] and maintaining a _____% on-time shipping record.

❏ Handle various production functions, ensuring a smooth and timely work-flow process [from raw materials to finished goods], including [assembling products/performing subassembly or preassembly of products/reading and following assembly sketches/applying labels/collating materials/quality testing/belt setups/product packaging/recommending quality improvement changes/other: _____], adhering to all performance standards and meeting or exceeding all required deadlines.

❏ Approve pricing of merchandise components to ensure best quality, price, and delivery schedules, and their timely delivery.

❏ Coordinate and manage sorting _____ [type of] products by _____ [what method(s)?].

❏ Schedule jobs on various _____ [type of] machines, depending on job type and production quantity by _____ [how do you do this effectively?].

❏ Perform financial analysis of new _____ [type of] lines to determine cost-effectiveness of final product—covering [materials/labor/packaging/shipping/other: _____] expenses.

Increasing Productivity and Streamlining Operations

❏ Increased [production/productivity] by [$_____/_____%] through effective means of _____ [state achievement], which resulted in _____ [how it was beneficial].

❏ [Streamlined operations/Increased production] by _____% and decreased errors by _____% by [running machines at their full potential/maintaining proper running condition/servicing machines more regularly/producing better-quality end products/other means: _____].

❏ Spearheaded the corporate-wide initiative to _____ [do what?], which realized production gains of _____% with no additional labor expenses.

❏ Increased [daily production/overall production efficiency] [by _____%/from _____ (#) to _____ (#)] without raising overhead by [streamlining manufacturing organization and procedures/developing results-oriented programs designed to motivate staff/other: _____].

❏ Increased productivity by training and developing _____ [#] quality production personnel in the production and manufacturing of [high-quality raw and finished goods/other: _____].

Step 6

❑ Increased daily production from _____ [#] to_____ [#] units without raising overhead by _____ [doing what?].

❑ Increased production by _____% by _____ [doing what?].

Reducing Production and Related Costs

❑ Decreased annual production costs in excess of $_____ [through selection of more cost-effective vendors/by training all employees on product features and benefits/by implementing effective quality-control procedures/other: _____].

❑ Streamlined in-house operations and increased production accuracy by _____ [doing what?], resulting in a reduction of productivity costs by $_____.

❑ Reduced purchasing costs in excess of $_____ annually by establishing a(n) _____ [what negotiation or initiative?] to _____ [do what?].

❑ Evaluated and modified [manufacturing/production/other: _____] procedures and overall facility operations by _____ [doing what?], resulting in _____ [what benefits?].

❑ Streamlined production and decreased final product turnaround time by $_____ annually by _____ [doing what?].

❑ Successfully implemented a _____ [type of] cost-reduction program by evaluating [manufacturing/production/ business/other: _____] bottlenecks.

❑ Reduced _____ [which?] fees by $_____ annually by spearheading the construction of a _____ [type of] facility for _____ [purpose], which resulted in _____ [what benefit?].

❑ Designed and implemented business forecasting and analysis models, which generated a cost savings of [_____%/$_____] after executing new production and training programs.

Production Equipment and Scheduling Workloads

❑ Introduced new CNC equipment to manufacturing process and developed _____ [type of] system for monitoring productivity, which resulted in _____ [benefits].

❑ Developed levels of productivity to _____% and contributed to _____% of this firm's business growth by successfully leading the firm's _____ [state initiative].

❑ Forecast workloads and schedule staff around production dates to ensure sufficient manpower coverage at all times, especially during heavy periods.

❑ Handle multiple projects simultaneously—from _____ [#] to _____ [#] raw, finished, and bulk products.

(continued)

PRODUCTION AND MANUFACTURING BULLETS *(continued)*
System and Procedural Improvements

❑ Developed systemized programs to monitor tracking of customer orders, resulting in a _____% on-time delivery ratio.

❑ Established and successfully implemented company-wide procedures for [an electronic production schedule/Merchandise Availability Report/other: _____], which was [a company first/implemented company-wide].

❑ Established a(n) [electronic data interchange software/other: _____] program to facilitate the production of orders, resulting in increased customer satisfaction due to [a more efficient way of shipping accurate orders on time/other: _____].

❑ Saved $_____ annually and increased customer satisfaction level from _____% to _____% at a value of $_____ by [establishing a state-of-the-art _____ (type of) program/reducing staff by _____ (#) without affecting production levels/other: _____].

❑ Produced a trackable work-order system utilizing a _____ [type of] software system, and set it up for manufacturing _____[what?].

Increasing Business/Sales

❑ Increased overall business from $_____ to $_____ in revenue in a _____[#]-year period by implementing a _____ [type of] program involving [all aspects of quality production/other: _____].

❑ Increased sales and profitability by [$_____/_____%] by [introducing new lines to coincide with customer purchasing trends/ introducing _____ (type of) equipment to the manufacturing process/evaluating equipment suppliers and developing cost-return analysis/leading a majority of capital equipment projects/other: _____].

Quality Control and Compliance

❑ [Perform/Oversee] _____ [what?] to ensure quality control of _____ [what?] by _____ [doing what?].

❑ Ensure all procedures are followed with quality control and deadlines in mind by [taking hourly production counts/handling mechanical difficulties/overseeing quality control personnel's functions/other: _____].

❑ Perform [quality control/quality assurance/compliance/validation/other: _____] in the areas of _____, _____, and _____.

❑ Conduct [first piece, in-process, or final inspections/inspections of all production phases/other: _____], ensuring compliance with all [regulations/state and federal laws/procedures/other: _____].

❑ Inspect [materials/assemblies/products/processes/data/other: _____] through _____ [what means?].

❑ Conduct monthly audits of all finances and inventory, including [raw goods/product stock/inventory and analysis of P&L statements to ensure profitability/other: _____].

Step 6

Developing Quality-Control Product Review Processes/Programs

❏ Established and successfully implemented quality-control procedures for _____ [what?], which benefited the company by _____ [doing what?].

❏ Initiated employee incentive programs, such as _____ for meeting production standards, which resulted in _____ [what benefits?].

❏ Developed a _____ [type of] quality-control product review process for _____ [what process?], which entailed _____ [what control functions?] to ensure _____ [what end result?].

Troubleshooting and Correcting Production Problems

❏ Troubleshoot and correct _____ [type of] production problems by _____ [doing what?], resulting in _____ [what benefits?].

❏ Identify and resolve quality problem areas by _____ [doing what?] to ensure high-quality final products.

Decreasing Final Product Turnaround Time

❏ Decreased final product turnaround time through means of _____ [methods you used], which benefited production by _____ [results].

Other Achievements

❏ Restructured and made profitable the acquisition of a distressed manufacturing facility. The facility previously employed _____ [#] people to produce _____ [#] tons of finished product daily; reduced staff to _____ [#] and increased production to _____ [#] tons daily.

❏ Raised safety performance levels to _____ [#] from previous incident rate of _____ [#] by _____ [doing what?].

❏ Contributed to success of company by recruiting, training, and developing skilled employees to deliver quality workmanship at all times.

❏ Forecast workloads and schedule staff around installation dates to ensure sufficient manpower coverage at all times, especially during heavy periods.

Step 6

SALES AND MARKETING BULLETS

Review the following fill-in-the-blank Resume ClipBullet™ samples to see whether any of the functions and achievements apply to your work. Fill in the blanks and adjust the wording as appropriate. Incorporate the bullets into your resume where applicable.

The following Resume ClipBullets™ are excerpted from Evelyn Salvador's profession-specific *Resume ClipBullets™ for Sales and Marketing Professions* book (Creative Image Builders), which you can order using the form at the back of this book.

What You Manage

❑ Direct and coordinate all aspects of [sales and marketing/new business development/strategic planning/cost management/brand management/other: _____], including [mergers and acquisitions/joint venture development/extensive _____ (type of) support programs/manufacturer and vendor relations/other: _____] for the _____ [what?] division of this $_____ _____ [type of] firm.

❑ Oversee and manage all facets of [sales and marketing/new program development/client relations budgets/other: _____] for this recognized [national/world] leader in _____ [what genre?].

❑ [Manage/Supervise/Oversee/Coordinate] all [advertising projects/marketing campaigns/promotional programs/creative planning/sales efforts/other: _____], including _____, _____, and _____.

❑ Direct and oversee [worldwide/nationwide/regional/local] sales and marketing activities, including [advertising campaigns/trade shows/direct-mail efforts/other: _____] and the strategic direction of products, taking the [firm/division/region/department] from $_____ to $_____ in annual sales.

❑ Manage and direct overall sales for the _____ [region] division, which specializes in _____ [which?] market by _____ [doing what?].

❑ Direct regional sales of all _____ [type of] products, including _____ to _____ [type of] markets.

❑ Manage and direct a team of _____ [#] [sales/marketing/creative/other: _____] personnel, and inspire teamwork among staff to develop measurable outcomes resulting in _____ [results of your initiatives].

Types of Products or Services You Sell

❑ [Manage and oversee/Perform] [local/regional/national/global] sales of _____ [what products or services?] for this $_____ _____ [type of] firm specializing in _____.

❑ Sell _____ [what?] to _____ [type of] [companies/consumers] via [canvassing/cold-calling/telemarketing/other sales methods: _____].

❑ Successfully present and sell _____ [what?] [products/services/other: _____] to _____ [type of] [businesses/consumers] through effective _____ [selling methods] for this [multimillion-dollar/$_____] _____ [type of] company.

Step 6

Sales Functions You Perform

❏ Present _____ [type of] [programs/campaigns/other: _____] to major _____ [type of] companies, including _____, _____, and _____ [Fortune 100 or 500 company names—if not a breach of confidentiality].

❏ Prepare and submit [sales budgets/revenue expectations/other: _____] to upper management, consistently attaining all revenue achievements for company.

❏ Create and present _____ [type of] proposals, conduct contract negotiations, and develop [multimillion-dollar/$_____] [marketing/sales/other: _____] budgets.

❏ Manage expenses associated with planning, training, rollout, and management for _____ [type of] programs.

Marketing Functions You Perform

❏ Manage the development of ideas for expanding promotional concepts, including _____ [what initiatives?].

❏ Conduct market research for _____ [what?] and establish _____ [#] [key accounts/strategies/other: _____] by _____ [doing what?].

❏ Conduct competitive, sales, and pricing analyses as well as product creation and analyses of _____ [what products?].

Launching New Products or Brands

❏ Successfully [marketed/sold] the "_____" [what product?], which _____ [does what?] by [recruiting a better sales force/training personnel/establishing new and expanding existing distribution channels/establishing relationships with several _____ (type of) manufacturers/other: _____]. Sales quota was $_____; achieved $_____.

❏ Spearheaded the _____ [which?] initiative(s) for establishing the _____ [type of] brand, which resulted in _____ [what benefits?].

❏ Launched the first of its kind _____ [product] for _____ [purpose], resulting in _____ [benefit to company].

❏ Working in conjunction with national sales force, launched many new products to market, including _____.

New Campaigns or Programs You Developed and Implemented

❏ Developed various sales and marketing programs, including [presentations/corporate images/sales incentive programs/product brochures/presentation materials/other: _____], which resulted in _____ [benefits].

❏ Played a major role in the creation of _____ [type of] programs involving _____ [what process or actions?], which resulted in _____ [benefits to company].

Step 6

(continued)

SALES AND MARKETING BULLETS *(continued)*

❏ Developed and implemented all facets of the _____ [type of] program, including the structuring and development of [a detailed business plan/market analysis for _____ /other: _____].

❏ Designed and created the _____ [marketing/advertising/sales] **campaign,** [establishing brand recognition/increasing firm's competitive edge in the marketplace/developing consumer awareness/increasing sales by $_____ /other benefit or results: _____].

❏ Developed new _____ [type of] program to secure preferred- and exclusive-provider contracts with _____ [whom?], resulting in increased sales of $_____ .

New Business-Development Initiatives

❏ Spearhead proactive business development of _____ [type of] products and services with concentration in the _____ [regions].

❏ Prospected and developed untouched new territory simultaneous to handling exitsing account base, including _____ , _____ , and _____ [Fortune 100/500 companies].

Increasing Sales/Profitability/Market Share

❏ Increased sales in the _____ [type of] marketplace [by _____%/from $_____ to $_____] and profits from $_____ to $_____ by creating a _____ [type of] program that enabled _____ [what?].

❏ Increased [sales/profitability/market share] by [$_____ /_____%] in _____ [#] years—from $_____ to $_____ —by [offering personalized service/promoting a consumer-sensitive approach/increasing product and customer needs awareness/developing effective marketing strategies/launching direct-mail campaigns/developing promotions that encourage up-selling higher-priced items or add-on sales/attending client functions/creating and presenting creative presentations/attending trade shows/networking/selling trust/educating consumers/offering community outreach programs/persistent follow-up/effective cold-call sales/securing numerous preferred-provider arrangements/converting numerous competitive accounts via buybacks and sell-downs/loyal customer service/other method: _____].

❏ Elevated sales with a _____ [#]-year compounded annual growth of _____ % and net income with a _____ [#]-year compounded annual growth of _____ % through effective use of _____ [what method?].

❏ Sold _____ [#] of _____ [what?], resulting in $_____ in new business using various methods, including _____ .

Step 6

Increasing Account Base

❏ Increased account base by [_____ (#)/_____%] over previous year by [concentrating on higher-end sales/increasing loyalty of existing client base/obtaining repeat customers/gaining increased referrals/problem-solving customer problems/other method: _____].

❏ Increased profitability of account base from _____% to _____% by _____ [what methods?].

Your Sales Performance

❏ Turned singular sales into multiple sales, increasing the average dollar transaction from $_____ to $_____ per client by _____ [what methods?].

❏ Produced the highest sales in company, selling _____ [#] _____ [type of product or service] in _____ [time period] and winning numerous awards for top sales by _____ [state how accomplished].

❏ Achieved highest sales quotas [company-wide/district-wide/nationwide] by [providing superior levels of service/using a consumer-sensitive approach/filling specific needs/promoting coordinating products/cross-selling other services/other achievement: _____].

❏ Exceed all monthly _____ [unit] sales quotas by an average of _____%.

❏ Continually outperform sales quotas and provide superior levels of service, exceeding overall expectations by _____ [doing what?].

❏ Elevated average [weekly/annual] sales by $_____ by [proactively presenting new items/other achievement: _____].

❏ Configured, proposed, and closed sale of _____ [what?] for _____ [what or whom?], resulting in $_____ in increased sales.

❏ Consistently ranked as top performer in the _____ [which?] department for developing new client relationships achieved by [actively uncovering and matching needs of _____ (type of) clients to _____ (type of) products/other means: _____].

Successful Sales Methods You Use

❏ Qualified sales leads and generated new business from [direct mail/advertising campaigns/industry trade shows/telephone inquiries/other methods: _____].

❏ Established and maintained a new account base of _____ [#] via _____, _____, and _____ [state methods].

❏ Generated a _____% sales increase in a _____[#]-year period by _____ [what methods?] for this leading _____ [type of company].

❏ Develop and service a customer base of _____ [#] via extensive cold calling on prospective customers within _____ [which?] regions.

❏ Utilize point-of-sale material to increase consumer awareness and sales, which resulted in _____ [benefits].

❏ Followed up on sales inquiries, closed sales, and finalized paperwork, receiving a high client referral rate for _____ [type of service].

(continued)

SALES AND MARKETING BULLETS *(continued)*

❏ Represented company at various major trade-show events, including _____, _____, and _____ [name of trade show, convention, or seminar], which resulted in _____ .

❏ Created sales and marketing campaigns designed to _____ [do what?], which resulted in _____ .

❏ Gained new business through [effective sales techniques/handling all customer associations in a positive, professional manner/building a rapport/cold calling on professionals in the community/other: _____].

❏ Networked and set up a referral base, developing proposals at a fair price [within guidelines] to win over clients from competition.

❏ Built a rapport with _____ [whom?], which allowed _____ [what?] and resulted in new business.

Establishing Market Leadership or National Presence

❏ Rapidly established company's national presence in the _____ [which?] marketplace by _____ [achievements that promoted presence].

❏ Increased sales of products and services to the _____ [which?] market while positioning company as a market leader in _____ [what discipline?].

❏ Spearheaded company's entrance into the _____ [type of] market environment through effective use of _____ [what methods?].

❏ Grew a previously untapped _____ [type of] market in the _____ [what?] area, increasing sales of _____ [what items?] by $_____ annually.

❏ Secured preferred-provider arrangements with _____, _____, and _____ [companies], allowing company to become the recognized leader in the sales of _____ [type of] products.

Product Visibility You Improved

❏ Expanded product visibility by _____% in just _____ [#] months through [market research/marketing campaigns/attending all trade shows and events in the industry/other achievement: _____].

Working with People

❏ Acted as team leader, successfully leading and supporting _____[#] [consultants/manufacturers/distributors/vendors/other: _____].

❏ Worked directly with key _____ [type of] personnel [identifying sales opportunities and new product concepts/participating with research and project specialists on all phases of development/other: _____].

Step 6

❏ Worked as a team with specific goals for each of us, which resulted in increased sales of $_____ within _____ [time period].

❏ Established lines of communication between and networked among _____ [type of] vendor firms from initial prospect contacts through to start of projects.

❏ Worked as a team with _____ [whom?] to increase company's sales from $_____ million to $_____ million by developing and implementing _____ [which?] products designed to _____ [do what?].

Increasing Service Levels

❏ Through regimented disciplines including [frequently reviewing product lines/enhancing computer programs to monitor inventory levels/ consistent client and vendor interface/other: _____], increased _____ [which?] service levels from _____% to _____% efficiency.

Developing New Products/Remerchandising Existing Ones

❏ Successfully [spearheaded the development and implementation of the new/remerchandised the existing] _____ [type of] products through effective use of _____ [what means?].

Decreasing Company Costs

❏ Successfully decreased _____ [which?] costs by [introducing a new _____ (type of) concept/implementing cost-reduction methods/improving employee morale/reducing turnover and training costs/evaluating business bottle-necks and turning them into assets/other method: _____].

❏ Decreased costs by _____% by [anticipating clients' needs and reducing return rates/other achievement: _____].

Developing Sales Staff

❏ Successfully coach, motivate, and mentor a winning sales team and develop loyalty in staff through effective use of _____ [type of] [incentive programs/motivation efforts/other: _____].

Increasing Employee Morale and Minimizing Turnover

❏ Minimized turnover by increasing employee morale and staff loyalty by [using morale-building techniques/creating a positive and proactive atmosphere/developing reachable but challenging goals/treating all employees fairly/offering praise when due/providing equal opportunity for promotion/enforcing company guidelines/other: _____].

Step 6

SERVICE POSITION BULLETS

Review the following fill-in-the-blank Resume ClipBullets™ samples to see whether any of the functions and achievements apply to your work. Fill in the blanks and adjust the wording as appropriate. Incorporate these bullets into your resume where applicable.

The following Resume ClipBullets™ are excerpted from Evelyn Salvador's profession-specific *Resume ClipBullets™ for Business Professions* book (Creative Image Builders), which you can order using the form at the end of this book.

The Type of Services You Manage, Supervise, or Provide

❑ [Manage/Supervise/Conduct] _____ [type of] services, including _____, _____, and _____ [what?], to provide _____ [whom?] with _____ [what services?] and aid in their ability to _____ [do what?].

❑ Provide _____ [type of] services to _____ [whom?] with _____ [what means?] to help them _____ [do what?].

❑ Perform specialized _____ [type of] work in _____ [what area?] focusing on _____ [what?].

❑ Provide [consultation/support/education/instruction/counseling/other: _____] using _____ [type of] techniques to _____ [do what?].

❑ Teach _____ [what?] to _____ [whom?] in a manner that benefits [clients/students/patients/other: _____] through _____ [what means?].

❑ Act as advocate for _____ [whom?], providing _____ [what?] services and assisting them with _____ [what means?] for the purpose of _____ [ways your services help].

What You Develop to Facilitate Services

❑ Develop and implement multifaceted _____ [type of] [services/care/support/guidance/other: _____] to _____ [whom?] in all areas of _____.

❑ Create, implement, and maintain the _____ [program/procedures/other: _____] and its related procedures, which benefit _____ [whom?] by _____ [how?].

❑ Establish _____ [type of] objectives and coordinate _____ [efforts/responsibilities/workflow/other: _____], ensuring _____ [what?].

❑ Create and facilitate _____ [type of] programs, including _____ to _____ [purpose], resulting in _____ [what benefits?].

Step 6

Proven Methods, Techniques, and Strategies You Use

❏ Use _____ [what?] [method/technique/strategy] to _____ [do what?], resulting in _____ [what benefits?].

❏ Utilize various _____ [type of] strategies to assist _____ [whom?] with _____ [what?], which has served to _____ [do what?].

❏ Using _____, _____, and _____ [type of] techniques, enabling _____ [whom?] to _____ [do what?].

❏ Incorporate _____, _____, and _____ [what?] to help _____ [whom?] gain a solid understanding of _____ [what?].

Functions/Projects You Coordinate or Manage

❏ [Coordinate/Manage/Supervise] _____ [type of] functions, including _____, _____, and _____ [what?] for the benefit of _____.

❏ Manage various projects, including _____, which benefits _____ [whom?] in the areas of _____.

❏ Coordinate and schedule _____ [type of] [programs/workshops/seminars/other: _____], including _____, and _____ [topics].

❏ [Oversee/Recommend] the selection, coordination, and organization of _____ [what?], including _____ [what?].

Those with Whom You Work to Benefit Your Clients

❏ As a member of the _____ [what?] team, present assessment results, make recommendations, and develop _____ [type of] plans designed to _____ [do what?].

❏ Work with _____ [whom?] to help clients _____ [do what?], including _____, _____, and _____ [ways your services help].

❏ Meet with all members of the _____ [what?] team to develop _____ [what?] for _____ [purpose].

❏ Liase with _____ [what agencies or professionals] for the purpose of _____ [what?].

❏ Establish and maintain solid relationships with _____ [whom?], which has served to _____ [do what?].

❏ Develop a rapport and network with _____ [type of] professionals for _____ [purpose].

❏ Work with _____ [whom?] to develop, implement, monitor, and modify _____ [type of?] programs for _____ [whom?].

❏ Communicate and collaborate with _____ [whom?] to determine _____ [what?].

Step 6

(continued)

SERVICE POSITION BULLETS (continued)
Who You Help

☐ [Provide/Assist] _____ [whom?] with _____ [what tools?], to help and encourage them to be able to _____ [do what effectively?].

☐ Help _____ [whom?] [develop/identify/improve] _____ [what?] by providing _____ [what?].

☐ Using _____ [what skills or techniques?], help _____ [what group?] effectively utilize their _____ [what?] by _____ [doing what?].

☐ Encourage _____ [what group?] to participate in _____ [type of] activities by _____ [doing what?].

☐ [Counsel/Work with] _____ [whom?] to help them with _____ [what?], which has resulted in their ability to _____ [do what?].

☐ Assist _____ [whom?] with _____ [what?] to help them _____ [achieve what?].

Assessments and Evaluations You Make

☐ Perform accurate _____ [type of] assessments and develop _____ [what?], resulting in _____ [what benefits?].

☐ Assess, evaluate, and determine clients' [needs/requirements/capabilities/other: _____] associated with _____ [what?] and perform _____ [type of] services for _____ [what purpose?].

☐ Prepare findings and make recommendations concerning the appropriate _____ [type of] program for each client based on his or her needs.

☐ Monitor, assess, and record _____ [what?] progress to ensure _____ [what?] and adjust _____ [what?] as needs dictate.

☐ Assess and diagnose _____ [what?] and notify _____ [whom?] of findings and recommendations, following up to ensure _____ [what?].

Planning for Future Needs

☐ Research, analyze, and plan for future _____ [type of] needs by _____ [doing what?].

☐ Analyze _____ [type of] procedures, make recommendations for improvements, and provide _____ [what?] for _____ [whom or what purpose?].

Step 6

step 7

Write Your Cover Letter

- What Makes a Successful Cover Letter?
- Writing Your Cover Letter
- Cover Letter Foundations and Examples

WHAT MAKES A SUCCESSFUL COVER LETTER?

A successful cover letter does a number of things:

✔ Entices the reader to want to read your resume.

✔ Provides a human touch so that the reader can get a feel for the applicant, which cannot be done with a resume alone.

✔ Summarizes your major achievements in brief statements that make an impact, with only bottom-line information to whet the prospective employer's appetite to know more about how you might be able to do the same for them.

✔ Shows you will be an asset to their firm and will be able to improve their bottom line or otherwise help their business grow.

✔ Compels them to call you in for an interview. Well-written cover letters might, in fact, do this before the resume is even read!

WRITING YOUR COVER LETTER

 note If there is a compelling reason why your cover letter should be longer than one page, try not to exceed one-and-a-half pages so that you don't lose your readers!

 note Because all of the cover letter foundations in this chapter are equally effective, you should be fine with whichever one you select based on what you feel is your own best fit.

Your cover letter should be a comfortable one page with approximately four to six paragraphs:

✔ The first few sentences should entice the reader with your general qualifications right up front (a benefit-driven statement will have the most impact) and an indication about what type of position you are applying for and why you would be an asset to the firm.

✔ The middle paragraphs substantiate why you are a qualified applicant for this particular (type of) position and include some heavy-hitter achievements as proof.

✔ The last paragraph states your call to action (what you plan to do next or want the reader to do—for example, you will follow up in a week or wait for them to call you) and thanks the reader for his or her consideration.

This step includes cover letter templates that almost anyone can use as a foundation for their cover letter, no matter what profession they are in. After you have completed your cover letter, it will be customized to you personally. I have used these foundations time and again with excellent results.

 note For complete information on every facet of and the development of each paragraph in your cover letter, refer to *Step-by-Step Cover Letters: Create an Outstanding Cover Letter Using Personal Branding*, the companion book to this one.

However, do not overlook any other major compelling information that you can think of. If you feel you have additional important information to include and there is not a specific section in the template that covers it, work it in. This could include your feelings about your sincere interest in the profession for a particular reason and why you are drawn to the position, a compelling story that prompted you to enter the profession, why you would like to work for that particular firm, how a similar job you had precisely matches what the employer seeks, or the like.

COVER LETTER WORKSHEET

Think about what type of important information a prospective employer might want to know about you. How can you convince them you are the best candidate for the position?

What would you like employers to know about you?

_____

_____

_____

_____

Why would you be an asset to their organization?

_____

_____

_____

_____

In what ways can you help them or their clients?

_____

_____

_____

_____

What is your mission in this field?

_____

_____

_____

_____

Why should recruiters consider you over others who are applying for the same position?

_____

_____

_____

Is there anything else of importance you think an employer might need to know?

_____

_____

_____

_____

Be sure to use this information in your cover letter as appropriate.

COVER LETTER FOUNDATIONS AND EXAMPLES

These cover letter foundations are available in Word format on the CD at the back of this book.

Dear Human Resources Professional (**OR** Executive Committee):

As a successful _____ [type of] professional, I bring to your organization more than _____ [#] years of progressively responsible experience in _____, _____, _____, and _____ for the _____ [type of] industry. My expertise lies in _____ [what areas?] and developing proactive programs designed to drive and sustain revenues. My resume is enclosed for your consideration.

I have a **proven track record** of [increased sales/increased profits/decreased costs/streamlining operations/increased productivity/other: _____]. Notable achievements include _____, _____, and _____ [your most significant accomplishments]. (Please see attached resume for details.)

Complementing my ability to _____ [do what?] and effectively _____ [do what?] are equally strong qualifications in _____, _____, _____, and _____ [other significant targeted areas].

I am able to provide strategic direction for _____ [what?] with appropriate tactical action plans to meet those needs while responding to the constantly changing demands of the _____ [type of] industry. I lead by example and provide strong [decision-making/problem-solving/staff development/other: _____] skills.

I am confident that the experience and drive I can bring to your organization will prove to be an asset. I would appreciate hearing from you regarding any existing or future openings you might have, and would welcome the opportunity to discuss a possible relationship that would prove to be mutually beneficial.

Thank you for your time and consideration.

Sincerely,

Step 7

Figure 7.1: Cover Letter Foundation 1 for an established professional or manager with several years of experience.

Dear Executive Committee:

As a successful manufacturing executive, I bring to your organization 13 years of progressively responsible experience in P&L direction, operations, finance management, marketing, labor relations, project management, and economic and business development for the paper manufacturing industry. My expertise lies in multimillion-dollar cost reductions and developing proactive programs designed to drive and sustain revenues. My resume is enclosed for your consideration.

I have a proven track record of increased sales, increased profits, and decreased costs. Notable achievements include spearheading the acquisition of 11 facilities, increasing gross annual sales from $350 million to more than $1 billion, decreasing purchasing costs by $3.5 million, and increasing profits by $150 million. (Please see attached resume for details.)

Complementing my ability to identify areas of weakness and establish effective and profitable solutions are equally strong qualifications in information technology direction, engineering, quality assurance, statistical process control, contract manufacturing, and employee relations.

I am able to provide strategic direction for driving manufacturing and production initiatives with appropriate tactical action plans to meet those needs while responding to the constantly changing demands of the manufacturing industry. I lead by example, am results-driven, and provide strong decision-making, problem-solving, and project management skills.

I am confident that the experience and drive I can bring to your organization will prove to be an asset. I would appreciate hearing from you regarding any existing or future openings you might have and would welcome the opportunity to discuss a possible relationship that would prove to be mutually beneficial.

Thank you for your time and consideration.

Sincerely,

Figure 7.2: A sample cover letter for a manufacturing executive using Foundation 1.

Step 7

Dear Human Resources Professional:

I believe my broad experience in all phases of _____ [what?] coupled with my [Master's/Bachelor's/Associate's] degree in [_____] would uniquely qualify me for a _____ [title or type of] position in your firm. I am enclosing my resume for your consideration.

During my ___ [#] years of _____ [type of] experience, I have been involved in just about every facet of _____ [primary responsibility]—from _____ and _____ [what functions?] to _____ [what functions?], including _____, _____, and _____ [primary functions]. I have utilized my _____ [type of] skills to successfully _____ [do what?].

_____ [what mission?] is my number-one criteria, and I have done so in various types of settings, including _____, _____, and _____. Working with _____ [whom or what?] has enhanced my personal growth and perspective in many ways. I have developed the ability to _____ [do what?]. (Please see resume for details.)

I find that my _____, _____, and _____ [your primary attributes] is a perfect combination for the _____ [type of] field. These are some of the reasons I feel confident I can apply my skills to work well within your firm.

I would very much like to discuss a _____ [title or type of] position within your company, and would appreciate hearing from you regarding any existing or future openings you might have. Thank you for your time and consideration.

Sincerely,

Figure 7.3: Cover Letter Foundation 2.

Step 7

Dear Human Resources Professional:

I believe my broad experience in all phases of corporate training coupled with my Master's degree in psychology would uniquely qualify me for a Corporate Trainer position in your firm. I am enclosing my resume for your consideration.

During my nine years of corporate training experience, I have been involved in just about every facet of training—from program design and instruction to monitoring and follow-up of its application in the real world. I have utilized my communication, listening, and presentation skills to successfully and effectively train at all employee and management levels.

Ensuring that my training results in the highest retention levels possible is my number-one criteria, and I have done so in various types of settings, including new-hire orientation, departmental retooling, and senior executive retreats. I find that by making the classes enjoyable, adding humor, and relating lessons to real business situations enables me to help trainees put into practice what is learned in class. I always make a point to get to know my trainees so that I can take them from where they are comfortable and bring them forward—whatever the subject matter.

I believe that training cannot stop in the classroom. It is critical that what is taught in class be carried through in business practice; so evaluating and monitoring results, and making modifications as necessary, are essential.

I find that my public speaking, people orientation, and effective team building is a perfect combination for the training field. These are some of the reasons I feel most confident I can apply my skills to work well within your firm.

I would very much like to discuss a corporate training position within your company, and would appreciate hearing from you regarding any existing or future openings you might have. Thank you for your time and consideration.

Sincerely,

Figure 7.4: A sample cover letter for a corporate trainer using Foundation 2.

Dear Human Resources Professional,

I am interested in exploring _____ [type of] opportunities within your firm and have enclosed my resume for your consideration. I believe my _____ and _____ experience coupled with my ability to _____ and _____ [do what?] could assist your firm in meeting its _____ [type of] goals.

My solid experience in _____ and _____ would serve your [firm/clients/patrons/other: _____] well in the areas of _____.

As _____ [title] for _____ [company name] for the past __ [#] years, I have _____ [state your accomplishments]. I [oversee/manage/perform/develop/other: _____] _____ [your primary functions].

Additional areas of expertise include _____ and _____.

I have a proven track record for [decreasing company costs/increasing sales and profits/streamlining operations/increasing productivity/other: _____] for my employers.

I believe my _____ [type of] expertise, _____ [type of] abilities, and _____ [type of] skills are a perfect combination for a _____ [type of] professional. I am confident that the enthusiasm and experience I can bring to your organization will prove to be assets in achieving your firm's goals as they have been for others.

Thank you in advance for your time and consideration. I look forward to hearing from you for a personal interview at your earliest convenience, and would welcome the opportunity to meet with you.

Sincerely,

Step 7

Figure 7.5: Cover Letter Foundation 3.

Dear Human Resources Professional,

I am interested in exploring Graphic Design opportunities within your firm and have enclosed my resume for your consideration. I believe my design and production experience coupled with my ability to manage special projects and create innovative and unique collateral pieces could assist your firm in meeting its graphic design goals. My solid experience in layout and design, four-color processing, prepress and photo retouching would serve your clients well.

As Graphic Designer for the ABC Advertising Agency for the past two years, I have designed and produced brochures, four-color ads, newsletters, and logos, and have overseen all file output and prepress for print production. Additionally, I have assisted in website design and development.

Additional areas of expertise include creating magazine layouts, developing effective advertising campaigns, and creating direct-mail pieces using Mac and various software programs, including Quark XPress, Adobe Photoshop and Illustrator, and Macromedia Dreamweaver.

I have a proven track record for assessing client needs, tackling difficult challenges, meeting tight deadlines, ensuring quality control, and utilizing creative Photoshop filters to design and produce high-end visual communications for my employers.

I believe my graphic design expertise, artistic abilities, and computer skills are a perfect combination for a design professional. I am confident that the enthusiasm and experience I can bring to your organization will prove to be assets in achieving your firm's goals as they have been for others.

Thank you in advance for your time and consideration. I look forward to hearing from you for a personal interview at your earliest convenience, and would welcome the opportunity to meet with you and show you my portfolio.

Sincerely,

Figure 7.6: A sample cover letter for a graphic designer using Foundation 3.

Step 7

Dear Human Resources Professional:

I believe my strong _____ and _____ [type of] experience, coupled with the ability to _____ [do or perform what?], makes me an excellent candidate for a(n) _____ [type of] position within your firm. With broad experience in all phases of _____ [what?], my forte is _____ [forte]. Based on my _____ [type of] success, I am confident I can be of considerable value to your firm. I am enclosing my resume for your review.

Currently as _____ [title] of _____ [company], I have taken the company from $_____ to $_____ in annual sales. Other achievements include _____ [list results of primary achievements].

My solid experience in _____ [what?] would serve your firm well in the areas of _____ [what?]. I have a proven track record for _____ [what achievement?].

Throughout my career, I have consistently demonstrated my ability to _____ [do or perform what?] by _____ [doing what?] to ensure attainment of goals. I have gained a solid reputation for _____ [what?], resulting in _____ [what benefit?] for my employers.

For all these reasons, I feel I would be an asset to your firm. I would welcome the opportunity to discuss my background and accomplishments with you in greater detail and to learn more about your company and its goals. I will contact you next week to answer any questions you may have.

Sincerely,

Figure 7.7: Cover Letter Foundation 4.

Step 7

Dear Human Resources Professional:

I believe my strong design and development experience, coupled with the ability to integrate new software programs and cutting-edge technology with basic engineering and mechanical design principles, makes me an excellent candidate for an Electronic Engineer position within your firm. With broad experience in all phases of running a tight business, my forte is systems integration. Based on my entrepreneurial success, I am confident I can be of considerable value to your firm. I am enclosing my resume for your review.

Currently as president and a founder of XYZ Company in 1999, I have taken the company from startup to $4.5 million in annual sales. Both XYZ Company and I have been the recipient of various awards for being one of the fastest-growing systems integrators in the country.

My solid experience in digital design, embedded systems, microprocessors/microcontrollers, mechanical design, and electronic/mechanical integration would serve your firm well in the areas of costing, new product development, increased productivity, quality control, and increased profits. I have a proven track record for decreasing company costs, streamlining operations, increasing production and manufacturing efficiency, and procuring profitable contracts for my employers.

Throughout my career, I have consistently demonstrated my ability to revitalize the production strength of an organization by identifying problem areas, devising and implementing effective manufacturing controls, and supervising all daily activities to ensure attainment of goals. I have gained a solid reputation for integrity, reliability, and skill in coordinating all internal functions, resulting in strong profits and expanded product lines for my employers.

For all these reasons, I feel I would be an asset to your firm. I would welcome the opportunity to discuss my background and accomplishments with you in greater detail and to learn more about your company and its goals. I will contact you next week to answer any questions you may have.

Sincerely,

Figure 7.8: A sample cover letter for an electronic engineer using Foundation 4.

Step 7

step 8

Create a Personal Brand for Your Job Search

- The Key to Your Success
  - What Is Personal Branding?
  - The Benefits of Identifying Your Personal Brand
  - What Can Personal Branding Do for You?
  - Personal Branding Exercise
  - Ways to Promote Your Personal Brand
- Visual Branding
  - Occupational Icons
  - Graphic Elements
  - Color
  - Font Selection
  - Charts and Graphs
  - Work Samples
- Verbal Branding
  - Personalized Slogans
  - Testimonials
  - Mission Statements
  - Success Stories and Case Studies
- Combining Branding Elements
- Branding Worksheets

This chapter is excerpted from Evelyn Salvador's Personal Branding How To *book on CD (Creative Image Builders, $39.95). It includes numerous personal branding ideas, techniques, tips, and strategies to create your personal brand and "wow" recruiters. You can order the complete book using the form on the last page.*

Personal branding is unquestionably critical in today's world of work. Understand branding and you will be in the top 2 percent of job candidates applying for positions. Ignore it and you will be in the other 98 percent

note If you need more help with personal branding, this book's companion title, *Step-by-Step Cover Letters*, goes into more detail.

of the general public. Most job candidates do not know what personal branding means and, as a result, have not capitalized on their own unique personal brands. Knowing your personal brand, developing it, and using it is a trade secret that will increase your odds of getting hired many-fold. Including your personal brand message in your resume will help you achieve success. Employers will seek *you* out.

Let's start with a definition of personal branding. Then you'll go into a personal branding exercise to develop your own unique brand and learn how to illustrate it within your resume.

THE KEY TO YOUR SUCCESS

Everybody has a personal brand, whether they are aware of it or not. It is who you are, what you are known for, and how you've made a difference. Identifying your personal brand and writing and designing your resume and cover letter around that brand will help put you among the top candidates considered for positions and will also help you increase your salary potential.

Your personal brand consists of the following:

- ✔ Your **assets**
- ✔ Your **benefits**
- ✔ Your **competitive edge**
- ✔ Your **value proposition**
- ✔ Your **return on investment** to prospective employers

All of these elements, compiled together and written in marketing-savvy language, make up your personal brand.

A business brands itself through promotional marketing materials and corporate identity pieces. Likewise, personal branding is the way in which you present and market yourself to develop your niche in your market—the prospective employers in your field—to build name recognition and set you apart from other job seekers. It is how your marketing materials (your resume, cover letter, Web resume or online career portfolio, thank-you letter, letterhead, business cards, and other promotional materials) define your competitive edge in your industry through content and presentation.

This chapter addresses personal branding through content, résumé design, occupational icons, graphic elements, color, charts and graphs, work samples, and other verbal and visual branding.

What Is Personal Branding?

In short, it is the KEY TO YOUR SUCCESS. It is the way in which you market yourself that results in name recognition in your field. It is how your marketing pieces define your competitive edge in your industry through content and presentation. Just like companies have brand recognition and sell their competitive edge, it is important for applicants to brand themselves in their professions.

Let's start by defining Personal Branding. There is no one definition for Personal Branding, so I've included several. My definition is a derivative of many:

> ## Personal Branding
>
> "An essential career and reputation management marketing tool that creates a successful, credible identity so that hiring managers who view your brand know your value proposition and return on investment to them and seek you out."

The Benefits of Identifying Your Personal Brand

Developing a strategy that uniquely positions you differently from your competition helps to establish you as an expert in your own professional niche and thereby increases your notoriety and builds a solid reputation in your field.

To successfully brand yourself, you must first establish and define what your personal brand identity is, determine the benefits of your assets *(features)* that help you solve problems within your field, and then focus that message on what you stand for (your benefits and value proposition). Then you must repetitively get the word out to others. This and the next chapter will show you how.

If you've convinced hiring managers that you are the best at what you do in your particular field and niche, they will seek you out. The benefits and value proposition you bring to the table can help them solve their problems, meet their challenges, increase their bottom line, or otherwise contribute to their firm—in a way no one else can or will do as well as you.

What Can Personal Branding Do for You?

Personal branding can do several things for the job seeker:

- ✔ Your resume will instantly and significantly stand out from the crowd of bland white resumes that all blend together.
- ✔ Employers will immediately recognize what position you are seeking.
- ✔ Your resume will invite your reader in and make him or her want to read it and learn about you because it will be a joy to read.
- ✔ Your resume will help make you known in your industry.
- ✔ It will be difficult to loose your resume in a pile of human resources papers.
- ✔ You will get many more calls for interviews, will take less time to secure a position, and will have a much higher probability of receiving the position you want—with higher salary-negotiation bargaining power!

Clients have told me that their resumes get passed around the human resources office for others to look at, and then they get called for interviews. Recruiters have told them that theirs is the best resume they have ever seen. Others have said that when recruiters have been reviewing hundreds of faxes from people applying for the same position, they stop at theirs and immediately call.

In the rest of this step, you will explore visual layout and design—because your resume presentation is what will first grab attention (or not)—and how you can brand yourself through your resume content.

Personal Branding Exercise

The following exercise will help you develop your personal brand. It covers all of the components of your brand identity. After you have identified each of them, you will write a statement containing all of them. This statement becomes your personal brand message. This statement shows what makes you unique from your competition and sells you to prospective employers ahead of other job candidates.

You will include your brand message as a paragraph in your cover letter and write your resume around this brand, ensuring that you include all of your achievements that relate to your value proposition and return on investment to employers.

YOUR ASSETS/FEATURES

From the "Your Primary Attributes" list you developed in Step 1 (pages 6–7), identify three of the most significant attributes and explain how they help you on the job. Your answers are the benefits of hiring you.

Asset 1: _____

How this asset helps you on the job: _____

_____

_____

_____

Asset 2: _____

How this asset helps you on the job: _____

_____

_____

_____

Asset 3: _____

How this asset helps you on the job: _____

_____

_____

_____

YOUR BENEFITS

In addition to your assets and features, explain any other benefits you may have to offer a prospective employer. They can be in the form of knowledge, qualifications, expertise, certifications, or anything else that helps you do your job well.

Benefits of hiring you: _____

_____

_____

_____

_____

_____

_____

_____

_____

_____

Step 8

YOUR COMPETITIVE EDGE

Compare yourself to coworkers or other candidates in similar positions, and ask yourself:

In what ways do I excel? What do I do that is better, faster, of higher quality, more innovative, or other that the next job candidate might not?

Your competitive edge: _____

_____

_____

_____

_____

_____

_____

YOUR VALUE PROPOSITION

In what way can you add value to an organization? How does what you do well help contribute to your employer's success?

Your value proposition: _____

_____

_____

_____

_____

_____

_____

YOUR RETURN ON INVESTMENT

Based on your qualifications and past achievements, what promise can you make to a prospective employer? Examples include elevating sales, increasing productivity, cutting costs, and so on. Put dollars and percentages to your ROI.

Your return on investment: _____

_____

_____

_____

_____

_____

Step 8

YOUR PERSONAL BRAND MESSAGE

Write a statement that includes all of the above:

1. Assets/Features

2. Benefits

3. Competitive Edge

4. Value Proposition

5. Return on Investment

This becomes your personal brand message. Be sure you include it in your cover letter, and write your resume around that brand, including all applicable achievements.

Here's an example of a personal brand message:

As an innovative, strategic Marketing Specialist with excellent communication and problem-solving skills **(assets/features)**, I develop creative marketing campaigns and promotional materials that meet my employers' target audience's direct needs **(benefits)**, thereby putting them a cut above their competition in the marketplace, increasing their market share, selling more widgets, and developing them into major full-service firms **(value proposition)**. I accomplish this through effective market research and new market identification, knowledgeable e-Marketing, creative multimedia presentations, and strategic public relations initiatives **(competitive edge)**. Achievement examples include expanding audience reach 65%, elevating brand awareness and product visibility 45%, increasing market share 26.5%, and driving annual sales $1.5 million **(return on investment)**.

Here's the foundation you can use to create your own personal brand message:

As a(n) _____, _____ **(your assets/features)** _____ [your job title] with excellent _____ skills and _____ abilities **(additional assets)**, I [develop/perform/direct/other: _____] _____ [what?] that meets my employers' _____ [which?] needs **(your benefits)** thereby _____, _____, and _____ [doing what?] **(your value proposition).** I accomplish this through effective _____ [what?], knowledgeable _____ [what?], creative _____ [what?], and strategic _____ [type of] initiatives **(your competitive edge).** Achievement examples include _____, _____, _____, _____, and _____ **(your return on investment).**

Your personal brand message: _____

_____

_____

_____

_____

_____

_____

Step 8

YOUR RELATED ACHIEVEMENTS

Based on all of the information you compiled, select achievements you have performed that showcase your brand.

Related achievement 1: _____

_____

_____

_____

_____

_____

What actions did you take and what challenges did you overcome?

_____

_____

_____

_____

_____

How did this accomplishment benefit your employer?

_____

_____

_____

_____

_____

Related achievement 2: _____

_____

_____

_____

_____

What actions did you take and what challenges did you overcome?

_____

_____

_____

_____

_____

_____

Step 8

(continued)

YOUR RELATED ACHIEVEMENTS *(continued)*

How did this accomplishment benefit your employer?

_____

_____

_____

_____

_____

Related achievement 3: _____

_____

_____

_____

_____

What actions did you take and what challenges did you overcome?

_____

_____

_____

_____

_____

How did this accomplishment benefit your employer?

_____

_____

_____

_____

_____

Now that you have a good idea of what your unique personal brand is, you can continue by writing, editing, designing, and focusing your resume around that brand. Be sure to include your brand message within your cover letter as its own separate paragraph or within various paragraphs.

Ways to Promote Your Personal Brand

There are many ways to brand yourself. This chapter explores various options from which you may select for your own print and Web resumes. Here are 19 ways to get your resume noticed and read—all of which can help you in the ever-important branding process:

- ✔ **Occupational icons** denoting your profession work like business logos.
- ✔ **Personalized slogans** can sell your greatest benefits to an employer.
- ✔ **Graphic elements** include the use of shapes, designs, shading, and so on.
- ✔ **Using a color on your resume** that is appropriate for your profession helps to further brand you.
- ✔ **Font choice** is important in a resume, and the font you choose should be professional-looking.
- ✔ **Graphics** can illustrate your resume content or define your field.
- ✔ **Photo images** can exemplify your profession at first glance.
- ✔ **Testimonials** about your work performance, experience, or character give credence to your resume and let someone else brag about you.
- ✔ **Mission statements** can show why your field is important to you, what you plan to accomplish, what you do that works, or some other statement that makes an impact about your profession.
- ✔ **Success stories** about clients or others whom you have helped are another excellent way to showcase your abilities.
- ✔ **Case summaries** and scientific studies you have performed are ways of showing an employer that you can do the job well.
- ✔ **Scanned images** of work you have performed or products you have developed or sold into your resume give credence to the saying "a picture is worth a thousand words."
- ✔ **Portrait shots** might help in your profession and resume design. (There are some do's and don'ts, which are explained in *Personal Branding How To.*)
- ✔ **Work-in-action photos** are shots of yourself immersed in your work; they create another visual way of showing an employer you can do the job.
- ✔ **Portfolios** are terrific interview showcases.
- ✔ **Charts and graphs** showing increased sales or performance levels, for example, can highlight your most significant achievements and tell an important story by themselves.
- ✔ **Letterhead design** for your cover letter and interview thank-you letter creates instant name recognition (personal branding) for you.
- ✔ **Matching business card designs** make the perfect interview leave-behind.
- ✔ **Published articles** or books you may have written show your expertise in your field.

This chapter defines some of the options from the preceding list that pertain to your resume presentation and provides samples. At the end of the chapter, you will see how a number of branding elements can come together to promote your own personal brand. Explore the various options and samples to see if they would be appropriate for you. You may even think of some additional ideas you'd like to incorporate.

Complete the Personal Branding Worksheet to start to incorporate your own personal branding elements into your resume.

Step 8

VISUAL BRANDING

This section of the chapter discusses many visual ways in which you can brand your job search documents.

Occupational Icons

A company's icon or logo—even just its shape—can immediately bring to mind the company or organization with which it is associated. For example, when you see the familiar yellow shell, you think of Shell Oil. When you see the "golden arches," you think of McDonalds. Personal branding through the use of occupational icons—illustrations related to your profession—can help do the same for you and is one of the many ways you can start to create your own personal brand. Companies that brand themselves well are remembered. The same holds true for your resume presentation.

Give this some thought: If you were going to put an icon next to your name, what might that be? Can't think of one offhand? How about another type of image…a color or texture, perhaps? Maybe a photo of a product or service? A chart, graph, or illustration of some sort? Work samples? There are many ways to develop your personal brand.

Here are some personal branding examples through the use of "occupational icons." You can use clip art related to your associated field (see figure 8.1 for examples), or if you are creative, you can design your own.

- ✔ An airplane for a pilot or flight attendant
- ✔ A hardhat for a construction worker
- ✔ Tax forms for an accountant
- ✔ A scale for an attorney or paralegal
- ✔ A prepared meal for a chef
- ✔ A satellite for a telecommunications professional
- ✔ A computer, chip, disk, or motherboard for an IT specialist
- ✔ A camera for a photographer
- ✔ Keys for a locksmith
- ✔ A color palette or an easel for an artist
- ✔ An easel for a training or marketing specialist
- ✔ A stethoscope for a doctor or a nurse
- ✔ Pill bottles for a pharmaceutical consultant
- ✔ _____
- ✔ _____
- ✔ _____
- ✔ _____
- ✔ _____
- ✔ _____

Once you've selected an icon that works for you, stick with it, or your personal brand-building will be compromised (because the "image recall" will be lost).

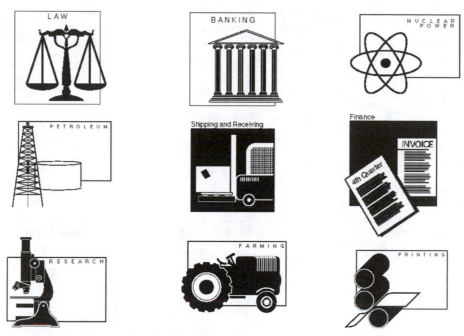

Figure 8.1: Sample occupational icons.

Graphic Elements

Designing promotional pieces using graphic elements is another way to set your resume apart from others. Using these elements in resume design requires more subtle use than perhaps other promotional pieces to keep it professional. All the sample resume designs in this book and on the CD use graphic design in some form or another, so you will find plenty of samples.

Here are some examples of graphic elements you can use to make your resume distinct. Be sure to keep them simple.

✔ Rules	✔ Rectangles
✔ Boxes	✔ Shades of gray
✔ Repeated shapes	✔ Triangles
✔ Patterns	✔ Gradation
✔ Bars	✔ _____
✔ Stripes	✔ _____
✔ Margin graphics	✔ _____
✔ Headers	✔ _____

The resume designs in figure 8.2 utilize various graphic elements. Each of these sample designs is included on the CD at the back of this book.

Experience has shown that clients get rave reviews on their resumes through the use of graphic design alone. Their resumes were pulled from hundreds, even thousands; applicants were remembered and called for interviews before their peers; and they received extremely high success rates on their resumes.

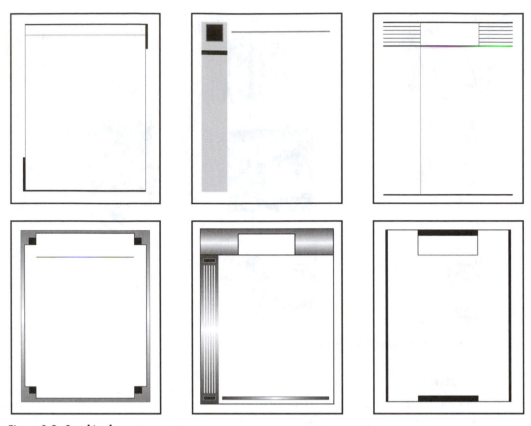

Figure 8.2: Graphic elements.

Color

Color attracts interest. It is physical and emotional, and it evokes feelings. When kept professional and suitable for your field, color can enhance your resume's readability. In the advertising world it has been proven that color increases readability seven-fold. I advise you to use color sparingly—such as in headings.

Font Selection

The fonts you select for your resume must be professional. I have two thoughts here for you to consider:

1. Keeping in mind that you want your resume to stand out in a professional way, if you are using a resume with a lot of design elements (such as the ones on the accompanying CD), you can use a standard typestyle such as Arial or Times New Roman. Because the design has already captured interest, you will not need to use a fancy font to do so. Also, a standard font style will not compete with the design.

2. If you are using a nice, professional format but not a designed resume, you can be a little more elaborate with your font choice, but stay professional. Instead of Times or Times New Roman, you can go with Garamond, Palatino, Book Antiqua, Bookman, or Korinna, for example. These are considered *serif fonts* because the tops and bottoms of the letters are capped with small horizontal lines (called serifs). Or you can use a sans serif font. Instead of the basic Arial or Helvetica font, you can go with Eras, Optima, Verdana, or Century Gothic, for example. Both serif and sans serif fonts work well.

Step 8

SERIF OR SANS SERIF FONT?

Different people have different opinions on which type of font is more easily read—serif or sans serif. This contradiction is due to the fact that serif fonts are what early typesetters used and people became accustomed to reading them. Some say sans serif fonts are easier to read because they are plainer and more like the text people learn in elementary school. So using either is a safe bet, and I wouldn't be concerned with which type you select, as long as the font you select is professional and readable.

 note Font names vary somewhat from the PC to Macintosh and from brand names to re-created fonts, so your font name may be titled a little differently. (For example the same font may be called Optima, Optimum, or Optane depending on what type of computer you have.)

HEADINGS AND BODY COPY FONTS

To organize your information and add interest to your resume presentation, you can use the same font for your text and headings, but make it larger and bold in the headings. Or you can use a bold sans serif font for headings and a plain serif font for body copy, or vice versa. Generally, the headings should be at least one or two font sizes larger than your body copy.

FONTS FOR ELECTRONIC RESUMES

More important than anything, however, is how you will be using your resume. If you plan to only print your resumes from your own computer and mail or hand them out, you can skip this part. But chances are you will want to e-mail your resume to prospective employers as well.

If you e-mail your resume as an attachment (Microsoft Word is the program of choice for recruiters), font choice is limited. If you select a font other than Arial or Times New Roman, you are taking a chance that the person at the receiving end might not have the same fonts on their system. If they do not, your resume will become unformatted and appear incorrectly at the recruiter's end. I recommend playing it safe and using Arial or Times New Roman. Another option is to convert your resume to a PDF (Portable Document Format) using Adobe Acrobat and attaching that version to the e-mail as well.

POINT SIZE

I suggest setting your cover letter in 11-point type and your resume in 10- or 11-point type, depending on how well the copy fits on the page. If you are using Times or Times New Roman, you can go up one-half to a full point size because the letters in these fonts print smaller. You can make your section headings one or two full point sizes larger than the body copy.

Figures 8.3 and 8.4 show examples of some of the most popular fonts for resumes.

Step 8

This is Arial bold in 12-point type—for headings

This is Arial Black in 10-point type—for headings

This is plain Arial in 10-point type—for body copy

This is Arial italic in 8-point type—for company information following employer and job title

This is Tahoma bold in 12-point type—for headings

This is plain Tahoma in 10-point type—for body copy

This is Tahoma italic in 8-point type—for company information following employer and job title

This is Eras Bold ITC in 12-point type—for headings

This is Eras Medium ITC in 10-point type—for body copy

This is Eras Medium ITC italic in 8-point type–for company information following employer and job title

This is Verdana bold in 10-point type—for headings

This is plain Verdana in 9-point type—for body copy

This is Verdana italic in 7-point type—for company information following employer and job title

---

Figure 8.3: Sans-serif fonts.

This is Times New Roman bold in 12-point type—for headings

This is plain Times New Roman in 11-point type—for body copy

This is Times New Roman italic in 8-point type—for company information following employer and job title

This is Garamond bold in 12-point type—for headings

This is plain Garamond in 10-point type—for body copy

This is Garamond italic in 8-point type—for company information following employer and job title

This is Palatino Linotype bold in 12-point type—for headings

This is Palatino Linotype in 10-point type—for body copy

This is Palatino Linotype italic in 8-point type – for company information following employer and job title

This is Book Antiqua bold in 12-point type – for headings

This is plain Book Antiqua in 10-point type – for body copy

This is Book Antiqua italic in 8-point type – for company information following employer and job title

---

Figure 8.4: Serif fonts.

Charts and Graphs

Another way to add visual interest to your resume presentation and exemplify your achievements is through the use of charts or graphs. If you keep in mind that the most important part of your resume is your achievements, think how much impact it would have if your achievements spoke for themselves. Instead of the prospective employer having to wait until reading that portion of your resume, one of the very first things they could see, for example, is how much you increased sales from year to year (see the sample for a sales vice president on the next page), or how you took on larger and larger projects over the years (see construction project manager sample).

You can use bar graphs, pie charts, graphs, or any type of visual that shows your achievements in numbers. Your chart or graph could show profits, sales increases, project timelines, client number increases, number of products sold, livestock farmed, and so on. Think of your greatest achievements, and think of various ways you can exemplify them by a chart or graph.

tip

Keep in mind that one of the first things a reader sees is the caption under an illustration of any kind. Be sure not to waste that opportunity. Indicate what you are showcasing through a caption or short story about your achievement. If you use a short story, be sure to include your challenge, action, and result (employer benefit).

Step 8

Following are some profession samples using graphs.

Sample for a Sales VP

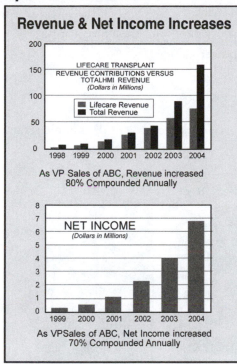

Sample for a Construction Project Manager

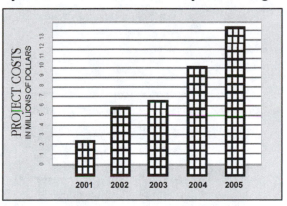

Figure 8.5: Profession samples using graphs.

Work Samples

You've heard it said that "a picture is worth a thousand words." Showcasing your accomplishments by exhibiting work samples is another excellent and very personalized way of branding yourself. It's one thing to *say* you are a great photographer (or designer, or architect, and so on), and yet another to *show* that you are!

Most professionals have some sort of work they can exhibit in their resume as an addendum (the second or third page of their resume), in a portfolio, or included within the layout of the resume. You can scan and incorporate into your resume presentation work sample images or photos of you actually performing the work, for example.

The Minnesota Department of Economic Security, for one, suggests being proactive with your work samples. They state within their "Creative Job Search Materials" that incorporating work samples "builds self-confidence: the tangible evidence of what you have accomplished; diffuses potential discrimination; shows you have the experience and can accomplish the tasks; and proves you can do the job [which helps] overcome [any] perception that you [might] lack experience or are underqualified [for the position you seek]."

Here are some examples of work samples that people in various professions might include:

- ✔ Actual photos taken by a commercial photographer (could be product shoots, architectural photography, wedding portraits, panoramas, and so on)
- ✔ Before-and-after photos of room designs created by an interior decorator
- ✔ Photos of the restaurants a restaurant manager has managed
- ✔ Apparel designs created by a fashion designer
- ✔ Blueprints designed by an architect
- ✔ Scanned paintings or illustrations by a fine artist

✔ Before-and-after auto restoration photos from an auto body painter or mechanic

✔ Brochure layouts or logo designs created by a graphic designer

✔ Finished architecture managed by a construction project manager

✔ Newsletters, reports, or presentations prepared by a secretary or administrative assistant

✔ Photos of culinary creations by an executive chef or sous chef

✔ Scanned photos of a music teacher conducting a band

✔ Before-and-after landscape designs created by a landscape architect

Get the idea? To see how you can integrate work samples into your resume, look at the sample resumes on the following page.

Scenic photos taken by a Photographer for a Travel Agency:

Photo Composite & Photos By Evelyn Salvador

Challenge: *Client wanted to attract a new niche market of local clients by using unique photos of local scenery, something they couldn't obtain from the standard produced brochures they had for the greater metropolitan area.*

Photography Solution: *Shooting unique scenes from beautiful, less known local areas hit the mark.*

Result: *Travel agency sent out revised brochures and obtained additional clientele in their specific niche.*

Project sites built by a Construction Manager:

Licensed Stock Photography (Photo Disc "World Commerce & Travel" CD)

Project Costs: $10.5 million $22 million $6 million

Illustrations or paintings by a Fine Artist:

Digital Paintings by Evelyn Salvador

Exhibited in: *ABC Exhibit*   *XYZ Gallery*

Step 8

Teacher and student photos for a Teacher:

Although Timmy always tried hard, his fine motor skills posed a problem for him. Once we discovered painting was a way for him to enjoy working on these skills, he became more confident in other areas as well.

Cooperative learning has proven a fun way to bring creative energy, enthusiasm, participation, and enhanced learning retention into the classroom.

Although the morning rush may seem the least impor- tant part of the day, ensuring the safety and positive energy of students is of utmost importance.

My Second Grade
Special Ed Inclusion Class

Licensed Stock Photography (Photo Disc "Business Occupations" CD)

Logos created by a Graphic Designer or Art Director:

Designs By Creative Image Builders, Inc.

Types of natural habitats an environmental conservationist is accustomed to working in:

Licensed Stock Photography

Types of work performed by a carpenter:

Licensed Stock Photography
(Photo Disc "Retail Shopping" CD)

Step 8

VERBAL BRANDING

There are many ways to use words to help establish your brand. This section discusses the various ways in which you can do this.

Personalized Slogans

Just about any business you can name has a slogan that they use to represent their business and try to capture their target market. The concept in developing a slogan for your resume is the same.

When pondering a slogan for yourself, think in terms of what your greatest benefit would be to sell to a prospective employer. What would get them excited? What benefits of your product—you—would you like them to know about? When it feels right, use it. Job search is all about persuasive selling, and your slogan is no exception.

You can put your slogan in quotation marks and set it off from the rest of your resume by using a different font or putting it in its own section. You can also use it as a header or caption in your resume and other personal marketing pieces.

To get your creative juices flowing, here are some sample slogan possibilities for various professions:

- ✔ Construction superintendent: "Bringing Projects in On Time and Within Budget…Every Time!"
- ✔ Sous chef: "Serving Dining Patrons Since 1990" or "From Gourmet Appetizers…To Fine Desserts"
- ✔ Creative director: "Helping You Brand Your Clients Ahead of Their Competition"
- ✔ Charter pilot: "Flying from the Caribbean to Mexico (and Everywhere in Between)"
- ✔ Aviation mechanic: "There Isn't a Plane I Can't Repair!"
- ✔ Elementary teacher: "Creating a Trusting and Nurturing Learning Environment for All Students" or "Helping Students Take Positive Steps Toward Their Future" or "Gaining Enthusiasm, Participation, and Lesson Retention" or "Teaching Academics in a Classroom Conducive to Learning"
- ✔ Registered nurse: "Providing Caring, Professional Medical Care…From Infants to Geriatrics"
- ✔ Sales manager: "Successfully Uncovering and Fulfilling Customer Needs" or "Meeting Challenges, Overcoming Obstacles, and Closing Sales"

Get the idea? Now you try it. Brainstorm some important keywords in your profession and try joining them in an interesting context that summarizes who you are and what you can do.

Testimonials

Besides compelling resume writing and an attractive, professional resume presentation, there are a number of additional ways to grab and hold the attention of your prospective employer and add interest to your resume presentation. One such way is to include testimonials others have written about you or your work. Testimonials lend credence to your resume information; and they will pique the interest of employers to see what others have said about you.

Testimonials can include excerpts from letters of recommendation, reference letters, customer thank-you letters, vendor satisfaction letters, performance evaluation comments, internship summaries, staff memos, customer surveys, and other commendations.

Depending on how much good and varied information you have about your performance and how long your resume is, you can put your testimonials on a separate testimonials page,

 note In my private practice, I inform my clients that it is not necessary to include "References available upon request" on your resume; when an employer wants your references, they will ask for them. Some say including that statement signifies the end of your resume; personally I believe there is better use for that wasted line on your resume even if it is just white space.

 Step 8

in a Testimonials section at the end of your resume, or in callouts in the margin of your resume. Three testimonials is a good number.

Try to select comments from a variety of sources in your field, such as superiors, professors, customers or clients, vendors, even peers and subordinates, and others that speak to your various abilities.

Select some job-specific information that shows how well you performed your functions. If you don't have any letters of reference or recommendation, now may be a good time to obtain them. You will find that people are usually more than happy to write one for you.

Begin and end each set of comments with quotation marks. It is not necessary to include the full text. Review what you have and select the statements with the most impact (preferably those that speak to your targeted abilities or personal attributes).

When you leave out words or sentences, use ellipses (…) to connect thoughts and show that something was omitted. When you are paraphrasing (condensing thoughts) or changing words to better join sentences (without changing the meaning), use brackets around the rephrased words.

Following are some sample testimonials.

RESTAURANT MANAGER: (EXCERPTS FROM PERFORMANCE EVALUATIONS)

"Sandy is a strong leader. She bases decisions on what is best for the guests and creates a positive environment for employees."
James Turner, Regional Director, Stamford Brew House

"Sandy has an incredible awareness of all money spent and her budgetary constraints."
Alex Cook, Regional Director, Lakeville Cafe

"Sandy is an excellent trainer and team worker. She shows dedication and commitment in all she does."
John Jones, Area Director, Pasta Grill Restaurant

COLLECTIONS SUPERVISOR (FROM CUSTOMER LETTERS AND A CUSTOMER SERVICE SURVEY)

(In a letter to superior) "My husband and I were very impressed and pleased with one of your employees…. Mary Smith helped us get back into a payment schedule. She is a very understanding person who does her job for the company but also takes the time to help and show concern for the customer."

(Response to a customer survey) "Mary Smith and her staff showed they truly cared about my needs and let me know they were there to help. I would recommend ABC Financial to anyone in need of financial assistance."

(In a loan-payoff letter) "Thank you very much for always being so helpful when we needed you most…. Enclosed is a check in the amount of $2,573 to pay off our account. It was always a pleasure dealing with you."

Step 8

CONSTRUCTION MANAGER

JAMES BAKER, Director of Engineering, NATIONAL HOME FOODS (Client Letter)
"I became acquainted with John when he was Construction Manager on a design-and-build project for a multimillion-dollar research laboratory and MIS facility. As the owner's rep, I worked closely with John throughout the project. I found him to be a most motivated individual, possessing good judgment and skills, whose main goal was to complete a successful project on time and within approved funding. John and I spent many on and off hours reviewing and developing plans to move the project forward. I personally attest to his commitment to get the job done and not compromise the contractual agreement. John relentlessly challenged and made contractors perform quality work on schedule…. John led this project to a very successful conclusion."

JOHN SHAKER, President, XYZ CONSTRUCTION MANAGEMENT, INC. (Staff Memo)
"Our congratulations go to John Baker and our construction group for their dedication in assisting our client… ABC Electric. As we progress through the construction phase, ABC management wrote to us: 'Your guidance and expertise in erecting this facility has been handled most professionally, and for that I salute you and your organization. It is refreshing to deal with a consultant that knows what they are doing.' We received this compliment because our clients noticed we care…. John represented us well."

Original letters available upon request.

Mission Statements

Including a mission statement in your resume presentation is another way to brand yourself. Writing and infusing mission statements into your resume presentation is a way to show that you are serious about your profession and career.

Generally, a mission statement used in a resume is a promise or a belief. Mission statements should be short and to the point and can be written for any position. A mission statement basically says what your mission is, specific to your targeted career goal—what you plan to do or have done, what you believe in (be sure it's something the prospective employer believes in, too!), why your profession is important to you, or another promise or belief of some sort that will pique the recruiter's attention and show your enthusiasm, contribution, and vested interest in your career.

Here are some ways to incorporate your mission statement into your resume:

✔ In the margin of your cover letter.

✔ At the end of your resume.

✔ On an attached addendum page, along with other supporting materials, such as work samples or testimonials.

✔ As a separate callout in quotation marks or alongside a career-specific illustration.

Here are some examples my clients have used in their resumes. Generally, instead of writing mission statements for my clients, I ask the clients to write them themselves because it must come from within.

Step 8

An effective Registered Nurse accurately assesses patients, provides care in a direct and management mode, and keeps a positive attitude at all times.

I believe the true quality of an excellent sales person is the ability to uncover a customer's needs and help him/her fulfill them.

"Each step a child takes in his life has an effect on his future. I would like to help students take positive steps by creating an educational experience conducive to learning."

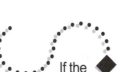

If the ◆ customer is happy and you are making a sale, it's a "win/win."

An *Executive Chef's talent lies in his ability to create innovative cuisine, instruct it masterfully, and wow his patrons.*

*"A successful **Travel Marketing Manager** is able to listen to and act on behalf of the client to offer the high-end customer service expected from an airline."*

An effective Case Manager takes time to listen, treats others the way she wants to be treated, inspires positive change in people's lives, and is accountable for her actions and reactions.

"I believe Housekeeping is a profession whereby quality, speed and care are its most important components— always bearing in mind the ultimate client your employer serves."

Mission Statement:
To provide complete IT solutions with dedication to service.

I believe the true quality of a good Service Manager is the ability to run an operation with an eye towards profitability while servicing the customer in a fair and honest way.

Figure 8.6: Sample mission statements.

Success Stories and Case Studies

What better way to show you can do the job than to actually prove it? Providing success stories and case studies is a way to add interest to your resume presentation and showcase your skills and abilities by providing challenges you were faced with, how you tackled them, and the end results—with real people, facts, studies, or other stories. (For confidentiality, the names you use can be changed.)

You can create a separate Case Studies or Success Stories page where the prospective employer can see first-hand how you have successfully employed your skills, abilities, and other achievements. Here you can incorporate how you have used your professional knowledge by providing summaries of some carefully selected success stories.

Select a few situations you feel especially proud of. Try to select different types of cases or stories in different settings, if possible, to show a variety of different skills. State the challenge with which you had to work and explain the actions you took to tackle the challenge and overcome any obstacles. Always provide an end result to show the benefit of your work and how you were successful.

You can design your page with graphics or clipart as shown on the following page; or you can list your cases on a separate page of your resume with captions and plenty of space between each case. Put your Case Studies page at the end of your resume. Chances are, your readers will flip through what you have sent and read this first!

Here are some examples of success stories that people in different professions might use:

✔ Case studies of client situations effectively handled by a social worker

✔ Success stories about terminally ill patients who required diverse care provided by a registered nurse

✔ Case studies about DNA, cloning, or environmental research, for example, performed by a scientist or research associate

✔ Success stories about an account executive winning over Fortune 500 clients

✔ Student stories of a special education teacher, indicating how he successfully taught students with learning disabilities

✔ Success stories of a sales manager showing how she turned around a flailing company and made it profitable

✔ Client stories of an art director illustrating how she tackled difficult advertising challenges and increased income for both her client and her employer

Following are some sample success stories.

Case Stories OF A SOCIAL WORKER

An adoptive adolescent with a tough exterior and intimidating mannerisms was in the Mercy Residential Treatment Center because of her negative behaviors. Though Jane was intelligent, she was told she had to attend until her behaviors improved. She wanted to leave at the end of the year to be mainstreamed into her district public school; however, during the year her behavior fluctuated. Although several counselors had chosen not to work with her, I found that by working on her conflicts and offering my client a working relationship built on trust, I helped empower her to focus on her behavioral and academic goals. At the end of the school year, Jane was mainstreamed back into her district high school.

1

A bipolar patient felt very upset when her mom yelled at or hit her. After inviting Mary's mom in for a meeting, I learned this means of discipline was part of their foreign culture.

After discussing with the mom the impact it had on her daughter and teaching Mary to communicate with her mom, Mary learned to express her feelings when she was upset, and her mom became more understanding of the impact she had on her daughter.

The relationship became more of a working one, and Mary responded better to treatment because she and her mom were talking things out.

2

3

Derk, a 15-year-old client with impaired intelligence, was to receive a prison sentence of 15 years to life for sexual offenses, which were learned from experiences he, himself, suffered as a child.

First I built up a relationship with his mother, who found it very difficult to deal with the situation, was preoccupied with her own life, and resisted putting in time. Together we worked on getting her son treatment instead of going to jail; and I found a parent support group for her to attend. I followed through with appropriate agencies so he could receive further psychiatric treatment while serving his time.

After receiving approval to move forward, I got a detailed report to the attorney to present to the judge before trial. Now, Derk is undergoing psychiatric care at the Children's Services Treatment Center with intense supervision for sexual abuse.

4 Jane, an alcoholic 17-year-old client who lived in a group home, had experienced difficulty living at home. Jane's mother saw her as shy and withdrawn and was afraid to have her home because she engaged herself in self-hazardous situations. My client didn't believe her mother listened to her side.

By creating a neutral environment during sessions and building trust by following up on issues, my client eventually disclosed her distrust for authoritative figures due to past experiences where she had been misled.

The counseling helped Jane come to terms with her alcoholism, which originated from her father and grandfather before her, and helped build a communicative relationship between mother and daughter.

Step 8

Figure 8.7: Sample success stories.

COMBINING BRANDING ELEMENTS

Collectively and without overdoing the end result, the use of various elements can become your personal brand. Combining several profession-specific elements in a subtle and professional way can really enhance your resume presentation. Always bear in mind that the final look must be of utmost professionalism.

The following examples demonstrate ways to combine various branding elements:

- ✔ For an architect, you could use a blueprint tint as a background, scanned images of completed or in-process structures you have designed, and an icon of an architectural element.

- ✔ For a fine artist, you could use a color-wash background, an occupational icon of a color palette, and scanned images of your work.

- ✔ For a pilot or a flight attendant, you can use photos of an island, the ocean, or the sky for the background, a plane illustration, and perhaps the "wings" icon.

- ✔ For a graphic designer, you could select or design your own graphic layout, include scanned samples of your work (such as brochures, logos, corporate identity, and direct-mail pieces), and design your own occupational icon.

- ✔ A photographer could select one of his or her photos, create it as a tint in Photoshop, and use it as a background image; add two or three photos within the layout of the resume; or include a half dozen on a separate page. You could even take a photo of your camera to use as your own unique icon (or scan in the one from your operating manual).

- ✔ For a Web site designer, you could select or design your own graphic layout, include captured Web site images and links from the Web sites you have designed, and select an appropriate occupational icon.

- ✔ For a fashion/apparel designer, you can use patterns as a tinted backdrop or in a border, along with scanned images of your unique designs. Take a design you are most proud of and convert it into a simplified black-and-white version; use this as your own unique occupational icon.

The following pages are sample resumes that show many of the branding elements described in this step.

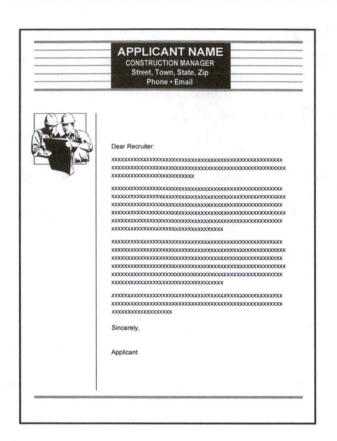

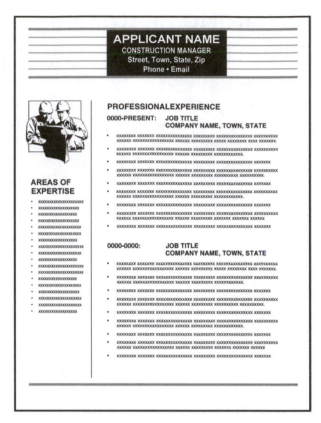

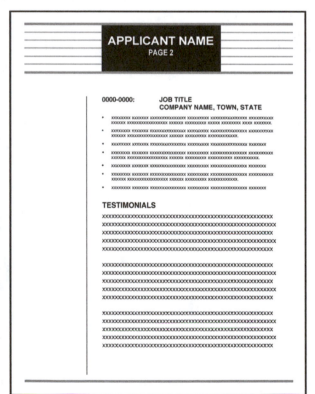

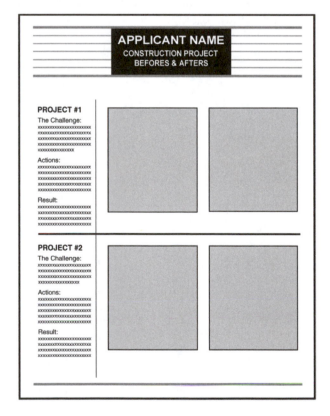

Figure 8.8: Sample branded resume for a construction manager.

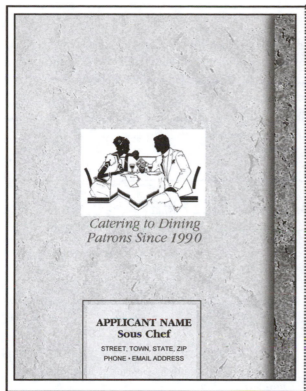

Catering to Dining
Patrons Since 1990

APPLICANT NAME
Sous Chef

STREET, TOWN, STATE, ZIP
PHONE • EMAIL ADDRESS

Résumé

APPLICANT NAME
Sous Chef

STREETADDRESS
TOWN, STATE, ZIP
PHONE • CELLULAR
EMAILADDRESS

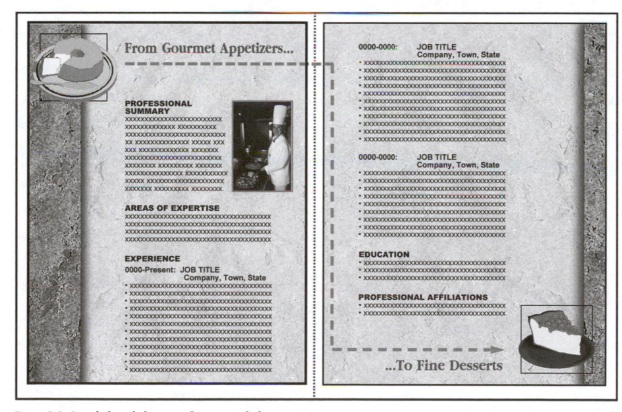

From Gourmet Appetizers...

PROFESSIONAL SUMMARY

AREAS OF EXPERTISE

EXPERIENCE

0000-Present: JOB TITLE
Company, Town, State

0000-0000: JOB TITLE
Company, Town, State

0000-0000: JOB TITLE
Company, Town, State

EDUCATION

PROFESSIONAL AFFILIATIONS

...To Fine Desserts

Figure 8.9: Sample branded resume for a sous chef.

BRANDING WORKSHEETS

The first worksheet in this section addresses the various personal branding elements discussed in this step. When completing this worksheet, it is best to brainstorm various ideas and jot down the first things that come to mind concerning your profession and position. After completing the worksheet, review your thoughts and ideas and select the ones that work best for your own unique resume.

If you have decided to use testimonials, or success stories or case studies, complete the Testimonials Worksheet and the Your Success Stories or Case Studies worksheet, which follow the Personal Branding Worksheet.

PERSONAL BRANDING WORKSHEET
Visual Branding

1. **Occupational icons:** Jot down a few types of occupational icons that might instantly bring to mind your profession.

_____

_____

_____

_____

2. **Graphic design:** Is your profession conservative, creative, or somewhere in between? Review the resume designs in Step 10 or on your CD and identify a few that you might be interested in using.

_____

_____

_____

_____

3. **Color:** What colors come to mind that could be associated with your profession?

_____

_____

_____

_____

4. **Fonts:** Will you be using a plain sans-serif font or a serif font, or both? Are there any fonts in particular that you prefer to use for your headings or body copy?

_____

_____

_____

_____

Step 8

5. **Charts or graphs:** Is there a chart or graph you could include that would exemplify your achievements, such as increased sales, project timelines, client number increases, or number of products sold? What would the chart or graph show? What achievement numbers could you illustrate?

_____

_____

_____

_____

_____

6. **Work samples:** What type of work samples do you have that might portray your abilities? Do you have or can you take photos of these items? Are they images you can retrieve from your computer or scan in? Or do you have clip art or stock photography that you can use to showcase them?

_____

_____

_____

_____

Verbal Branding

7. **Slogans:** What are some of the greatest benefits you could sell to an employer that highlight your competitive edge?

_____

_____

_____

Are there any keywords or profession-specific lingo that might be important to include in a slogan? List them here.

_____

_____

_____

Brainstorm a number of possible slogans you might want to use. Try to keep the thoughts within 10 words or less. Work on your slogan until you find something catchy that would intrigue a prospective employer.

_____

_____

_____

Step 8

(continued)

PERSONAL BRANDING WORKSHEET *(continued)*

8. **Testimonials:** Do you have testimonials from others about your performance? For now, list those who come to mind from which you have received compliments and others from whom you believe you can obtain a testimonial from. (A Testimonials Worksheet follows this one.)

_____

_____

_____

_____

9. **Mission statements:** If you were to write a mission statement of a belief or a promise specific to your career, what might that be? Jot some thoughts that initially come to mind. You can fine-tune it later. Here are some ideas:

- I believe the true quality of an excellent _____ [title] is the ability to _____ [do what?].
- To provide _____ [what?] to _____ [whom?] for _____ [what?].
- A(n) _____'s [targeted position title] talent lies in his/her ability to _____ [do what?].
- An effective _____ [your position title] _____, _____, and _____ [does what?].
- I believe _____ [profession] is a profession in which _____, _____, and _____ [what?] are its most important components.

Now write yours:

_____

_____

_____

_____

10. **Success stories or case studies:** Think about your greatest achievements. What type of challenges were you faced with? How did you tackle them (what actions did you take)? What was the end result of your efforts and the benefits to your employer? List several types of achievements you might want to develop a success story about. You'll develop this further at the end of this step.

_____

_____

_____

_____

11. **Other:** Is there anything else you can think of that can help brand you in your field and create "image recall" when a prospective employer sees your resume? What method might you use to portray this in your resume?

_____

_____

_____

_____

Step 8

12. **Bringing it all together:** Now that you have read many of the possible ways you can brand yourself and have completed the worksheet with a number of ideas you might want to use, reconsider all of them, and list the ones you want to include in your resume presentation.

_____

_____

_____

_____

13. **Resume design layout:** Now go back and review each of the resume layouts in Step 10 or on the accompanying CD and determine which ones would work best in your profession, for your target audience, and for you personally. Which is your final selection?

_____

_____

_____

Step 8

TESTIMONIALS WORKSHEET

Name _____ Title _____

Company _____ , Town _____ , State _____

_____

_____

_____

_____

_____

_____

Name _____ Title _____

Company _____ , Town _____ , State _____

_____

_____

_____

_____

_____

_____

Name _____ Title _____

Company _____ , Town _____ , State _____

_____

_____

_____

_____

_____

_____

Name _____ Title _____

Company _____ , Town _____ , State _____

_____

_____

_____

_____

_____

Step 8

YOUR SUCCESS STORIES OR CASE STUDIES

Success Story 1

Your challenge: _____

_____

_____

_____

_____

_____

Your actions: _____

_____

_____

_____

_____

_____

_____

The end results: _____

_____

_____

_____

_____

_____

_____

Success Story 2

Your challenge: _____

_____

_____

_____

_____

_____

Your actions: _____

_____

_____

_____

_____

_____

(continued)

Step 8

YOUR SUCCESS STORIES OR CASE STUDIES *(continued)*

The end results: _____

_____

_____

_____

_____

_____

Success Story 3

Your challenge: _____

_____

_____

_____

_____

Your actions: _____

_____

_____

_____

_____

_____

The end results: _____

_____

_____

_____

_____

Step 8

step 9

Pull Together, Edit, and Design Your Resume

- Pull It All Together
- Edit Your Final Resume
- Add Descriptive Adjectives and Adverbs
- Designer Resumes: The Secret to Getting Noticed
- Format and Design Guidelines
- Select Your Resume Design
  - The Resume Designs on the CD
  - Select a Template Design
- Designer Resume Gallery Templates

In this final resume writing step, you will add your Resume ClipBullets™ responsibilities and achievements from Step 6 and any additional resume-branding options you selected from Step 8 and then edit and design what you have to prepare your final resume.

PULL IT ALL TOGETHER

To pull together all of the elements for your resume, follow these steps:

1. Add the Resume ClipBullets™ you checked off and worked up from Step 6 under their appropriate job titles, listing the most important functions first.

2. Compare the information from your Resume ClipBullets™ to what you completed in your first resume draft in Step 5. Check for duplication of information or similar functions that you already addressed in the first draft. Select the bullets that best describe what you performed or achieved, or combine and edit them into one bullet.

3. Add any additional options you selected from Step 8 (such as testimonials, case studies, mission statements, product samples, charts or graphs, and so on). These can go on a separate page, or they can be part of the resume. Here are some guidelines for determining where each additional element should go:

   • **Testimonials:** If the testimonials you have are a few lines each, you can incorporate them into the margin of your cover letter or resume. If they are several lines each, you can make Testimonials a separate heading at the end of your resume. If you have some great referrals and want to use them in their entirety, you can put them on a separate page.

   • **Case studies:** I suggest putting these "interest stories" on a separate (last) page of your resume.

   • **Mission statement:** Use this as a callout in the margin of your cover letter or at the bottom of your resume.

   • **Product Samples, Charts, and Graphs:** The most appealing way to add these is to include them within your resume presentation, generally at the end of the resume. If your resume is already a full two pages, put them on a separate page.

EDIT YOUR FINAL RESUME

Now that all of your resume text is in place, it's time to edit it down to the most essential elements. Here are some tips for doing so:

1. **Remove personal pronouns.** The subject (I, me, or my) is understood in your resume and you should leave it out of each sentence. If your resume contains any of these words, delete them and restructure your sentences if necessary.

2. **Check for action verbs.** Be sure each bullet in your Professional Experience section starts with an action verb or adverb preceding the action verb. Also be sure to include all main action verbs you circled in Step 3 that are targeted to your profession.

3. **Delete redundant or superfluous words.** Review each sentence or bullet and delete any words that your sentence reads fine without, such as "the" and "that," as well as unnecessary "fluff" words. Edit down to the most concise sentence possible without omitting any important content, such as achievements.

4. **Include personal attributes.** Double-check that your primary attributes (from Step 1) are included in your "Professional Summary" section and cover letter and that you didn't leave out any important ones.

5. **Ensure that all pertinent, targeted qualifications are included.** Go back to Step 1, where you identified your Job Related Information, and check that you have correctly problem-solved your resume—that is, met your original objective to target it correctly to the positions you are seeking. If in Step 1 you included some criterion that you have performed but have not included in your resume, include it now.

   Then check Step 2 to be sure that all your primary areas of expertise are included in your Areas of Expertise section and in your resume bullets under the jobs where you performed these functions.

6. **Prioritize your bullets.** Review your responsibilities and achievements in each position and move the more important and targeted ones closer to the top under each position.

7. **Remove irrelevant information.** Check to ensure that anything irrelevant or not directly related to your targeted goal is minimized, put toward the end, or omitted altogether so that your resume includes more relevant information.

8. **Subdivide and categorize bullets.** If you have many responsibility and achievement bullets under each position (say, more than 10), you can divide them into two categories ("Responsibilities" and "Achievements") and subtitle them as such under each position for easier reading.

9. **Check for quantifying information.** When reviewing your sentences, ask yourself, "Did I include how many, how much, how often, how big, how fast, how well, and so on?" If not, go back and check Step 3 for this information and edit your sentences.

10. **Verify that "CAR" and benefit info is included.** Do your achievements include the **C**hallenge you faced, the **A**ction you took, and the **R**esult? Be sure you show how well you performed these functions and *always* include the benefit(s) to the company.

11. **Vary bullet line length.** Try for a good mix of line lengths. Bullets are effective when they are a combination of one, two, and three typed lines. Because it is important to show not only what you did, but also how well you did it and what the benefits were to the company, information should be concise without sacrificing content or meaning. In this way, you will have an action-packed, achievement-oriented resume that is tightly and concisely written.

12. **Check grammar, punctuation, and spelling.** Spell-check your document in your word-processing program. Proofread several times. Be consistent in your use of capitalization and hyphenation. Be sure you have used correct grammar and punctuation. If this is not one of your fortes (and it isn't for many people), give your completed resume to someone you trust to proofread it for you.

13. **Add more descriptive adjectives or adverbs where applicable.** Review the examples and "Descriptive Adjectives" and "Descriptive Adverbs" lists later in this step and check to see whether you can infuse any additional descriptors that show how well you performed your job functions.

14. **Get a professional resume critique:** If you would like to receive a professional opinion in the form of a resume critique before you send out your resume and cover letter, e-mail your resume to me at CareerCatapult@aol.com or fax it to (631) 698-0984 using the order form at the back of this book along with your credit-card payment of $39. Be sure to put "CRITIQUE" in the subject line.

ADD DESCRIPTIVE ADJECTIVES AND ADVERBS

A properly placed word can answer the "How well?" question. After you document your responsibilities and achievements starting with an action verb, take a look at each function/accomplishment to see whether you can add an occasional adverb in front of an action verb or adjective in front of the noun to show how well you performed a particular function. Here are some sample adverbs and adjectives.

Step 9

ADVERBS (Answer the Question "How Well?"):

- <u>Creatively</u> develop…
- <u>Actively</u> network with…
- <u>Significantly</u> surpassed…
- <u>Accurately</u> prepare…
- <u>Regularly</u> maintain…
- <u>Appropriately</u> allocated…
- <u>Diplomatically</u> negotiate…
- <u>Efficiently</u> conduct…
- <u>Patiently</u> cater to…
- <u>Effectively</u> enhance…
- <u>Concisely</u> edit…
- <u>Thoughtfully</u> address…
- <u>Warmly</u> greet and receive guests…
- <u>Vividly</u> demonstrate…
- <u>Fruitfully</u> negotiated with…
- <u>Corroboratively</u> tackle…
- <u>Encouragingly</u> assist…
- <u>Lavishly</u> but <u>tastefully</u> decorate…
- <u>Succinctly</u> write…
- <u>Professionally</u> greet…
- <u>Successfully</u> transitioned…
- <u>Consistently</u> attain…
- <u>Dramatically</u> reduced…
- <u>Persistently</u> follow up on…
- <u>Quickly</u> intervene…
- <u>Persuasively</u> upsell…
- <u>Strategically</u> forecast…
- <u>Carefully</u> inspect…
- <u>Diligently</u> perform…
- <u>Successfully</u> spearheaded…
- <u>Thoroughly</u> review…
- <u>Voluntarily</u> serve…
- <u>Finitely</u> detail (or define)…
- <u>Virtually</u> eliminated…
- <u>Expediently</u> route…
- <u>Analytically</u> review…
- <u>Intriguingly</u> captivate…
- <u>Intuitively</u> foresee…

ADJECTIVES (Show "How Well" by Describing "What Type?"):

- Develop <u>creative</u> lesson plans…
- Prepare <u>accurate</u> records…
- Conduct <u>regular</u> compliance reviews…
- Allocate <u>appropriate</u> resources…
- Conduct <u>timely</u> negotiations…
- Prepare <u>essential</u> reports…
- Create <u>vogue</u> fashions…
- Make <u>analytic</u> recommendations…
- Write <u>succinct</u> outlines…
- Implement <u>seasonal</u> planograms…
- Create <u>vivid/vibrant/captivating/intriguing</u> presentations…
- Implement <u>successful</u> new policies…
- Negotiate <u>diplomatic</u> relations…
- Develop <u>effective</u> solutions…
- Make <u>thorough</u> recommendations…
- Perform <u>standard</u> maintenance…
- Develop <u>contemporary</u> programs…
- Make a <u>visible</u> difference…
- Offer <u>encouraging</u> support…
- Showcase <u>attractive</u> displays…
- Present <u>stimulating/insightful</u> ideas…

Step 9

DESCRIPTIVE ADJECTIVES LIST

Here is a list of descriptive adjectives from which you can select to describe your work performance, projects, and so on, and infuse into your Professional Summary, Professional Experience bullets, and cover letter.

Strategically interspersing descriptive adjectives and adverbs into your resume will help illustrate how well you performed your job functions and accomplishments and help quantify your information. However, be careful not to use too many adjectives. Doing so might come off as egotistical and might obscure your tangible skills and expertise that employers really want to see.

❏ Accelerating	❏ Certifiable	❏ Controllable	❏ Diligent
❏ Acclimating	❏ Challenging	❏ Converging	❏ Diplomatic
❏ Accommodating	❏ Changing	❏ Convincing	❏ Discreet
❏ Accompanying	❏ Collaborative	❏ Cooperative	❏ Dispensable
❏ Accumulative	❏ Collective	❏ Coordinating	❏ Disputable
❏ Accurate	❏ Communicative	❏ Correct	❏ Dissipating
❏ Adaptable	❏ Community-oriented	❏ Corroborative	❏ Distinguishable
❏ Adaptive	❏ Compassionate	❏ Creative	❏ Distributable
❏ Aesthetic	❏ Competitive	❏ Critical	❏ Diversifying
❏ Allowable	❏ Complete	❏ Cultivating	❏ Dramatic
❏ Ambitious	❏ Comprehensive	❏ Customized	❏ Dynamic
❏ Analytic	❏ Computerized	❏ Cyclical	❏ Economizing
❏ Animated	❏ Conceivable	❏ Debating	❏ Educative
❏ Appealing	❏ Conceptual	❏ Deciphering	❏ Effective
❏ Appropriate	❏ Concise	❏ Decisive	❏ Efficient
❏ Artistic	❏ Conditioned	❏ Declining	❏ Elective
❏ Assuring	❏ Configurative	❏ Decorative	❏ Elevating
❏ Attainable	❏ Confirmable	❏ Deliberating	❏ Eluding
❏ Attentive	❏ Conforming	❏ Delineating	❏ Embellishing
❏ Attractive	❏ Consenting	❏ Deliverable	❏ Embracing
❏ Authoritative	❏ Consistent	❏ Demonstrative	❏ Empowering
❏ Automated	❏ Constrictive	❏ Demystifying	❏ Enabling
❏ Balanced	❏ Constructive	❏ Depreciating	❏ Enamoring
❏ Bridging	❏ Consultative	❏ Descriptive	❏ Encouraging
❏ Brief	❏ Containing	❏ Detachable	❏ Encumbering
❏ Calculative	❏ Contesting	❏ Detail-oriented	❏ Enduring
❏ Candid	❏ Continuing	❏ Diagnostic	❏ Enhancing
❏ Captivating	❏ Contrasting	❏ Differentiating	❏ Enlightening

(continued)

Step 9

DESCRIPTIVE ADJECTIVES LIST *(continued)*

- Enlivening
- Enriching
- Entertaining
- Enticing
- Entrusting
- Enveloping
- Equalizing
- Equitable
- Escalating
- Essential
- Evaluative
- Evolving
- Excavating
- Exchangeable
- Exciting
- Excusable
- Executive
- Expeditious
- Experimental
- Expressive
- Extenuating
- Fair
- Familiarizing

- Final
- Flexible
- Flowing
- Focused
- Genuine
- Healthy
- Helpful
- Identifiable
- Impartial
- Inclusive
- Increasing
- Individualize
- Influencing
- Innovative
- Insightful
- Inspiring
- Intriguing
- Intuitive
- Logical
- Maintainable
- Marketable
- Methodical
- Meticulous

- Morale-building
- Mutual
- Nonjudgmental
- Objective
- Ongoing
- Open-minded
- Optimistic
- Persuasive
- Political
- Positive
- Practical
- Precise
- Proactive
- Problem-solving
- Productive
- Professional
- Prompt
- Realistic
- Reasonable
- Reflective
- Regular
- Reliable
- Resilient

- Resourceful
- Respectfully
- Results-oriented
- Seasonal
- Sensible
- Service-oriented
- Sincere
- Standard
- Stimulating
- Strategic
- Succinct
- Supportive
- Systematic
- Technical
- Thorough
- Thoughtful
- Understanding
- Versatile
- Vibrant
- Visible
- Visionary
- Vivid
- Warm

Step 9

DESCRIPTIVE ADVERBS LIST

❏ Accurately	❏ Confidently	❏ Enticingly	❏ Persuasively
❏ Actively	❏ Conscientiously	❏ Equitably	❏ Politically
❏ Aesthetically	❏ Consistently	❏ Expediently	❏ Precisely
❏ Analytically	❏ Constructively	❏ Expeditiously	❏ Proactively
❏ Appealingly	❏ Contrastingly	❏ Expressively	❏ Productively
❏ Appropriately	❏ Convincingly	❏ Fairly	❏ Professionally
❏ Approvingly	❏ Cooperatively	❏ Flexibly	❏ Promptly
❏ Artistically	❏ Corroboratively	❏ Fruitfully	❏ Quickly
❏ Assertively	❏ Courteously	❏ Genuinely	❏ Realistically
❏ Assuringly	❏ Craftily	❏ Healthily	❏ Reasonably
❏ Attentively	❏ Creatively	❏ Helpfully	❏ Reflectively
❏ Attractively	❏ Cyclically	❏ Identifiably	❏ Regularly
❏ Authoritatively	❏ Decisively	❏ Impartially	❏ Resiliently
❏ Briefly	❏ Decoratively	❏ Inclusively	❏ Resourcefully
❏ Calmly	❏ Deductively	❏ Increasingly	❏ Respectfully
❏ Candidly	❏ Demonstratively	❏ Independently	❏ Sensibly
❏ Captivatingly	❏ Descriptively	❏ Innovatively	❏ Strategically
❏ Carefully	❏ Diagnostically	❏ Insightfully	❏ Succinctly
❏ Caringly	❏ Diligently	❏ Intriguingly	❏ Supportively
❏ Categorically	❏ Diplomatically	❏ Intuitively	❏ Systematically
❏ Characteristically	❏ Discreetly	❏ Lavishly	❏ Tactfully
❏ Collaboratively	❏ Distinguishably	❏ Logically	❏ Tastefully
❏ Collectively	❏ Dramatically	❏ Methodically	❏ Technically
❏ Communicatively	❏ Economizingly	❏ Meticulously	❏ Thoroughly
❏ Compassionately	❏ Effectively	❏ Objectively	❏ Thoughtfully
❏ Competitively	❏ Efficiently	❏ Observantly	❏ Understandingly
❏ Comprehensively	❏ Electively	❏ Open-mindedly	❏ Visibly
❏ Conceivably	❏ Embracingly	❏ Optimistically	❏ Vividly
❏ Conceptually	❏ Empathetically	❏ Patiently	❏ Voluntarily
❏ Concisely	❏ Encouragingly	❏ Perceptively	❏ Warmly
❏ Conditionally	❏ Enthusiastically	❏ Persistently	

Step 9

RESUME COMPLETION CHECKLIST

Review your finalized resume to determine the following:

❑ Is your resume targeted to the position you seek? Would it match up with the required skills and expertise listed in a job description of this position?

❑ Does it focus on fulfilling an employer's needs? Have you included all of your applicable skills and expertise to meet those needs?

❑ Is all or almost all of the information you included relevant to your job objective? Does your resume content support the position you seek?

❑ Are there any required areas in which you have experience or skills that are not included?

❑ Is your resume heavily achievement-oriented as opposed to task-oriented? Are your resume bullets written in CAR (challenge-action-result) statements?

❑ Do your content, format, grammar, punctuation, fonts, spacing, and so on show consistency?

❑ Is your final resume a persuasive document? Have you convinced the reader that hiring you would be a sound decision that would provide them with a high return on their investment?

❑ Have you edited your resume down to the "lowest common denominator"? Weigh all words. Have you eliminated superfluous or redundant words? Does every word have impact?

❑ Is your resume content rich and powerful? Think in terms of advertising copy; has it addressed all the benefits of hiring you?

❑ Have you provided enough evidence to sell yourself as the perfect candidate for the position?

Step 9

DESIGNER RESUMES: THE SECRET TO GETTING NOTICED

Now that you've pulled together your resume and cover letter, you can move on to the formatting and design of your resume presentation. Just as the content of your resume is essential to get your foot in the door, the design and look of your presentation are important to ensuring that your resume gets noticed and read.

Here's a trade secret: The reason my clients get noticed well before their competition and gain significantly higher interview odds is that their resume presentation is visually appealing and stands out from the crowd in a very professional way. As a result, recruiters stop to read their compelling resumes, and clients get called for interviews a lot more frequently than their peers.

In a pile of bland resumes, the ones that get noticed first are the ones that attract the prospective employer's attention. And if after attracting their attention, the content compels them to call, you have met your goal of getting noticed; the resume has served its purpose: to get your foot in the door for an interview.

In this section (and on the accompanying CD), I share with you dozens of my designs for designing your own resume presentation. Some designs are conservative, whereas others are more creative. There's a reason for this. Not all designs are appropriate for all fields. Some fields require a more conservative look, whereas applicants in other fields can be more creative. You can select one and use it for your resume or create your own.

These resume designs are the crème de la crème of distinctive, creative, professional, and cutting-edge resume designs for everyone from college graduates to high-level executives. Coupled with expert professional writing, these designs have helped my clients obtain interviews at a much higher percentage than the norm.

Experience has shown that design choice is dependent on several factors including the market, the position or profession, its receiving audience, and the individual. The next two pages outline the steps for formatting and designing your resume. Later in this step you'll read guidelines for selecting a design.

FORMAT AND DESIGN GUIDELINES

Use the following instructions when you are formatting and designing your resume, whether you are using a design from the disk or creating your own. Keeping it organized, crisp, and clean looking is the key.

1. **Use good organization.** Organize your information so that it is easy to read and easy to find. Refer to the designs at the end of this step and on the CD to see how section headings should be set up, the order things should go in, and so on.

2. **Boldface important information.** Boldface your header/contact information (name, address, phone number, and e-mail address), all section headings, and subtitles, such as your position title and company name.

3. **Use italics to set information apart.** Use italics to separate out subordinate information, such as a second set of dates for promotions or awards under one employer, subheadings for breaking out your Responsibilities and Achievements into two sections under each position, parenthetical information, page numbers, and so on.

4. **Use white space effectively.** Don't cram the page with a lot of text. Make it comfortable for the employer to read by giving your resume large margins and sufficient space between sections. You want your readers to *want* to read your resume, not try to *force* themselves to read it...they won't.

5. **Use graphic elements to group information.** Review the sample designs to see how you can use rules, bars, and other graphic elements to separate, highlight, or frame certain information. Use these elements in a way that they enhance your resume rather than clutter it.

6. **Consider using clip-art images.** I have included a few design samples that use designer clip art. Use art poignantly, not in a haphazard fashion. You want the art to make a subtle, professional statement. You don't want your resume to look like a hodgepodge school newsletter with art images all around. Adding "occupational art" creates a profession-specific image, much as a logo does for a business.

Be sure to use the same type of stationery on your post-interview thank-you letters. This promotes "image recall" when the recruiter sees another piece of correspondence from you. It's a way of branding yourself (remember, you are the product you are selling).

7. **Be careful with colored boxes.** If you want to use a design with a gray or colored box, be sure that there is no critical information in a gray box. Most faxes today can handle shaded resumes, but older faxes will distort the images, making them either pure black or pure white—and unreadable.

8. **Don't worry about the one-page myth.** Most resumes I prepare for my clients are two pages—even entry-level resumes, because I work up their knowledge and proficiencies in the same concrete fashion used in this book. Human resources managers are very comfortable with two-page resumes. They generally scan over the first page on the first screening and read the resume fully when it is time to determine who they will be calling for interviews. Adjust your spacing to fit, but do not try to cram everything on one page; it will not be read. Management and high-tech resumes can be as long as they must be to include all of your achievements in a concise format; three and four pages are very acceptable.

9. **Choose an appropriate font.** Keeping in mind that you want your resume to stand out in a professional way, if you are using a resume design (from the disk at the back of this book or one you created yourself) or if you plan to e-mail your resume, you should use a standard typestyle such as Arial or Times New Roman. Because the design has already captured the reader's interest, you will not need to use a fancy font to do so. Also, a standard font will not compete with the design. If you are using a nice, professional format and not a design (and you are not planning to e-mail your resume), you can be a little more elaborate with your font choice…but stay professional.

 **note** If you are using Times New Roman, you can go up one-half to a full point size more because the letters in this font print smaller than the letters in other fonts.

10. **Use the right point size.** Format your cover letter in 11-point type and your resume in 10-point type (larger for headings) to start. If you need to make the content fill the page better, you can go up a half a point on both. If your cover letter does not fit on one page, you can set it at 10 points to make it fit better. Do not use a smaller font size than 10 points for your cover letter or resume— it will be difficult to read.

11. **Break pages as well as possible.** End your pages with full paragraphs if you can. Also, try not to divide up positions from one page to the next. You can adjust your font size and line spacing to help break your pages at the best places.

12. **Make your contact information readable.** Be sure your contact information is clear and large enough to read on your cover letter and the first page of your resume (14 to 16 points works well for your name, and 12 points works for your address and phone number). Your name should appear on all pages. And double-check all your contact information; that's the place that most people skip over—I have seen resumes go out with the wrong contact phone number!

13. **Mail it professionally.** I recommend mailing your resume and cover letter without folding them in a large white or ivory 9″ × 12″ envelope. You can also first insert your resume and cover letter in a clear plastic folder. This makes for a clean presentation and a professional look, and prevents your resume pages from being separated. Don't staple the pages together.

SELECT YOUR RESUME DESIGN

To make the most of your resume presentation and other personal branding materials, make them unique, professional, and in keeping with your profession and target audience to capture interest and invite the reader in to want to learn more. The following design templates from *Evelyn Salvador's Designer Resume Gallery* (Creative Image Builders) include 24 resume layout design ideas, from conservative to more creative. The black-and-white resume design samples included on the accompanying CD incorporate graphic elements, texture, gradations, and other professional design elements.

The Resume Designs on the CD

The resume design templates on the accompanying CD are suitable for printing, e-mailing, and faxing.

Each design template is provided as a Microsoft Word document and contains three pages—for a cover letter and two-page resume. You can easily add or subtract pages as needed. Also, each design template includes carefully aligned text boxes for name and address information, and resume and cover letter body copy. Some contain margin text boxes to maximize text area and enhance the design while maintaining white space. You can add or delete text boxes to further customize the resumes to suit your needs.

tip — When you e-mail a resume to a prospective employer, copy and paste the resume text into the body of the e-mail (see Step 10 for tips on doing this correctly). Then also attach the MS Word document or a PDF. In this way, the recruiter can use the text document for their database and can also print the designed one.

You can further enhance the design templates by incorporating various additional branding elements, as discussed in Step 8. Additional notations on the templates indicate where you might want to consider placing profession-specific clip art, callouts, photos, testimonials, mission statements, success stories, and other personalized elements. You can also add text or picture boxes in other places.

The "Guidelines for Selecting Your Resume Design," "Designer Resume Gallery Templates," and "Sample Resume Layouts" included in this step and contained on the accompanying CD were excerpted from Evelyn Salvador's Designer Resume Gallery Deluxe *8-CD set of 300 resume design templates created for MS Word and available as Web-ready images in JPG and GIF formats (Creative Image Builders). The complete set of 300 black-and-white and full-color design templates can be ordered using the form at the end of the book.*

Select a Template Design

When selecting a design that is appropriate for your profession, consider the following:

- **The nature of your field:** Is your field conservative by nature, highly creative, or somewhere in between? The level of conservatism or creativity in your chosen field is the first indicator as to whether you should select a conservative design or a more creative one. For example, more conservative fields include legal, banking, accounting, finance, pharmaceutical, and biotechnology. Creative fields include advertising, sales, marketing, fashion design, interior decorating, teaching, travel consulting, culinary, photography, and the like. Fields that fall somewhere in between could include social work, retail, construction, restaurant and hospitality, transportation and logistics, agriculture and farming, and a host of others. The creativity of some fields could depend on your position title, such as those in general business. (For example, if you are a vice president of sales for an automobile dealership, your resume can be somewhat more creative than if you work in the corporate world.)

- **Your target market:** Who is your target market—your prospective audience? Who will actually be reading your resume? Are they generally young or old? Do they think outside the box or stick with what's worked? Obviously, you won't always know this in advance, but your experience in your profession might be a good indicator as to who your average audience might be. For example, if you are a graphic designer or an art director, you would know that your audience is generally young and must think outside the box. In this case, a more creative design might be suitable. Manufacturing hiring managers might be older, more experienced people who have come up the ranks; you may want to use a more conservative design in this case.

- **Your actual position title:** What is your position title? Are you an executive or entry-level? A marketing specialist or number-cruncher? An innovative sales manager or a research associate? Your position itself may be one that is conservative in nature or highly creative. Choose your design accordingly.

Step 9

- **Location and logistics:** Where are you looking for work? Do you seek employment in the suburbs or in a big city? If you are seeking work in the city, for example, you might want to go with a more corporate look than you would for the suburbs. Is it a fast-paced environment or slower-paced one? For the stock market, for example, hiring professionals will want to read something quickly, so your resume should be very organized, easy to read, and not too elaborate.

- **Your own unique personality:** What is your personality like? Are you quiet by nature? Outgoing and sociable? Enthusiastic and energetic? If you are an energetic, gung-ho type of person, you might want to select a design that reflects that part of your personality—something more creative or colorful, perhaps, if it is appropriate for your profession.

DESIGNER RESUME GALLERY TEMPLATES

The following 24 resume designs come from my *Designer Resume Gallery Deluxe* CD. You will find each of these design templates on the accompanying CD under Design Templates.

Following are thumbnails of the resume design templates on the accompanying CD.

Step 9

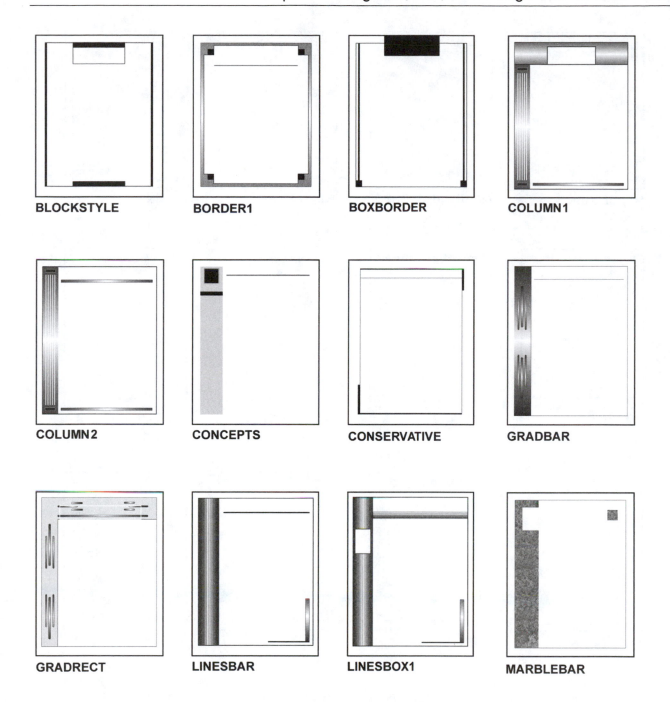

BLOCKSTYLE

BORDER1

BOXBORDER

COLUMN1

COLUMN2

CONCEPTS

CONSERVATIVE

GRADBAR

GRADRECT

LINESBAR

LINESBOX1

MARBLEBAR

Step 9

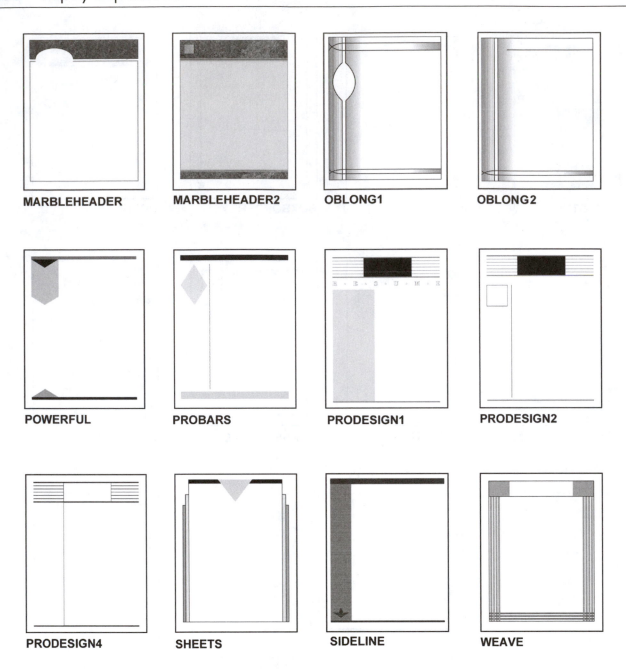

MARBLEHEADER

MARBLEHEADER2

OBLONG1

OBLONG2

POWERFUL

PROBARS

PRODESIGN1

PRODESIGN2

PRODESIGN4

SHEETS

SIDELINE

WEAVE

If you would like to purchase the full version of the Designer Resume Gallery Deluxe *CD, which contains 300 MS Word design templates, call Creative Image Builders at (631) 698-7777, e-mail CareerCatapult@aol.com, or complete and fax the form at the back of this book to (631) 698-0984.*

Step 9

step 10

Ready Your Resume for Job Boards and E-mail

- Creating the Print Version of Your Resume
- Creating the E-mail Version
- Posting Your Resume to a Job Board or Aggregator
- Creating a Web Resume or Web Portfolio

Once your resume is complete, you will need to prepare several formats so that you can print it (for mailing or handing to prospective clients), e-mail it (as a .doc/.docx file, a PDF file, and an e-mail file), post it to online job boards, and put it directly on the Internet as a Web resume or Web portfolio. This step shows you how to convert and use your resume in all of these ways.

Though each topic has specific steps to be taken, creating the various resume formats is really quite simple and will take you no time at all.

First and foremost, be sure to save and title each resume version (file) separately, so that you do not mistakenly overwrite your original resume and lose it. The best way is to set up your additional files before you work on any of the resume versions. Make five copies of the original. The files will come up named as –copy 1, –copy 2, –copy 3. Then go into Windows and change the titles of the five copies, as follows:

- **Printed version:** *(Your Name) Resume.doc* or *Resume of (Your Name).doc*
- **PDF version:** *(Your Name) Resume.pdf* or *Resume of (Your Name).pdf*
- **Text version:** *(Your Name) Text Resume.txt* (Note that you cannot convert a resume to this format simply by changing its name. You must save your document as .txt from the .doc file.)
- **E-mail version:** *(Your Name) E-mail Resume*
- **Web resume:** *Your Name.com* (You must purchase a domain name from a service provider, and using your name as the domain name is a good idea.)

CREATING THE PRINT VERSION OF YOUR RESUME

The resume and cover letter you have been creating throughout this book as an MS Word .doc file is the version you will be using for printing.

When printing, select paper that is heavier than standard 20-pound copy paper (for example, 24-, 28-, or 32-pound weight). The paper should have a grain and be white or ecru. Personally, I recommend the 28-pound; it makes a very nice impression. You can find resume paper in your local office-supply store or online. Southworth carries a wonderful line of resume papers, and there are other brands equally suitable to print your resume. Southworth is also affiliated with the National Resume Writers' Association (NRWA) and includes helpful resume writing in each package, prepared by the NRWA.

Once you print your resume to send to prospective employers or recruiters, I recommend that you enclose it (without stapling) in a 9″×12″ envelope, unfolded. It makes a nice presentation to receive it without folding. Enclosing your resume in a larger envelope also helps it to stand out from others.

 tip Be sure to save a copy of your e-mail resume (as well as your printed version) in your e-mail's Sent folder for use on all e-mailed resumes. When you're ready to send your resume to another prospective employer, you can resend the same e-mail by just changing the recipient's e-mail address and/or any targeted information/subject matter of the position sought. Save each sent resume separately so that you'll have a record of where you've sent resumes.

CREATING THE E-MAIL VERSION

The resume version you will use for pasting into an e-mail message is an ASCII—or plain-text—version of your resume in a standard font. Whenever you e-mail your resume to a prospective employer, paste the ASCII version (plain copy) right into your e-mail. Attach the pretty (print) version to your e-mail so that the hiring manager can download and save it.

You create an ASCII version by separately saving your file in Microsoft Word in ".txt" format. Once you've saved the new file, close and reopen it. When it opens, you will see that all formatting has been removed and you will have plain text to work with.

Of course, when you save your resume as a .txt file, the boldfacing and italics drop out. However, most e-mail programs are now capable of receiving boldfacing and italics intact. So you have the option of adding those type enhancements back to your resume once you've pasted it into the body of the message. Follow these steps:

1. Boldface all headings and make them all caps.
2. Boldface and capitalize all job titles.
3. Boldface employer names (but do not capitalize them).
4. Add two returns between section headings and one or two returns between each job.
5. Make sure that you are using a standard font (such as Arial, Helvetica, Verdana, Times New Roman, or Garamond) and font size (10- or 11-point).

Even if the hiring manager's e-mail program can't receive boldfacing, using all caps for headings and job titles will help make your resume easily readable for him or her.

FIRST & LAST NAME
(Optional Title or Profession)
Street Address, Town, ST 00000
Home: (000) 000-0000 • Cell: (000) 000-0000
E-mail: xxxxxxxxxxxxx • Web Portfolio: YourName.com

PROFESSIONAL SUMMARY

XXXXXXXXXXXXXXXXXXXXXXXXXXXXXXXXXXXXXXXXXXXXXXXXXXXXXXXXXXXXXXXXXXXXXXXXX
XXXXXXXXXXXXXXXXXXXXXXXXXXXXXXXXXXXXXXXXXXXXXXXXXXXXXXXXXXXXXXXXXXXXXXXXX
XXXXXXXXXXXXXXXXXXXXXXXXXXXXXXXXXXXXXXXXXXXXXXXXXXXXXXXXXXXXXXXXXXXXXXXXX
XXXXXXXXXXXXXXXXXXXXXXXXXXXXXXXXXXXXXXXXXXXXXXXXXXXXXXXXXXXXXXXXXXXXXXXXX

AREAS OF EXPERTISE

- XXXXXXXXXXXXXXXX
- XXXXXXXXXXXXXXXX
- XXXXXXXXXXXXXXXX
- XXXXXXXXXXXXXXXX

- XXXXXXXXXXXXXXXX
- XXXXXXXXXXXXXXXX
- XXXXXXXXXXXXXXXX
- XXXXXXXXXXXXXXXX

- XXXXXXXXXXXXXX
- XXXXXXXXXXXXXX
- XXXXXXXXXXXXXX
- XXXXXXXXXXXXXX

PROFESSIONAL EXPERIENCE

0000–present: **JOB TITLE IN CAPS**
                     Employer Name, Town, ST

- XXXXXXXXXXXXXXXXXXXXXXXXXXXXXXXXXXXXXXXXXXXXXXXXXXXXXXXXXXXXXXXXXXX
  XXXXXXXXXXXXXXXXXXXXXXXXXXXXXXXXXXXXXXXXXXXXXX.
- XXXXXXXXXXXXXXXXXXXXXXXXXXXXXXXXXXXXXXXXXXXXXXXXXXXXXXXXXXXXXXXXXXX
  XXXXXXXXXXXXXXXXXXXXXXXXXXXXXXXXXX.
- XXXXXXXXXXXXXXXXXXXXXXXXXXXXXXXXXXXXXXXXXXXXXXXXXXXXXXXXXXXXXXXXXXX
  XXXXXXXXXXXXXXXXXXXXXXXXXXXXXX.
- XXXXXXXXXXXXXXXXXXXXXXXXXXXXXXXXXXXXXXXXXXXXXXXXXXXXXXXXXXXXXXXXXXX
  XXXXXXXXXXXXXXXXXXXXXXXXXXXXXXXXXXXXXX.
- XXXXXXXXXXXXXXXXXXXXXXXXXXXXXXXXXXXXXXXXXXXXXXXXXXXXXXXXXXXXXXXXXXX
  XXXXXXXXXXXXXXXXXXXXXXXXXXXX.

0000–0000:   **JOB TITLE IN CAPS**
                     Employer Name, Town, ST

- XXXXXXXXXXXXXXXXXXXXXXXXXXXXXXXXXXXXXXXXXXXXXXXXXXXXXXXXXXXXXXXXXXX
  XXXXXXXXXXXXXXXXXXXXXXXXXXXXXXXXXXXXXXXXXX.
- XXXXXXXXXXXXXXXXXXXXXXXXXXXXXXXXXXXXXXXXXXXXXXXXXXXXXXXXXXXXXXXXXXX
  XXXXXXXXXXXXXXXXXXXXXXXXXXXXXXXXXXXXX.
- XXXXXXXXXXXXXXXXXXXXXXXXXXXXXXXXXXXXXXXXXXXXXXXXXXXXXXXXXXXXXXXXXXX
  XXXXXXXXXXXXXXXXXXXXXXXXXXXX.
- XXXXXXXXXXXXXXXXXXXXXXXXXXXXXXXXXXXXXXXXXXXXXXXXXXXXXXXXXXXXXXXXXXX
  XXXXXXXXXXXXXXXXXXXXXXXXXXXXXXXXXXXXXXXXXXX.
- XXXXXXXXXXXXXXXXXXXXXXXXXXXXXXXXXXXXXXXXXXXXXXXXXXXXXXXXXXXXXXXXXXX
  XXXXXXXXXXXXXXXXXXXXXXXXXXXXXXXXXXXXX.

0000–0000:   **JOB TITLE IN CAPS**
                     Employer Name, Town, ST

- XXXXXXXXXXXXXXXXXXXXXXXXXXXXXXXXXXXXXXXXXXXXXXXXXXXXXXXXXXXXXXXXXXX
  XXXXXXXXXXXXXXXXXXXXXXXXXXXXXXXXXXXXXXXXXXXXX.
- XXXXXXXXXXXXXXXXXXXXXXXXXXXXXXXXXXXXXXXXXXXXXXXXXXXXXXXXXXXXXXXXXXX
  XXXXXXXXXXXXXXXXXXXXXXXXXXXXXXX.
- XXXXXXXXXXXXXXXXXXXXXXXXXXXXXXXXXXXXXXXXXXXXXXXXXXXXXXXXXXXXXXXXXXX
  XXXXXXXXXXXXXXXXXXXXXXXXXXXXXXXXXXX.
- XXXXXXXXXXXXXXXXXXXXXXXXXXXXXXXXXXXXXXXXXXXXXXXXXXXXXXXXXXXXXXXXXXX
  XXXXXXXXXXXXXXXXXXXXXXXXXXXXXXXXXXXXXXXXXXX.

EDUCATION
- XXXXXXXXXXXXXXXXXXXXXXXXXXXXXXXXXXXXXXXXXXXXXXXXXXXXXXXXXXXXXXXXXXXXXXX
- XXXXXXXXXXXXXXXXXXXXXXXXXXXXXXXXXXXXXXXXXXXXXXXXXXXXXXXXXXXXXXXXXXXXXXX

And so on…

Step 10

POSTING YOUR RESUME TO A JOB BOARD OR AGGREGATOR

Online job boards and aggregators allow you to upload Microsoft Word resumes (generally up to 250K in size). Alternatively, they provide a text box for you to paste your entire resume into. If the resume file you used for your printed version is larger than 250K (as some of the Designer Resume Templates on CD at the back of this book are), you can simply click on the background image and delete it, which will immediately decrease the file size so that you can then post it online.

Looking up jobs on a job board is a lot easier than posting your resume there, as anyone who has done it can tell you. It requires cutting and pasting your resume information into boxes, often into separate sections, as dictated by the job board's programming. Doing the same thing on various sites could take you numerous hours or days to complete.

I recommend that you use **indeed.com** as your primary online job search portal because it is an aggregator that pulls together job postings from many different job boards and company sites. When you post your resume there, you can use it to apply for jobs that are posted all over the Internet.

caution

When job boards ask you to type your resume information directly into a provided box, *do not* just type the information. There is no spell-check, and typos will cause the HR rep to relegate your resume to the proverbial trash. Instead, copy and paste it from your text version directly into the provided spot. If you do have to hand-type anything, be sure to proofread what you write three times: once for reading legibility, a second time for proper grammar use and spelling, and a third to make sure you did not miss anything.

If you prefer to work with individual job boards, which also might include a place to upload your resume for employers to search, here is a list of some of the top boards (the top boards are boldfaced):

BilingualCareer.com

Career.com	JobShouts
CareerBuilder	LocalHelpWanted.net
CareerExposure.com	**Monster**
CareerJournal	myCareerSpace
CareerMag.com	NationJob
CareerPark	**Net-Temps**
CollegeJobBoard.com	NowHiring
CollegeRecruiter.com	ProHire
Employment Guide.com	QuintCareers.4Jobs
Employment911	Recruiters Online Network
freshjobs.com	Registerjobs.com
Futurestep	**SimplyHired**
Hound	SnagAJob.com
Indeed	Thingamajob.com
Interview Exchange.com	**TopUSAJobs.com**
Job Search Shortcut	TrueCareers
JobBank USA	**USAJOBS**
JobCentral	Vault
JobGuru.com	Yahoo! HotJobs

Step 10

CREATING A WEB RESUME OR WEB PORTFOLIO

If you are not familiar with developing Web sites or Web resumes, you will need the services of a professional Web resume designer or developer to prepare your Web Resume or Web portfolio for the Internet. They can take your resume and post it to the Internet in an attractive format that looks like your printed resume. Or they can include your resume as a download from a Web portfolio, which is a Web site that showcases your personal brand, expertise, credentials, and additional information.

Here's an example of a Web portfolio for a Nurse Manager.

Deborah James
NURSE MANAGER

| INTRO | CAREER HIGHLIGHTS | RESUME | CASE STUDIES | CONTACT |

Professional Summary

Deborah James is a compassionate results-oriented Nurse Manager with progressive and diversified experience in shift management and patient care /coordination in acute care settings. She provides meaningful advocacy for patients and families in Medical/Surgical, Respiratory/Ventilation, Surgical Step-down and Telemetry settings. Deborah possesses excellent interpersonal, critical thinking, and assessment skills coupled with the ability to put individuals at ease.

Proficient in telemetry monitoring, performing cardiac monitoring and catheterization, administering medications, and starting IVs, Deborah has planning and organizational adeptness and the ability to maintain superior levels of quality care under all types of circumstances.

The tenacity to successfully complete assignments and the flexibility to adapt to changing situations and requirements—even in pressure situations—are a few of Deborah's attributes.

Medical/Surgical
Respiratory / Ventilation
Surgical Step-down
Telemetry
Patient Assessments
Staff Supervision & Development
Team Building

123 MAIN STREET, TOWN, ST 00000 · (631) 698-7777 · EMAIL: CAREERCATAPULT@AOL.COM

Web Resume by DesignerWebResumes.com

Following are more samples of Web portfolios I have created for my clients in various professions.

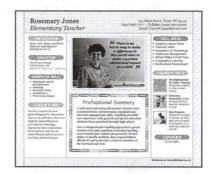

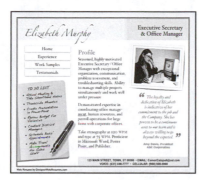

To view these samples full screen, go to www.CareerImageBuilders.com and click on Web Resume Development.

You can also build a basic and simple online resume and portfolio at VisualCV (www.visualcv.com). You can't get too fancy with the design, but you can link to examples of your work and include references. And it's free.

Another way to get your credentials online is to join the business networking site LinkedIn and build your profile there. Again, this site is free, and it enables you to leverage your business contacts as you look for work.

Appendix

Sample Resumes

Following are more sample resumes and cover letters covering various positions, showing how to incorporate resume components, including Areas of Expertise, Action Verbs, Professional Summary, Resume ClipBullets™, cover letters, resume designs, and other elements of your resume covered in this book.

The samples also exemplify how you can use different professional designs to make an immediate impact. The use of graphic design, occupational art, mission statements, testimonials, and so on will further wow your potential employer. These design elements are incorporated into the following samples.

I do not recommend that you copy any of the resumes to prepare your own. As I mentioned earlier, the more your resume and cover letter are geared to who you are with your own unique qualifications, the better your resume will be and the more appropriate your fit will be to an organization looking for your qualifications. Instead, look to these resumes for inspiration in putting together your own.

Many thanks to the professional resume writers who contributed examples to this appendix:

Laurie Berenson, CPRW
Phone: (201) 573-8282
www.SterlingCareerConcepts.com

Dawn S. Bugni, CPRW
The Write Solution—Resume Writing and Career
   Advising
Phone: (910) 540-0544
E-mail: dawn@write-solution.com
www.write-solution.com

Phyllis G. Houston
The Résumé Expert, Mobile Service

Angie S. Jones, CPRW, CEIC
Haute Resume & Career Services LLC
Toll-free phone: (866) 695-9318
www.ANewResume.com

Abby Locke, MRW, NCRW, ACRW, CPBS
Premier Writing Solutions
Phone: (425) 608-7200
E-mail: alocke@premierwriting.com
www.premierwriting.com

Tina Kashlak Nicolai, PHR
President | Career Strategist | Writer
Resume Writers' Ink, LLC
Phone: (407) 578-1697
www.resumewritersink.com

Don Orlando, MBA, CPRW, JCTC, CCM, CCMC, CJSS
The McLean Group
Phone: (334) 264-2020
E-mail: yourcareercoach@charterinternet.com

Reya Stevens, MA, MRW
STANDOUT RÉSUMÉS
Phone: (617) 524-0912
E-mail: reya@standoutresumes.com

Kelly Welch, CPRW, MA, GPHR
Phone: (919) 744-8866
E-mail: kelly@yescareerservices.com
www.yescareerservices.com

RESUME

Richard Clemmings

123 MAIN STREET
ANY TOWN, STATE 00000
Phone: (000) 000-0000
Fax: (000) 000-0000
Cellular: (000) 000-0000
E-Mail Address

•

NEW BUSINESS DEVELOPMENT

SALES & MARKETING CAMPAIGNS

DISTRIBUTION MANAGEMENT

P&L RESPONSIBILITIES

SALES BUDGETS

•

EXECUTIVE SUMMARY

• A senior-level pharmaceutical / biotech sales executive with expertise in sales management, managed care, and distribution of new biotech products.

• Twenty years sales management experience in the healthcare field with a proven track record of driving substantial sales and profitability increases.

• Expert at recruiting strong sales talent for specific disease states and directing a national sales force to procure numerous preferred provider agreements and launching many new biotech products.

• Extensive experience in identifying strategic mergers and acquisitions.

• Superior client and patient customer support focus, before and after sale.

• Developer of internal disease management protocols and value added services to new pharmaceutical products.

• Competitive, profitability-conscious, and results-oriented sales management professional who is customer-service-oriented, goal-driven, and deadline-conscious.

• Proficient in ACT, Goldmine, Microsoft Word, Microsoft Outlook, QS-1, HBS pharmacy systems, and PowerPoint.

Resume Brochure Style (Cover)

Areas of Expertise

- Pharmacy Case Management
- Disease Management
- Prescription Benefit Management
- Plastic Card Adjudication Market
- Chronic Disease States Management
- Formulary Management
- Internet Pharmacy Services
- Global Health Costs
- Drug Utilization Review
- Drug Use Evaluation
- Patient Compliance and Noncompliance
- e-Commerce
- Specialty Mail Order Pharmacy
- Rebates
- PMPM Costs
- Genomic Treatment Plans
- MCOs, PPOs, HMOs
- Physician Hospital Networks
- Independent Physician Associations
- Third Party Administrators
- Self Insured Employers
- Integrated Delivery Systems
- Biotech
- Big Pharma

Experience

2004–present: XYZ Specialty Pharmacy, Inc., Anytown, State
VICE PRESIDENT, BIOTECH BUSINESS DEVELOPMENT

- Direct and coordinate all aspects of sales, marketing, and new business development for this $3.5 billion dollar pharmaceutical / biotech firm, including mergers and acquisitions, joint venture development, extensive pharmacy support programs, and drug manufacturer company relations.

- Catapulted firm to a nationwide biotech leader by launching many new products to market and working in conjunction with national sales force.

- Secured $12 million wholesale distribution agreement for Cytogam used in IVIG substitution therapy by developing a specialty pharmacy and distribution program.

- Implemented pharmacy distribution and support program for major biotech company for launch of new drug for pancreatic cancer which increased annual sales by $5 million.

- Launched the first monoclonal antibody indicated for the prevention of RSV in premature infants—the most successful in biotech history— by implementing pharmacy and laboratory support campaigns.

- Developed new biotech programs to secure preferred and exclusive provider contracts with managed care organizations.

- Created and initiated pharmacy support program for dialysis centers nationwide.

1998–2004: Acme Drug Distribution, Inc., Anytown, State
VICE PRESIDENT, BUSINESS DEVELOPMENT *(2003-2004)*

- Managed and oversaw all facets of sales and marketing, new program development, client relations, and budgets for this recognized national leader in Intron-A retail, Sandimmune/Neoral, Neupogen, and Infertility (Pergonal, Metrodin) retail sales.

- Increased annual sales by $3.5 million by implementing preferred provider agreements.

- Developed various programs for multiple disease states.

VICE PRESIDENT, SALES *(1998-2003)*

- Recruited, trained, and developed a talented and aggressive national sales force to reach goals to meet our vision.

- Increased sales with a seven-year compounded annual growth of 80% and net income with a seven-year compounded annual growth of 70%.*

- Increased sales of services and products to transplant market by 55% while positioning company as a market leader in pre- and post-transplant drug therapies.

See Revenue and Income Charts, Page 4.

Resume Brochure Style (Inside Left)

Experience *(Continued)*

- Rapidly established company's national presence in the transplant and infertility specialized markets.

- Increased annual sales from $12.5 million to $115 million in six years by introducing new chronic disease state programs and by securing numerous preferred provider arrangements with biotech partners.

- Coordinated development of marketing and sales budgets with CFO.

- Secured additional preferred provider arrangements with CDF Labs, GHI Pharmaceuticals and JKL Labs allowing our sales force to become the recognized leader in the sales of Intron-A, Sandimmune/Neoral, Neupogen, Serostim, Pergonal, Metrodin, and Synagis.

- Created and presented proposals, and conducted contract negotiations.

- Developed and produced sales and marketing tools including brochures and presentation materials which drove sales up $2.5 million.

1994–1998:   ABC Health Reimbursement Corp., Anytown, State
PRESIDENT, Health Reimbursement

- Oversaw all facets of company operations for providing specialized reimbursement, clinical support, and product distribution services to ABC Laboratories and XYZ Pharmaceuticals.

- Contracted with the Center for Special Immunology, a multi-state physician practice affiliation and health care organization, specializing in patients with immune system disorders.

- Secured exclusive contracts with Eastern University Hospital, Northwestern Medical Center, New York Medical Center, and the National Transplant Center, increasing annual sales by $17 million.

- Secured preferred provider agreements with Mount Sinai Medical Center, Bayles University Medical Center, Westchester County Medical Center, and San Antonio Transplant Center.

- Developed business plan and a $2.5 million budget for transplant program.

- Provided customized services to drug manufacturers, physicians, hospitals, and insurers within Lifecare Program.

- Leveraged Clozaril patient management facilities to expand into new transplant referral sources.

- Established and merged comprehensive transplant marketing program into managed care arena.

Areas of Strength

- Competitive Analysis
- New Market Identification
- Business Plans
- Sales Forecasting
- P&L Responsibility
- Sales Budgets
- M&A Activity
- Pharmaceutical Pricing
- Distribution Management
- Strategizing Client Needs
- Sales & Marketing Campaigns
- New Business Development
- Public Speaking
- Trade Shows
- Presentations
- Internet Marketing
- Coaching, Motivating, and Developing Winning Sales Teams
- Account Management

Education

NEW YORK STATE COLLEGE
Anytown, NY
Bachelor of Science Degree in
Business Administration

STATE UNIVERSITY OF
NEW YORK, Anytown, NY
Computer Training Certification

Resume Brochure Style (Inside Right)

Professional Affiliations

- North American Transplant Coordinators Organization
- International Society for Heart and Lung Transplant
- American Association of Transplant Surgeons
- Transplant Recipients International Organization
- United Network for Organ Sharing *(Transplant Administrators Forum)*
- American Kidney Fund

- American Association of Transplant Physicians
- American Association of Kidney Patients
- International Transplant Nurses Society
- Society for Heart and Lung Transplant Social Workers
- National Kidney Foundation
- Liver Transplant Social Workers
- American Liver Foundation

> **" *I believe the most important leadership qualities of a Pharmaceutical Sales Executive are the ability to set future vision and develop a high performance sales team to achieve the goals to meet that vision.* "**

Sample Accomplishments

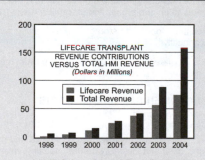

As VP Sales of Acme Drug Distribution, Revenue Increased 80% Compounded Annually

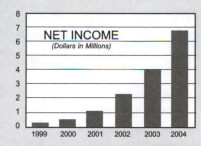

As VP Sales of Acme Drug Distribution, Net Income Increased 70% Compounded Annually

Resume Brochure Style (Back Cover)

Mark F. Bergfield
123 MAIN STREET
ANY TOWN, STATE, 00000
(000) 000-0000

GOAL

Seeking a **Pharmaceutical Sales or Sales Management** position where I can apply my unique combination of education, lab research, and successful sales experience to increase sales and profits in the pharmaceutical field.

PROFESSIONAL SUMMARY

- Three years sales and sales management experience, including setting sales goals, sales training, strategic planning, and sales merchandising.
- Sales abilities in cross-selling, overcoming objections, and closing the sale.
- Thorough understanding of laboratory techniques and biological functions.
- Skilled in operations management, quality assurance, inventory control, auditing, buying and purchasing, cash control, and productivity improvement.
- Excel in personnel management, and coaching, motivating, training and developing staff.
- Proficient in IBM and Macintosh operating systems, word processing and d-base.

EDUCATION

Syracuse University, College of Arts and Sciences, Syracuse NY
Bachelor of Science in Biology – 1996
Course Profile:
- *Cell Biology / Laboratory*
- *Population Biology*
- *Developmental Biology*
- *Genetics*
- *Microbiology / Laboratory*
- *Molecular Genetics*
- *Immunobiology*
- *Biochemistry*
- *Organic Chemistry / Laboratory*

LABORATORY EXPERIENCE

- **Cell Biology Lab** – Studied several types of microscopy, including light field, dark field, phase contrast, UV/immunoflouresence, and electron.

- **Microbiology Lab** – Studied several species of bacteria and bacteriophage. Learned various laboratory techniques including plaque analysis, gel electrophoresis, and aesthetic techniques. Found an unknown bacterium through analysis of metabolic pathways, resistance to drugs, and physical characteristics.

- **Anthropology Lab** – Analyzed and input data regarding several excava-tion sites. Participated in a mock dig. Cross-mended broken artifacts; and analyzed fauna.

SALES MANAGEMENT EXPERIENCE

**1996 – Present: Acme Retail Corp., Anytown, NY
MANAGEMENT TRAINING PROGRAM**
(Annual Revenue: $20 million, Direct Reports: 20, Indirect Reports: 100)

- Selected for Executive Training Program working in the positions of Area Manager and Customer Service Manager; and selected to manage Fixture Liquidation for the local Caldor store.

- Increased sales and decreased employee handling time through effective implementation of innovative merchandising techniques and by reorganizing stockroom access.

- Oversee merchandising, distribution center, and stockroom departments to ensure proper flow of retail items to isle display.

- Eliminated need for off-site storage trailers, saving company $20,000 annually.

- Direct and facilitate sales and safety meetings with managers, associates, sales and operations staff.

CUSTOMER SERVICE MANAGER
(Annual Revenue: $20 million, Direct Reports: 50, Indirect Reports: 100)

- Monitored, tracked and reviewed sales, service and productivity, promotions, cash and inventory control, auditing, and training.

- Oversaw front-line operations, scheduled cashiers and service desk, and responsible for store opening and closing.

Two-Page Resume Variation

Mark F. Bergfield
(PAGE 2)

TESTIMONIALS

" *Mark has shown great inner drive and resolve. His willingness to do whatever needs to be done to achieve his goals is commendable....He works hard to ensure proper communication with his supervisors and associates... a positive presence on our team since his arrival.* "

John Smith, Operations Manager
Acme Corporation, Deer Park, NY

" *Mark is a very dedicated and loyal individual. His daily job performance exceeds all company standards as he strives for excellence in his job responsibilities. Mark will succeed in all aspects of any endeavor he chooses.* "

Thomas Jones, Store Manager
Acme Corporation, Melville, NY

" *During my working relationship with Mark, he developed from an executive in training to a mature professional. Mark always exhibits the highest personal standards toward achieving excellence and expects the same from his direct reports...Mark's strong leadership skills will benefit any team that he is associated with.* "

Daniel Fisher, Store Director
Acme Corporation, Pelham Manor, NY

- Promoted positive "can do" attitude and team effort amongst staff which increased employee morale and overall productivity.

- Ensured customer satisfaction and increased sales through fast and friendly check lines and quick resolution of customer concerns.

- Conducted sales training and awareness programs for sales associates and front-line personnel, which increased staff productivity and promoted a friendly shopping atmosphere.

- Reduced cash shortages from .073% to .016% and increased profitability through effective staff counseling and retraining, strong follow-up, and implementation of company standards.

- Recipient of "Manager of the Month" award.

AREA MANAGER
(Annual Revenue: $22 million,
Direct Reports: 10, Indirect Reports: 100)

- Set unit sales goals, and trained staff to meet and exceed those goals.

- Oversaw merchandising, planogram implementation, store maintenance, weekly circulars, and special events.

- Resolved customer service concerns through effective research and communications, resulting in repeat and referral business.

- Effective time management helped increase store productivity, planogram implementation, and inventory control.

- Recipient of "Manager of the Month" award.

VOLUNTEER WORK

Volunteer Firefighter, Galliston Fire Department, Anytown, NY
Volunteer, Memorial Hospital, Anytown, NY

" *I believe the true quality of a sales professional is the ability to overcome all objections and obstacles.* "

Getting into pharmaceutical sales without prior pharmaceutical experience can be difficult. To give this client an edge, we emphasized his sales management experience and laboratory research education, then went a little further to "wow" recruiters with a "Testimonials" section and a mission statement.

REGISTERED NURSE

NICOLE MACKEY

- Intensive Care Unit
- Surgical ICU
- Telemetry Monitoring
- Cardiac Monitoring
- Pulmonary Monitoring
- Open Heart Recovery
- Peritoneal Dialysis
- Catheterizations

NURSING

PROFESSIONAL SUMMARY

- Nine years of nursing experience in hospital and nursing home settings, including ICU, Telemetry, Open Heart Recovery, Emergency Room, and SICU.
- Proficient in telemetry monitoring, administering medications, making physical assessments, inserting IVs, performing cardiac monitoring, pulmonary monitoring, catheterizations, peritoneal dialysis, endotracheal, tracheostomy, and SICU care.
- Make appropriate medical decisions and know when to defer to a physician.
- Innate ability to create a positive working atmosphere for staff and patients alike.
- A self-motivated professional nurse who works well under pressure, enjoys new challenges, is a team player, and is dedicated to the profession.

EDUCATION

1995–1997:   **St. Mary's Hospital School of Nursing, Anytown, MA**
- Registered Nurse Diploma – 1997 • GPA 4.0 • Dean's List
- Second Honors in Nursing Theory and Nursing Skills

Additional Training:
- Coronary Care – Mercy Medical Center, Rockville Centre, NY
- ACLS – Stony Brook Hospital, Stony Brook, NY

CERTIFICATIONS / MEMBERSHIPS

- Certified Registered Nurse – Licensed in MA and NY
- Licensed Practical Nurse
- Member, New York State Nurses Association
- Member, American Association of Critical Care Nurses

PROFESSIONAL EXPERIENCE

2003–present: **REGISTERED NURSE, SICU**
                            Massachusetts University Hospital, Anytown, MA

- Provide patient care and monitor intracranial pressure monitors, ventriculostomies, and status of post-neurological surgeries requiring ICU monitoring.
- Assisted with lumbar punctures and caring for patients in Halo/cervical traction.
- Interpret ABGs and perform tracheostomy and endotracheal suctioning.
- Assess adventitious breath sounds and monitor patients during weaning off ventilators, intubations, extubation, and tracheostomy and bronchoscopy procedures at bedside.
- Check patients in ARDS and administer and monitor O2 therapy.
- Assist in chest tube placement and removal at bedside including air leak troubleshooting.
- Assist physician with insertion of Swan Ganz catheters and central venous lines.
- Perform hemodynamic monitoring and lines maintenance.
- Provide care to patients requiring CVVHD, maintain AV Fistulas, and assist with insertion of Quinton Catheters.
- Monitor patients on multiple drip medications and perform dressing changes on surgical wounds.

123 MAIN STREET, ANYTOWN, STATE • (000) 000-0000 • E-MAIL ADDRESS

Resume Page 1

REGISTERED NURSE

NICOLE MACKEY

> *Nicole is an asset to any hospital. She makes the atmosphere more enjoyable. ...Her eagerness to learn is contagious and makes others eager to learn.*
> **Anette Davis, ANCC Days, St. Frances Hospital Anytown, MA**

> *Nurses like Nicole only come around every ten years. ...Nicole is an asset to any institution. She is dedicated and perseveres. (I believe) she will not only meet her goals, but supercede them.*
> **Mark Simon, Nephrologist NY Nephrology, Anytown, MA**

> *Nicole is an intelligent, success-driven individual and a professional, dedicated, and compassionate nurse.*
> **Mare Ranor, Head Nurse Sunrest Nursing Home Anytown, MA**

2001–2003: **REGISTERED NURSE, OPEN HEART RECOVERY**
Lenox University Hospital, Anytown, MA

- Staff Nurse in the Open Heart Recovery Room, Telemetry Unit, and step down of this prestigious hospital, which treats 1,250 patients daily.
- Performed nursing care for post CABG, MIDCABG and valve replacement patients, drew labs, and assisted with insertion and removal of arterial lines.
- Monitored ABGs, telemetry monitor, cardiac outputs, cardiac indexes, and SVO2 levels, and performed cardiac outputs.
- Monitored patients with Swan Ganz catheters and Epicardial pacing wires.
- Changed endotracheal tube tapings; performed endotracheal and tracheostomy care.

1998–2001: **REGISTERED NURSE, TELEMETRY**
St. Agnes Hospital, Anytown, MA

- Started as RN; asked to become ANCC due to dedication, fairness, creating a positive work environment, and thorough problem-solving abilities.
- Charge Nurse in a 21-bed Telemetry Unit. Performed telemetry, medical, cardiac, and pulmonary monitoring. Covered Emergency Room and ICU as needed.
- Monitored and administered medications, performed physical assessments, inserted intravenous, drew blood, and monitored central line access.
- Administered peritoneal dialysis, monitoring input and output for electrolyte balance.
- Monitored cardiac monitor, assessed lab values, and reported to physicians.
- Started patient discharge plans on admission and follow through, resulting in timely patient discharges and training.
- Made positive contributions at staff meetings regarding streamlining operations, continuity of care, teamwork, increasing patient satisfaction, and decreasing staff tension.

1995-1998: **HEAD NURSE**
Sunrise Nursing Home, Anytown, MA

- Starting as CNA, received promotions to LPN and Head Nurse in charge of 53 patients through hard work, dedication, staff member respect, and furthering my education.
- Scheduled and supervised nursing staff consisting of 7 CNAs and 2 LPNs.
- Assessed patient vital signs, performed physical assessments, and monitored wound care.
- Administered GT/NGT tube feedings, monitored lab values, administered medications, and performed male and female catheterizations.
- Created a positive atmosphere and working environment for staff and patients alike.
- Kept physicians abreast of changes in patient symptoms, offering accurate nursing assessments regarding patient progress and status.
- Accomplished all daily shift requirements by learning effective time management.
- Performed my best services for each patient through holistic nursing care and teamwork with nursing staff and patients.

123 MAIN STREET, ANYTOWN, STATE • (000) 000-0000 • E-MAIL ADDRESS

Resume Page 2

ALICA LaFONTAINE

12345 Rough Rider Lane ◆ Parkton, NC 28371 ◆ 910.555.1212 ◆ lafontaine@email.com

TECHNICAL RESEARCH

CELL CULTURES ◆ DATA ANALYSIS ◆ GENOTYPING ◆ BIOLOGY ◆ DATA ANALYSIS
STERILE ENVIRONMENT ◆ LABORATORY SAFETY ◆ PROTOCOL ◆ BUFFER, REAGENT AND SOLUTION PREPARATION

Energetic graduate ready to start career in bio-technical and research fields. Extensive experience managing multiple priorities by working full- and part-time positions throughout college career. Able to lead and mentor peers, deliver succinct instructions and follow long-term assignments through to completion. Competent in laboratory protocol with a strong ability to ensure safety, exercise stringent study control and properly document expected and unexpected results. Skilled problem solver, able to introduce new and improve existing procedures.

Willing to relocate for new opportunities

ACADEMIC EXPERIENCE

Studied Mendelian, molecular and human genetics and DNA structure, function and formation in pursuit of a biology degree. Carried out course-required laboratory experiments. Hypothesized study outcome, documented findings, researched anomalies and submitted written reports regarding experiment outcome.

- Learned science behind biochemical reactions and observed environmental effects on cell-level cultures. Recorded changes and drew scientific conclusions based on thorough research and analytical thought.
- Prepared and plated cultures, monitored growth and reported on changes. Used western blotting, gel electrophoresis, sterile culture and other methods to conduct DNA, human cell and polymerase chain reaction (PCR) studies, completing course assignments and building basic laboratory research fundamentals.

EMPLOYMENT CHRONOLOGY

Full- and part-time positions concurrent with other positions and full-time school attendance to fund degree

Shadow Volunteer, Fullerton Genetics Center, Asheville, NC (2008)
Reviewed counseling session notes and observed related activities for two weeks while conducting career research.

Western Carolina University, Cullowhee, NC
Registrar's Office (2008–2009)
Responded to general student questions and answered phones in a busy university office. Provided information while adhering to University privacy policies. Assisted with applications and transcript transfer supporting office flow.

- Created, organized and moved student files following University archive procedures. Ensured easy retrieval.

Orientation Counselor (2006–2008)
Selected as one of 30 counselors assigned to assist campus freshmen. Learned school history and gave campus tours to new students and parents during orientation week. Led group activities and responded to parent and student questions in formal group presentations and one-on-one.

- Sent monthly follow-up emails to approximately 50 students a semester, keeping them involved in school-sponsored activities and supporting a positive freshman year. Generated reports documenting communications.

Book Runner 2006–2008; Entourage, Chatty Cat programs (2007)

Wait Staff, Highlands Country Club (2006)
Provided buffet service support in a high-end country club. Processed payments against correct member accounts in a non-cash environment and assisted with setup and teardown for special events.

EDUCATION

Bachelor of Science—Biology, Western Carolina University (2009)
Pursuing **Phlebotomy certification,** Fayetteville Technical Community College *expected graduation 2010*

◆ ◆ ◆

Written by Dawn S. Bugni, CPRW

ERIC G. BROWN, PMP

> *Provide cost-effective technology solutions that streamline processes, improve productivity, and recapture revenue.*

Analytical and solutions-oriented **Business Technology Officer** with experience developing people and guiding organizations to improve efficiency, increase cost savings, and drive growth. "Go-to guy" with proven expertise in reengineering legacy systems and process improvement. Contribute strong project management, hands-on technical acumen, and business analysis skills to define business objectives and project scope. Effectively encourage team members through verbal and nonverbal feedback. Successfully bridge communication gap among business and technology groups.

Core Expertise includes

☑ Systems Reengineering & Change Management ☑ Process & Performance Improvement

☑ Strategic Business Planning & Merger Integration ☑ Project Scope & Management

☑ Business Analysis & Requirements Gathering ☑ Team Building & Communication

CAREER SNAPSHOT

STONE FINANCIAL, LLC, Los Angeles, CA   2003 to Present

Business Technology Officer (2009 to Present)

Identify cost and systems efficiencies within existing technology; support 125 professionals across 2 divisions, Financial Control (including Treasury and Billing) and Credit Risk, ensuring projects remain consistent with divisional/firm objectives; and identify new technology to enhance growth of business lines. Lead efforts to further company's environmental sustainability initiative and global finance vision.

ENTERPRISE IMPACT:

- *Achieved more than $2.5 million in annual cost savings* by implementing new IT infrastructure and resource cost validation procedures after conducting a thorough analysis of the firm's existing infrastructure and cost reporting framework.
- *Realized $300,000 of cost savings and increased operational efficiency* by adding headcount in a low-cost market. Chosen by CFO to lead strategic design and implementation of India-based finance team to support U.S. and UK processing, including process identification, documentation, training, and migration.
- *Sought approval and implemented first global firm-wide open source application deployment* to 30,000+ workstations across parent company and affiliate entities.

Vice President (2003 to 2009)

Department manager for 15c3-3 Customer/PAIB Reserve formulas, Federal Reserve, TIC, SHC, SHL, reporting, and disaster recovery; and Vice President of Process Improvement, Financial Control division. Managed comprehensive upgrade of regulatory systems used for reserve formula, net capital, balance sheet, and management reporting. Lead Paris-based team to enhance financial reporting, automate P&L close, and improve data integrity check. Strong record of performance recognized by the firm's Division Power Award (2005) and Leadership Conference Award (2007).

ENTERPRISE IMPACT:

- Achieved status of *first department with business-continuity and disaster-recovery plan* of each employee working from home through process and infrastructure changes.
- *Reduced non-contractual rebates processed by 50%* as Six Sigma project lead to reduce number of customer non-contractual rebates. Enhanced reporting capabilities and created stronger workflow and audit trail by managing CFO-mandated project to create paperless customer rebate process.
- *Increased revenue by $700,000 annually* through Six Sigma project to develop a process to track and charge clients for firm's contractual minimum revenue requirements.

Continued...

28 Rose Court   ✧   Beverly Hills, CA 90210   ✧   310-883-1198   ✧   eric_brown@msn.com

Written by Laurie Berenson, CPRW

ERIC G. BROWN, PMP

STONE FINANCIAL, LLC—*Continued*
- ***Recaptured $650,000/year in revenues*** by designing and implementing database to track and calculate short interest participation.
- ***Increased reporting accuracy and future system flexibility*** by reengineering 2 major regulatory reporting systems for compliance with SEC Rule 15c3-3.
- ***Reduced balance sheets by $2.5B,*** decreased FX exposure, and facilitated aggressive financial reporting deadlines by reengineering financial reporting systems for U.S. and UK entities.

MORGAN STANLEY, New York, NY   2001 to 2003
Assistant Vice President
Streamlined regulatory functions to automate procedures, reduce data collection time, eliminate redundancies, and reduce data-entry error. Managed 3-person team through full project life cycle for new Federal Reserve TIC S and B reporting requirements, including reporting analysis and interpretation, data and criteria selection, report design and testing, project documentation, and training.
ENTERPRISE IMPACT:
- ***Increased functionality and data volume, automated data retrieval,*** and further streamlined existing processes and reporting procedures by leading team to migrate existing Access database application used for data collection and reporting into a Web-based format.
- ***Reduced data processing time 20 hours/month*** by reengineering SEC Rule 15c3-1 capital reporting process to FINRA and other regulatory authorities.
- ***Eliminated 2 hours of manual calculation time*** by designing and implementing spreadsheet applications to import Securities Borrow/Loan and Repo/Resale daily transaction data from existing systems and calculate Net Capital exposure.
- ***Successfully created and tested application requirements*** as designated Change Manager for Regulatory Reporting disaster recovery project.

■■■

EARLY CAREER
Worked as a Senior Consultant at **Hudson Crossing, Inc.,** related to the design and integration of the financial systems architecture of a merging global bank with a $55B market capitalization. Started career as a Staff Accountant in the regulatory reporting and general ledger departments at **Merrill Lynch,** completing formal coursework at New York University related to broker/dealer regulatory reporting requirements and brokerage accounting.

EDUCATION & CERTIFICATIONS

MBA, Banking & Finance
UNIVERSITY OF SOUTHERN CALIFORNIA, Los Angeles, CA—2001

BS, Accounting with Minor in Computer Science
UNIVERSITY OF CALIFORNIA AT BERKELEY, Berkeley, CA—1994

■■■

Project Management Professional (PMP) Certification—2008

Six Sigma Green Belt Training—2005

28 Rose Court ✧ Beverly Hills, CA 90210 ✧ 310-883-1198 ✧ eric_brown@msn.com

Jerry Levine

(440) 347-5263 • jlevine@comcast.net • 5482 Meadow Wood Blvd., Lyndhurst, OH 44124

SENIOR EXECUTIVE PROFILE
Start-Up, Turnaround & High-Growth Organizations
Domestic & Overseas Markets

Delivering double- and triple-digit growth by attaining strategic goals, developing win-win business partnerships, and providing skillful, proactive leadership.

Innovative, hands-on, and results-oriented, with an unbroken track record of success:

- VersaFlex, Inc.: Reversed a 65% sales loss and achieved profitability in 2 years.
- Premier Materials: Grew sales by 468%.
- DuPont: Increased sales from $22M to $63M.

- P&L Management
- Sales
- Market Development
- Competitive Positioning
- Product Development
- Productivity Improvement
- Negotiations
- Team Leadership

PROFESSIONAL EXPERIENCE

VersaFlex, Inc., Cleveland, Ohio
Chief Executive Officer, 2006–Present

Recruited by chairman to transform a design/technology venture into a manufacturing and marketing operation serving the medical and consumer products markets. Brought company into the black from a $770K loss on $1.2M in sales. Also, increased gross margins to over 50% by implementing cost and efficiency improvements.

Sales, Marketing & Business Growth:
- Increased sales by 150% to $3M.
- Expanded customer base by more than 300%, including account development in China, Taiwan, and England.
- Entered new markets by developing and patenting new products.
- Negotiated higher credit line and mezzanine financing.

Sales
('06, '07, '08)

Financial & Operational Improvements:
- Boosted equipment utilization by 100%.
- Reduced plant floor space by 25%.
- Negotiated an 11% price reduction on primary raw material.
- Recruited rep agencies to extend marketing reach without significantly adding to overhead.

Strategic Planning & Positioning:
- Developed and implemented strategic goals to achieve turnaround.
- Conducted market research to determine direction of new product development and product promotion.
- Targeted—and won—multibillion-dollar companies as new customers.

Corporate Branding: Overhauled company brand including promotional materials and website.

ABC Corporation, Warrensville Heights, Ohio
Executive Vice President & General Manager—Automotive Products Division (2000–2006)
Vice President—Automotive Products Division (1995–2000)
Sales Manager—ABC Corporation (1992–1995)

Promoted to start up and head new Automotive Products Division for $145M supplier of foam-in-place laminates. Grew it to rank #2 in industry.

—Continued—

Written by Reya Stevens, MA, MRW

Sales & Marketing:
- Grew sales from $31M to $145M in 10 years.
- Increased market share of primary product from 17% to 43%.
- Promoted entry into new markets by developing new products.

Strategic Initiatives:
- Shifted the division from Tier 3 to Tier 2 supplier status by developing additional expertise in supply chain and quality management (ISO 9002/QS 9000).
- Created "buyer-supplier parks" by adding 2 new regional manufacturing facilities, locating them near major customers and encouraging business partners to lease space in these new facilities. Results: more efficient just-in-time (JIT) deliveries, lower overhead costs, and elimination of duplicated assets.

Joint Ventures & Partnerships:
- Initiated and negotiated long-term sales agreements with 3 of the industry's 4 Tier 1 suppliers.
- Developed strategic partnerships and purchasing agreements with major suppliers to expand product line, facilitate entry into new markets, and reduce costs.

Average Sales Growth (Over 10 Yrs)

DuPont, Wilmington, Delaware
Sales and Marketing Manager—DuPont AutoProducts (1987–1992)
Hired to run Automotive Fabrics business unit, which was operating at a loss, and brought it to profitability in first year. Directed national and international sales and marketing activities.

Sales & Marketing:
- Brought company from a $500K loss to a $4M profit in first 4 years.
- Grew sales by almost 200% in 5 years.
- Increased market share of primary product from 21% to 44%.
- Entered new market to achieve average sales increase of almost 12% in each of 5 years.

Average Profit Growth (1st 4 Yrs)

Joint Ventures & Partnerships: Negotiated a technology sharing/marketing agreement with a major Japanese supplier.

Product Development: Developed new product line in 1988, which accounted for nearly 40% of total sales by 1992.

Operational Efficiency: Reduced manufacturing costs by strategic outsourcing of specific manufacturing services to 1 supplier and purchasing new equipment.

EDUCATION

Master of Business Administration (MBA)   TULANE UNIVERSITY
Bachelor of Science (BS)   AMERICAN UNIVERSITY

PATENTS: Two patents awarded; 4 patents pending.

CIVIC AFFILIATIONS

Past Member, Board of Directors, Horizons for Youth, Cleveland, OH
Past Member, Board of Directors, Carroll Grove Homeowners Association, Carroll Grove, DE
Past Member, Board of Directors, Harahan Neighborhood Development Association, Harahan, LA

Jerry Levine   **Page 2 of 2**   **(440) 347-5263**

John Jaxson M.A., SPHR
"Leading leaders through courage, action, and relationships"

1226 Electra Ave., Apt. D111 ◆ Long Island City, NY 11111 ◆ 123.456.7890 ◆ jjaxbo@me.net

Seeking position as:

Human Resources Director

Experienced, driven, and results-focused Talent Management/Human Resources business partner brings **leadership**, **consultative support**, and **project management** for key talent-management initiatives. Areas of expertise include **staffing**, **competency assessment**, **career development**, and **Human Resource Generalist** functions. **Exceptional communicator** and **change agent**.

Key Accomplishments

- **Behavioral leadership development** and promotional support for 2 Regional Directors, 5 District Managers, and 6 territory leaders utilizing the ABC development coaching series.
- **Developed global succession plan model** for Field Retail Management Employees resulting in 54% increased retention.
- **Created and implemented 2,010 Recruiting Tips and Tools Program** for client usage to identify, attract, and recruit top-performing talent. Contained thousands of ideas for increased productivity.
- **Developed compensation matrix** to equitably pay field employees market-value wages for both salaried and hourly positions. No matrix or compensation structure existed upon taking on position.
- **Created comprehensive intranet policy/procedure manual** for business partners. Computer accessibility increased employee usage, which reduced on-the-job errors. Reduced paper usage, producing a savings of $650K annually.

Strengths Finder 2.0

Relator
Arranger
Self Assurance
Intellection
Communicator

Core Leadership Competencies

Drive for Results
Virtual Leadership
Managerial Courage
Intellectual Horsepower
Developing Direct Reports

Areas of Expertise

Leadership Training and Development: *Certified in ABC Leadership Development Program,* which is recognized internationally in 60 countries and by Fortune 100 organizations. Developed ongoing development planning for executive leaders focusing on organic strengths and position descriptors. Coached and counseled executives on *"building and benching"* future leaders. Designed coursework for classroom training sessions, including 15 members per session.

Employee Relations: 6+ years of experience in directing executive teams in mitigating employee relations. Acted as internal consultant and leveraged relationships with field business partners to *reduce and eliminate EEOC claims by 80%. Through skills of influence and sharing knowledge,* leaders embraced "best practices" and stepped up to course-correct employee issues in a nonthreatening, educational manner.

Strategic Innovation: Partnered with senior management to *develop and execute strategies* to hire, retain, and manage performance of management professionals. Received *Strategic Innovation Award for saving more than $1M annually* on cost-per-hire in 2009.

Recruiting: 6+ years of focused experience in full-cycle recruiting. *Created 4-step process,* which *decreased open-to-hire by 50%.* Increased awareness on the importance of developing recruiting strategies for diversity and inclusion to hire candidates with a broad range of experiences and skills.

John Jaxson | Page 1 of 2 | jjaxbo@me.net

Written by Tina Kashlak Nicolai, PHR

John Jaxson M.A., SPHR
"Leading leaders through courage, action, and relationships"

Professional Experience

ClothesU Inc., *Zone Director,* New York, NY *(2007–Present)*
Coffee Company, *Executive Recruiter,* New York, NY *(2004–2007)*
BQQ International, *Senior Human Resources Manager,* New York, NY *(2002–2004)*
Bull's Eye Corporation, *Human Resources Generalist,* New York, NY *(2000–2002)*

> *"...John is an extraordinary HR business partner. His engaging style, strategic vision, and direct communication style build trust and solid rapport. He is results-oriented and understands balancing human capital with business."* **—Billy K., VP, ClothesU Inc.**

Professional Development and Education

- SPHR Certification (HRCI and SHRM)
- ABC Leadership-Based Competency Certification
- Train the Trainer Certification
- OCCP Certification
- Project Management Professional Certification

M.A., Business Management and Human Resources | University of Pittsburgh | Pittsburgh, PA
B.A., Political Science | St. Vincent | Latrobe, PA

Professional Organizations

Society for Human Resource Management (SHRM)
American Society for Training and Development (ASTD)

Computer Technology

Windows and Mac platforms; Microsoft Word, Excel, PowerPoint, Outlook
Social Media Marketing and Recruiting

John Jaxson | Page 2 of 2 | jjaxbo@me.net

Kenneth J. Melba, MBA
Digital Solution Strategist

919-363-3970 • 114 Chertney Lane • Raleigh, NC 27613 • kennethjmelba@gmail.com • linkedin.com/in/kjmelba

Online Advertising • Lead Generation • Social Media • eCommerce Tactics

Core Expertise

Web 2.0 / Social Media
Analytics & Strategies

•••

Omniture

Google AdWords

Site Catalyst

Google Analytics

•••

Search Engine
Marketing

•••

Search Engine
Optimization

•••

Content Strategy

•••

**Brainstorming Client
Solutions**

•••

Keyword Analysis

•••

Meta Tag
Development

•••

Key Performance
Indicators

•••

Link Popularity

•••

E-mail Marketing

Career Profile

➢ Savvy creative leader and keen implementer of strategic communications.
➢ Customer experience enhancement via creative data analysis and solutions.
➢ Passion for helping clients envision the bigger picture.
➢ Excellent relationship skills and energy, with focus on results.
➢ Strengths in business acumen, communication, and team leadership.

"(Ken) has the rare ability to be both strategic and tactical depending on the need."
Client praise (enterprise software developer)

Value Proposition

"Clarify the confusing and unknown, develop actionable solutions, and drive improvement. Achieve this by analyzing data in the areas of usability, Web analytics, and online communication in conjunction with digital project management within user interface guidelines."

Professional Experience

SW Topix, Raleigh, NC • 2009 to 2010   **Business / Data Analyst**

Recruited to analyze high-level business requirements and develop key performance indicators (KPIs) in support of a strategic sales project. Defined, designed, and drove business intelligence (BI) solutions.

• Gauged success of online marketing campaigns using Omniture Web and Magic Draw (Visio) for data modeling.
• Proposed business intelligence solutions integrating data from multiple source systems and supplying cross-application reporting functionality.

AB Financial Bank, Raleigh NC • 2007 to 2009   **Online Channel Analyst**

Hand-selected to analyze and propose solutions for improving flow, increasing revenue streams, and decreasing operational costs.

• Lowered operational costs by streamlining online enrollment process, instituting ability to open new screens within the same window.
• Saved $40K/month; reduced call center volume by recommending security questions and creating temporary user names and passwords online.
• Implemented SEO best practices for Web page content, structure, internal linking and meta tags; increased online usage for stop-payment transactions.
• Compared Web analytic reporting to third-party PPC reports showing true report analysis to the detail level; counseled client accordingly.

Hanswi, St. Louis, MO • 2006 to 2007   **Search Marketing Campaign Manager**

Mined analytical data and keyword research; developed online campaigns for Fortune 500 clients to initiate and improve Web-driven business revenue. Managed Web search marketing programs for top-level accounts.

Continued...

Written by Kelly Welch, CPRW, MA, GPHR

Kenneth J. Melba page 2   kennethjmelba@gmail.com

- Organized campaign into "branded" and "non-branded" segments, increasing revenue 41% and reducing cost per acquisition (CPA) from $17 to $10.
- Coordinated vendor relationships for best-of-breed search marketing solutions for clients' online search campaigns.
- Improved user experience using market intelligence and Web analytics.
- Identified new business opportunities for clients.

MarketSmart Interactive, Morris, NC • 2004 to 2006   Manager, Interactive Marketing

Promoted three times in two years to Lead for enterprise team. Managed SEO campaigns, initiated business consulting, and marketing research and analysis.

- Transitioned client from a search engine optimization websource model to an interactive marketing agency model, yielding stronger online presence.
- Performed marketing, competitive, and keyword analyses and wrote articles on how to correctly measure for custom-tailored shirts.
    - Achieved top rankings 4 months into campaign for desired terms.
    - Increased unique site visitors from 0 to 400 daily.
- Developed targeted benchmarks to analyze online channel performance.
- Improved unique visitor traffic 15% and reduced cost per lead (CPL) to $28.

Early Career Experience

Launched career focus in sales, gaining indispensable customer relations experience. Moved through roles developing Web sites and Web marketing, regularly surpassing quotas and exceeding expectations.

Employers:

Renegade Office Solutions, Raleigh, NC • Cache Systems Inc., Raleigh, NC
Dargon Corporation, Raleigh, NC • HH&H Inc., Cary, NC

Profile

Value proposition:	Clarify the confusing and unknown, develop actionable solutions, and drive improvement, from analyzing data in the areas of usability, Web analytics, and online communication in conjunction with digital project management within user interface guidelines.
Education:	MBA–North Carolina State University; graduated with honors BA, History–Eastern Carolina University AAS, EE Technology–Beaufort County Community College
U.S. Navy:	Active duty and reserves
Published in:	pandia.com, searchenginelowdown.com, webrankinfo.com, searchengineguide.com, webrankinfo.com, & ezinedirector.com

Recognition & Involvement

Sales Awards:	Top Quarterly & Monthly Award, Out-of-the-Box Thinking
Navy Awards:	Sea Service Citation with Bronze Star, Expeditionary Medal
Associations:	TIMA (Triangle Interactive Marketing) • WAA (Web Analytics)

VACANCY ANNOUNCEMENT 2009-016SM

Martin A. Croft

24 Allendale Curve Drive, Leedsville, Virginia 20100
macroft@aol.com ☎ primary phone 202.555.5555 (cell) – 571.555.6666 (home)

> "Your exceptional leadership has been integral to providing the very best systems security solutions for some of our nation's most critical space assets."
>
> —Chairman, National Space Infosec Steering Council

WHAT I CAN CONTRIBUTE TO **THE TREASURY** AS YOUR **ASSISTANT SECRETARY FOR SECURITY**

- ❑ Vision to **define and reach** the **optimum security end state** by integrating expectations, requirements and needs. In short, to translate corporate vision into results.

- ❑ Leadership to **help people** to draw the straight line between what they do each day and how well we **perform our mission,** and to treat both as **personal points of honor.**

- ❑ Political savvy to **build constituencies** that help us win the **funds and consensus** we need to move our mission forward.

- ❑ Professional development to **exploit useful change** to **our advantage** and powerful enough to **frustrate the threats.**

- ❑ Approachability to hear, and **learn from,** the voices of **colleagues, leaders,** and **"customers."**

- ❑ Passion to **attract, hire,** integrate, and **retain professionals** with the same values you've just seen described.

RECENT WORK HISTORY WITH EXAMPLES OF PROBLEMS SOLVED

- ❑ **Systems Security Manager** *sought out by the Assistant Administrator for the Office of Security and Safeguards for promotion to* **Director, National Security Systems,** *then promoted to* **Director of the Security Management Division,** NASA Headquarters, Washington, D.C.   May 06–Present

  The administrative information you requested about this position:

Salary: $125,078	Hours worked per week: 40
Employer's name and address:	Supervisors' name and phone number:
Headquarters, NASA	Mark Hopkins—202.555.1111
300 E Street SW	Charles Amberly—202.555.2222
Washington, DC 20546	

  What my responsibilities are:

  I am NASA's key adviser on how we protect classified and sensitive, unclassified information across the voice, data, video, and communications spectra. It's up to me to ensure NASA's plans and policies meet customer requirements on time. I work with senior leadership to find potential threats to people, facilities, missions, information, and technology—in short, all our assets. (Additional elements are in the original résumé.)

  Examples of contributions I've made (described within the tight restrictions that apply to classified information):

  Chosen by senior leadership to handle **every security aspect** of the **largest** technical **recovery effort** in U.S. history: protecting human remains and exceptionally classified materials after the

More indicators of return on investment **Treasury** *can use …*

Written by Don Orlando, MBA, CPRW, JCTC, CCM, CCMC, CJSS

loss of the space shuttle *Columbia.* Coordinated the efforts of 600 teams and 25,000 first responders from 425 agencies for 100 days working in 680,000 acres. *Payoffs:* **Recovered and protected every sensitive component**—even though no one had ever supervised such an effort before.

Stepped forward to **transform the** communications security (COMSEC) **program I inherited.** Envisioned the capability our mission required and then compared it to our first solid inventory of accounts and assets. **Built trusting constituencies** at every level to help me champion my programs. Leveraged relationships I built earlier at the White House to help me build and demonstrate a secure prototype with voice, video, and limited data capability. *Payoffs:* **Senior leadership** went **from skeptics to converts.** Funding went from $0 **to $1M at once**—even outside the budget cycle. Our culture went **from** security **caretakers to** security **leaders.**

Built a **strong defense against cyberintrusion,** even though we were attacked more frequently than any other federal agency. For the first time, closely integrated formerly separated cultures: human counterintelligence and cyber counterintelligence. Leveraged WAN configuration control to **protect every network we had.** *Payoffs:* **Slashed** the number of **intrusions.** Got us **in compliance** with new, more complicated, stringent statutory requirements.

❏ **Telecommunications Specialist** *promoted to* **Communications Program Manager** *with additional duties as* **Communications Security Manager,** Department of the Treasury, Washington, D.C.   04–06

The administrative information you requested about this position:

Salary: $61,895	Hours worked per week: 40
Employer's name and address:	Supervisor's name and phone number:
Department of the Treasury	Charles Harmon (deceased)
1500 Pennsylvania Avenue NW	
Washington, DC 20220	

What my responsibilities were:

Managed the communications and computer systems of the Treasury, and particularly the Office of Intelligence Analysis, used to provide secure voice, data, video, and fax communications. Negotiated with every level of leadership and contractors, not just in Treasury, but the U.S. Secret Service, ATF, Customs, IRS, U.S. Mint, and other federal agencies. Evaluated our level of emergency preparedness and served on some six working groups regularly. Directed a technical staff, oversaw contracts, and wrote analyses and policy for the Department. Was the direct reporting official for 15 telecommunications professionals.

Examples of contributions I've made (described within the tight restrictions that apply to classified information). You will find **more detailed information** on many of these contributions **in the ECQs** and professional qualifications that are part of this package:

Played a key role helping the responsible manager **integrate Treasury's capabilities** and responsibilities into the **Continuity of Government Plan.** Armed him with just the information he needed on every subject from security architectures to required facilities, to the intricacies of required redundancies to connectivity. *Payoffs:* With my help, he **quickly built** vital, committed **relationships** with key **White House staff.** Our input was approved virtually without change.

❑ Previous related assignments as **Telecommunications Manager,** Science Applications International Corporation (05–06) and **Chief of the White House Telecommunications Certification Office (02–04)**

Detailed information on these and earlier positions available on request.

Security Clearances

❑ Top Secret/SBI   Current

Education

❑ AA, Technology Information Systems, Community College of the Air Force, Maxwell Air Force Base, Alabama   Apr 00

❑ AA, Williams College, Walnut Ridge, Arkansas   May 99

Earned this degree while working up to 20 hours a week while carrying a full academic load.

❑ Diploma, Poplar Bluff High School, Poplar Bluff, Missouri 63901   95

Recent and Relevant Training

❑ Introduction to the National Incident Management System, FEMA   Jun 06

(Full documentation of more than 150 hours on recent training was in the original document.)

IT Skills

❑ Expert in Access, ACT!, Adobe Acrobat, Dragon Naturally Speaking (speech recognition software), Entrust PKI (e-mail and **file encryption** software), Excel, Informed (**e-form** software), MS Project, MS Publisher, MS Streets & Trips, Norton Internet Security, Outlook, PC Anywhere, PCWebTabs (time and attendance software), PowerPoint, Quicken, TravelManager, and Word.

❑ Comfortable with advanced Internet search protocols.

Recent Professional Recognition

❑ Six Cash Performance Awards, NASA   00–07

❑ Certificate of Appreciation, National Space INFOSEC Steering Council   Mar 06

❑ Space Flight Awareness Honoree Award, NASA   Aug 04

(Additional professional recognitions included in the original résumé.)

Professional Affiliations

❑ Former member, 1600 Association   92–93
The Association's members are drawn from White House security and telecommunications professionals.

Administrative Information: (Included in the original document.)

RHONDA JOHNSTON-WOLFSON

✉ **1234 Smith St. NE**
Washington, DC 20002

☎ **202-123-4567**
✉ **johnstonw@comcast.net**

Career Summary

Highly motivated, enthusiastic, and dedicated educator offering strong academic credentials; the exceptional ability to establish cooperative professional relationships with staff, parents, and administrators; and a heartfelt commitment to student success to an institute of learning that is seeking a taskmaster who will create a challenging classroom environment that maximizes student potentiality to excel intellectually.

Professional Profile

Child & Youth Program Assistant
Army Child Development Center, Silver Spring, MD
October 2008–Present

- ☐ Assist in planning age-appropriate structured activities for children to foster individual and group activity development based on stated goals and curriculum plan. Conduct activities designed to stimulate and sustain interest of children.
- ☐ Increase reasoning skills through use of questions. Provide activities that promote cognitive development. Prepare activities contributing to recognition of colors, shapes, and letters. Encourage children to creatively express themselves through art, music, stories, finger play, puzzles, dramatic play(s), blocks, and other stimuli.
- ☐ Receive children from parents. Note any special instructions that parents may provide. Conduct daily health checks of children. Notify managing officials of marks or other signs that might indicate a suspicion of abuse or neglect. Ensure safety and sanitation of children through constant supervision, effective arrangement of space, and proper maintenance of equipment. Instruct children in health and personal habits such as eating, resting, and toilet habits. Employ knowledge of pertinent regulatory requirements affecting early-childhood development.
- ☐ Keep individualized records on children, including daily observations and information concerning activities, meals served, and medications administered. Identify signs of emotional or developmental problems in children and bring them to parents' or guardians' attention. Complete and submit required reports in an accurate and timely manner. Participate in conferences with parents and supervisor.

High School Teacher
Sean T. Zukaris High School, Bladensburg, MD
August 2004–September 2008

Academic Approach

- ☐ Taught world history to approximately 150 students daily. Emphasized growth and preservation of democratic society and world interdependency. Provided students with learning experiences to aid developing knowledge, values, and attitudes necessary for participation as citizens in a culturally diverse democratic society.
- ☐ Planned, organized, and presented instruction compatible with school- and system-wide curriculum goals. Facilitated students learning subject matter and skills that contributed to their educational development.
- ☐ Implemented personal teaching approach centered on active engagement and cooperative learning. Administered oral and written exams to determine students' level of understanding. Based on results, determined course weaknesses, made adjustments to course materials, and developed re-teach modules.
- ☐ Demonstrated ability spurring dramatic improvement in classroom performance and standardized testing. Achieved desired results by incorporating innovative learning principles into areas of instruction.

(continued)

Written by Phyllis G. Houston

RHONDA JOHNSTON–WOLFSON
☎ 202-123-4567 ⌨ johnstonw@comcast.net

Professional Development

Child Development Skill Level Training, March 2009
Child Development Foundation Training, March 2009
Child Development Full Performance Care-Giving Skills, March 2009
Intermediate Problem Solving, August 2009
Child Development Entry-Level Training, March 2009
Communicable Diseases, January 2009
First Aid/SIDS, December 2008
Infant/Child CPR, December 2008
Child Growth and Development, November 2008
Developmentally Appropriate Practices, November 2008
Parent and Public Relations, November 2008
Child Health, Sanitation, and Nutrition, November 2008
Safety and Emergency Procedures, October 2008
Child Abuse Identification, Reporting, and Prevention, October 2008
Special-Needs Awareness, October 2008
Food Handling, October 2008

Software Training

Word II, June 2006
Word I, December 2005
Introduction to MS PowerPoint, June 2003

Academic Showcase

M.A. in Teaching (Elementary Education/Social Studies)
Fisk University, Nashville, TN
December 2003

PETER L. SCHROEDER

1372 Clayton Street • Brooklyn, NY 11231 • (917) 304-5678 • plschroeder1@gmail.com

CAREER FOCUS: PROPRIETARY TRADING

"GAMBLING IS ENTERTAINMENT, INVESTING IS BUSINESS" – AUTHOR UNKNOWN

SUMMARY OF QUALIFICATIONS

An aggressive, success-driven, and highly collaborative entrepreneurial trader with 7 years of experience trading within financial markets. A disciplined investor with a passion for high-volume trading and a solid understanding of global markets. Skilled in developing and executing highly effective quantitative investment strategies, including systematic trading and correlation high-frequency trading. Deeply committed to the belief that exhaustive research is the key to success in generating superior risk-adjusted returns throughout the market cycle.

AREAS OF EXPERTISE

Quantitative Trading • Low/High Trading • Frequency Trading • Intraday Trading • Equity Long-Short
Portfolio Management • Quantitative Data Analysis • Risk Management • Forecasting / Market Trend Analysis
Technically savvy; proficient in real-time charting software and a variety of trading platforms

PROFESSIONAL EXPERIENCE

ENTREPRENEURIAL TRADER   2003–PRESENT

- Employ probability-based logic using valuation models and leading-edge technology to gain a competitive advantage in providing liquidity to the marketplace and exploiting market inefficiencies.
- Dedicated 2 years to building existing trading skills through consultation with industry experts, including John Ehler and Peter Steidmayer; tested new methodologies through sophisticated trading simulators; and attended various trade shows, seminars, and webinars with the goal of learning to become consistently profitable.

CAREER HIGHLIGHTS

- **Executed large-volume trades resulting in first-year profit of $80,000** using automated algorithms, adjusting trading strategies based on market conditions, analyzing post-process trade data, optimizing strategy parameters, and researching information relevant to the market.
- **Tripled profits the following year with less short-term value trading** having utilized the same strategy but incorporated application of technical indicators with comparisons, inverses, correlations, and defined spread research.

ANNUAL VOLUME	2003	2004	2005	2006	2007	2008	2009
LOW-FREQUENCY TRADING / INTRADAY TRADING	$165K	$1.6M	$3.2M	$465K			
HIGH-FREQUENCY TRADING					$1.42M	$13.6M	$19.7M

DEPARTMENT MANAGER   1992–2003
Best Deal Electronics—Monmouth, NJ

CAREER HIGHLIGHTS

- **#1 Ranked Sales Executive on the East Coast** and recipient of the Toshiba Award (BMW Z3) for exceptional sales performance.

PROFESSIONAL DEVELOPMENT

CES International Conference—Keynote speakers included John T. Chambers, Noel Lee, and Carly Fiorina.

Real Estate Wealth Expo—Donald Trump, Robert Kiyosaki, and Tony Robbins.

Traders Expo • Nanotech Conference • Mining Expo Conference • UN Convention on the Use of Electronic Communications in International Contracts

Written by Angie S. Jones, CPRW, CEIC

RAVIS WILLIAMS

201457 River's Head Lane ▶ Purcellville, VA 20132 ▶ Phone: 703-547-8587 ▶ E-mail: twilliams@yahoo.com

SENIOR MANAGEMENT EXECUTIVE

VISIONARY & INFLUENTIAL LEADER ▶ STRATEGIC THINKER & PLANNER ▶ ENERGETIC & COLLABORATIVE EXECUTIVE

"BEING A STRATEGIST AND ADVOCATE FOR THE MEMBERS"

Delivering Proven Strengths in Entrepreneurial/Organizational Leadership, Business Acumen & Relationship Management to Forge a Collective Vision of Success and True Partnership Among Active and Retired Players

RESTORE & INCREASE MEMBERSHIP • IDENTIFY REVENUE SOURCES & GROW BUSINESS • BUILD COHESIVENESS IN ORGANIZATION

Executive-level experience in leadership of member-driven organization—top performance in startup, high-growth, and turnaround management situations. Consistently successful in building consensus, exhibiting inclusive management style, and driving cooperative relationships with staff, board of directors, players, and industry leaders.

Core Leadership & Executive Management Competencies

Strategic Planning & Corporate Vision	Profit & Loss Management	Cross-Functional Team Leadership
Labor Contract & Union Negotiations	Human Resource Management	Corporate Sponsorship & Partnerships
New Program & Service Development	Marketing & New Business Development	Policy & Procedure Development
Public Relations & Media Affairs	Budgeting & Financial Management	Member Development & Retention

Entrepreneurial Ventures & Organizational Leadership Experience

PRESIDENT
International Tennis League Players Association, Washington, DC (2004 to 2010)

Leadership Impact: **Advocated and endorsed several organizational initiatives that reinforced organization's mission, charted course of action for new program development, and delivered resurgence in member interest, commitment, and participation.**

▶ Collaborated with executive director in overseeing the entire management of association operations including the development of long-term and short-term program objectives, marketing strategies, and operational policies.

▶ Functioned as chief spokesperson for ITL players at Board of Representative Meetings, Competition Committee Meetings, and Rookie Symposium; interfaced extensively with the Board of Player Representatives and Executive Committee on strategic planning efforts.

▶ Served as primary liaison between players and the union regarding critical issues such as salary negotiation, the collective bargaining agreement, and overall working conditions for its members.

Key Successes:

—Introduced new health and medical benefits programs that increased and expanded coverage for retired players.

—Initiated cardiovascular health study and acclimatization and hydration study that helped redefine the off-season and reconditioning programs for players.

—Formed series of strategic committees and alliances to strengthen member support and participation, restructure internal processes, and cultivate new programs and services.

—Instrumental in establishing open forum to encourage candid, productive communication between the players and the ITL Commissioner.

(continued)

Written by Abby Locke, MRW, NCRW, ACRW, CPBS

TRAVIS WILLIAMS ▸ 703-547-8587

COFOUNDER/MANAGING DIRECTOR OF BUSINESS DEVELOPMENT
ABC Business Solutions, Purcellville, VA (1998 to 2004)

Leadership Impact: Instrumental in the startup, launch, and rapid growth of national investment advisory, risk-management, business consulting services firm; contributed to company's portfolio expansion from zero to $95 million in assets under management.

▸ Conceptualized and executed key strategic market planning and business development initiatives that increased revenue growth, expanded market share, built company reputation, and solidified client relationships.

▸ Assumed lead role in developing innovative service and product offerings that gave company advantage in highly competitive industry. Routinely introduced and established sound operating policies for HR, client management, and marketing.

▸ Led multiple negotiations with Pershing, Lehman Brothers, AXA, and Lincoln Financial Services and evaluated viable opportunities with strategic partners, member firms, and advisors.

Key Successes:

—Provided decisive operating leadership with deep focus on employee empowerment that helped reduce employee turnover, encourage internal growth and stability, and elevate firm's overall performance.

—Steered company through volatile economic and market conditions—immediately following 9/11 disaster and subsequent financial market crash—while maintaining corporate vision and long-range business objectives.

—Leveraged business acumen, market expertise, and relationship-building strengths to optimize revenue performance and accumulate company portfolio.

—Drove development and market launch of new product offerings that strengthened company's long-term position.

CO-OWNER/MANAGING DIRECTOR
Visions Spa & Beauty Salon, Ewing, NJ (1989 to 1998)

Leadership Impact: Created a successful, profitable business from the ground up to $500,000 in annual revenues; secured partnership and distributor rights with an international leader in beauty products.

▸ Conceived operating plan, business infrastructure, marketing strategy, and feasible revenue projections that allowed business to continually generate positive net income during early startup years.

▸ Integrated print, broadcast, and Internet media to deliver high-impact multimedia marketing and advertising campaigns; efforts helped quickly build company and service reputation.

✱✱Education & Professional Development✱✱

Bachelor of Arts Degree in Liberal Arts
California State University, San Diego, CA

Executive Education Program
Kellogg School of Management – Northwestern University
Harvard School of Business – Harvard University, Cambridge, MA

Index

Want Your Final Résumé and Cover Letter to Be Perfect?

*Include all the information you need for your **specific profession**.*

Deluxe DIY Résumé Writing Kit
Customized to Your Profession

Contains:

- Step-by-Step Résumés book & CD
- Career Worksheet – CONVERT PROFESSION-SPECIFIC QUESTIONS AND ANSWERS INTO EASY RESUME BULLETS
- Résumé Keywords – INCLUDE ALL OF YOUR PROFESSION-SPECIFIC KEYWORDS
- Résumé ClipBullets™ – FILL IN THE BLANKS AND ADD TO YOUR RESUME
- 24 Résumé Design Templates

All for $59

Add:

- Final Résumé and Cover Letter Critique by Author

Critique: $39

Total: $98 *Plus $8 S&H*

ORDER FORM

Name: _____ E-mail: _____

Street Address: _____

Town: _____ State: _____ Zip: _____

Day Phone: _____ Eve Phone: _____

Profession or Job Title: _____

Please send me: [ ] DIY Kit: $59*   [ ] Kit without Book: $39   [ ] Critique: $39   [ ] All: $98*

*Plus $8 S&H

[ ] Visa [ ] MasterCard [ ] Discover – Credit Card #: _____

Exp. Date: _____ Signature: _____

CALL: (631) 698-7777 • FAX: (631) 698-0984 • EMAIL: CareerCatapult@aol.com

---

For detailed information on all résumé and career products, please visit CareerCatapult.com